TRANSFOCUS

ANTHOLOGY

A COLLECTION OF TRANS EXPERIENCES

...am.com/transfocus

 medium.com/transfocus

First Edition

Edited by Rori Porter

Introduction by Jacob Nash

TransFocus Publishing

Los Angeles

TRANSFOCUS

ANTHOLOGY

A COLLECTION OF TRANS EXPERIENCES

1st Edition Hardcover

TransFoc.us

Cover Design and Book Interior Design/Typesetting by RoriPorter.com

Names: Rori Porter, Editor | Susan Kolarik, Editor | Jacob Nash, Introduction

See page 358 for contributor bios

Title: TransFocus Anthology

Subtitle: A Collection of Trans Experiences

ISBN: 978-1-7947-1302-4

Subjects: Gender identity. | Transgender Identity. | Anthology.

Activism. | Sexual Minorities. | Gender expansive people. | Poetry.

Art. | Gender nonconformity. | Nonbinary identity. | Short non-fiction.

Typeset in Quasimoda 9pt,

Lettersoup Type Foundry

Printed and bound in the United States on Rainforest-Free Paper

DEDICATED TO MJ ECKHOUSE
& ABBY ROSE FIALA

YOU ARE MISSED

CONTENTS

 Denotes Sensitive Subject

PREFACES & APPENDICES

PART ONE: ESSAYS & EXPERIENCES

PART ONE: ESSAYS & EXPERIENCES (CONTINUED)

PART TWO: POETRY & FREE FORM

PART TWO: POETRY & FREE FORM (CONTINUED)

PART THREE: ART & ACTIVISM

- Rori Porter -

Editor of TransFocus

- FORWARD -
THEY TRIED TO DROWN US OUT

If you flip to page 330, you will see the comic "Rainforest" by Andy Passchier, which inspired the cover art I designed for TransFocus. Andy was kind enough to let us publish their comic for the first time in print, and I am extremely glad and honored that they did. This anthology exists because some of us found a way to take root and come together to make a forest. This work is a labor of love for all of those involved because we have all been in the place of having shallow roots, or maybe even having no roots at all. Sometimes, our roots have been trimmed unjustly by those around us to keep us from thriving. Other times, our roots never grew at all because our loved ones didn't nourish them. Sometimes we *think* our roots are deep, but coming out shows us how adrift in the world we really are. Or perhaps, the topsoil was too unstable for natural growth in the first place.

This metaphor resonates deeply with a lot of trans folks because roots often equate to home. When we speak of roots, we can be referring to family and the skills we learned from those who raised us to handle all that the world throws our way. But often, even the most loving home struggles or flat-out fails to prepare a trans kid for the realities of this world and what it means to walk the earth in trans boots. All too often for trans and gender expansive folks, home can be a place of conflict and hostility. Many of us face invalidation, attempts at conversion, disownment, violence, or worse from our families and the world around us. That's why the idea of taking transphobia and turning it into nourishment is so damned appealing. There is no shortage of bigotry and adversity in the world to drown us out, while love, security, and acceptance can

2

be far harder to come by. If we can be watered

instead of washed away by a deluge of hatred, if our roots can take hold in a hurricane of ignorance, then maybe we really are unstoppable forces of nature. In turning external hatred into self-love, we take away the power from those who wish to poison us, drown us out, and dull our shine. When we find a way to take pride in their shame of our transness, we become stronger than their hatred and, instead of drowning, our branches make way to the surface of a great flood. This all brings to mind one of my favorite quotes of all time, by American writer Maggie Nelson from her memoir The Argonauts:

> "I have long known about madmen and kings; I have long known about feeling real. I have long been lucky enough to feel real, no matter what diminishments or depressions have come my way. And I have long known that the moment of queer pride is a refusal to be shamed by witnessing the other as being ashamed of you."

Whenever I feel stripped naked by a lingering stare or degraded by a hateful comment on one of my articles, I think of that quote, and it pulls me back to the pride I feel in having learned how to not just survive as a nonbinary trans woman, but *thrive* in a world that let's me know every day that who I am is different. Marsha P. Johnson may have said it best with her tongue-in-cheek middle name: *"Pay it no mind."* When we shrug off hate like water off a duck's back, we will find that we are indeed free. When we pay no mind to haters, we take away their power over us.

In the community, the slang term for a closeted or repressed trans person is an "egg." We use this term to refer to those who have yet to break out of their shell. Some are merely closeted and are not yet ready to come out, while others may not even know they're trans yet, either because they don't have the words to describe their experience or their transness is too repressed for them to realize their truth. This slang is superbly compatible with the roots metaphor, as it is in the branches we create for ourselves where our baby trans eggs sit and we ourselves once nested until ready to fledge and flutter to the forest floor. Some won't be ready, and we'll lose them. Some will sink, some will swim. Some will fly without ever being told how. And others still will survive, but it will take time before they learn how to thrive.

If I have learned anything since coming out in 2017, it's that forming connections within the community is a life preserver when the water current becomes too strong to fight by ourselves. In those instances, we must swallow our pride or feelings of burden, admit that we need help and simply ask for it. Community is one of the most extraordinary things you can find when you're trans, as when our flesh and blood families are insufficient in their guidance on how to fight adversity (which is not necessarily to say unsupportive), we need our chosen families to take us by the hand so we can walk in the footsteps of those who have traversed this path before us.

Here in the pages of this anthology, you will find trans love, joy, contentment, and pride. But you will also find trans anger, fear, and pain. I'm not going to sugarcoat it for you: within these pages, you may find dragons. But the thing about dragons is, if you learn to tame one, you can ride it to the highest mountain tops. There is always a light if only you know how and where to find it. If you are sopping wet from the flood of hatred, may this book be a warm change of clothes in whatever fashion makes you feel like you.

And if nobody has told you you're loved today: *I* love you.

- Rori Porter

(she/they)

The Trans Lifeline hotline is available 24/7, the Mermaids UK hotline is open Monday to Friday, 9am to 9pm, and the Mermaids UK textline is open 24/7. If you are in crisis or need someone to talk to, make a call or text. You are worth it.

TRANS LIFELINE

US (877) 565-8860

Canada (877) 330-6366

translifeline.org

UK 0808 801 0400

or text MERMAIDS to 852557

mermaidsuk.org.uk

TRANSFOCUS

ANTHOLOGY

- Jacob Nash -

- INTRODUCTION -
THE METAMORPHOSIS

Storytelling and art have been a bedrock in all of civilization, reminding us of what happened in the past and how far nations, countries, cities and peoples have come. This is true even today—in order to see the progress that a community has made, their stories must be told and their art must be seen. TransFocus does just that, sharing the stories, artistry, and activism of diverse individuals within the trans, non-binary, and gender-expansive communities.

These stories, poems, and pictures, carefully chosen by the editor, bring to life an often-overlooked and misunderstood group of people. Through these glimpses into their lives, we hope to foster understanding of the courage and strength necessary for trans folks to survive and thrive.

May I tell you a story of change? People within the trans community often connect with the image of a butterfly expressing who they are. Many see themselves as plain and ordinary caterpillars that metamorphose into beautiful butterflies. These pages are full of stories of personal triumphs and tragedies, telling the growth and process of becoming the people they know themselves to be.

But here's the science project part of the story. How does the caterpillar actually BECOME the butterfly? We have to look at the caterpillar's past: while it develops inside its egg, it grows body parts that it will need as a mature butterfly. In some caterpillars those parts, called imaginal discs, stay dormant throughout the caterpillar's life; in others the imaginal discs start to take the shape of tiny adult body parts even before the caterpillar forms its cocoon. Some caterpillars walk around with tiny rudimentary wings tucked inside their bodies, though you would never know it by looking at them.

It's when the caterpillar initiates change by spinning itself into the cocoon that a rather messy process happens. First, the caterpillar digests itself, disintegrating all of its tissues except for the imaginal discs. Those discs then use the protein-rich soup all around them to feed the rapid breakdown required to form all features of an adult butterfly.

Why did I tell you this story, and what does it have to do with this book? I wanted to share a little bit about what we transgender, non-binary and gender expansive individuals go through. Just like butterflies, we are born with the knowledge that there is something different and extra that we carry around inside of us. Some of us are able to show that tiny part of who we are before we are able to become that beautiful butterfly, while others keep it hidden until it's ready to come out. Either way, we are still beautiful butterflies in the end.

Most people do not know the struggles and challenges that trans* people work through in order to emerge as the butterflies that they are. Some just see the caterpillar and see no further because of indifference, ignorance, or fear. Societal attitudes can make a challenging process even more difficult. Thus some individuals within the transgender, non-binary, and gender expansive community are not given the opportunity to climb out of their cocoons, so their true being never sees the light of day. Many continue to see themselves as caterpillars, even after the metamorphosis has occurred. Sadly, they are never able to escape the messiness of the change. Others have not been handled with care and have therefore lost the ability to fly freely and are left on the ground to try and figure out what to do next. Happily, some of us are given the care and attention we need to help us become those beautiful butterflies.

How will *you* help to change the narrative about transgender, non-binary, and gender expansive people of all colors? As you read the stories and poems and look at the art that has been shared, think about butterflies and what it takes for them to emerge triumphant. Think about the bravery and perseverance, and honesty necessary to undertake such a process of change. Do not dismiss or look away from the pain and messiness: see it, acknowledge it, and ask how you can be a supportive part of their process. Listen to their stories. Do not walk past; walk beside. Do not turn your head; look them straight in the eyes. Do not ignore them; face them. Help them to believe in their own strength, courage, and color! See the beauty before you!

If you yourself are a trans butterfly, thank you for sharing your beauty—please don't stop. Share your story so that others can share in your triumph. We are all beautifully and wonderfully made—you are no longer the caterpillar or the soup, so spread your wings, show off your beauty and fly! Thank you to all the wonderful individuals who became vulnerable and shared their stories, poems, and art.

I see you, and you are loved!

- Jacob Nash
He/Him

Jacob Nash

" WE DELIGHT

IN THE BEAUTY

OF THE BUTTERFLY,

BUT RARELY ADMIT THE CHANGES

IT HAS GONE THROUGH

TO ACHIEVE

THAT BEAUTY. "

- MAYA ANGELOU

- Rori Porter -

Editor of TransFocus

DEDICATED IN LOVING MEMORY
OF MJ ECKHOUSE

TransFocus is dedicated to my friend, MJ Eckhouse. MJ was a fierce and powerful force in the fight for trans equality in the United States, focusing on the Ohio trans community. He passed away on October 21, 2020, and fought right up until his body gave out. He has left behind numerous family members, friends, comrades in activism, and his loving partner, Lis, and his stepson, Kenneth. If you flip to page 192, you can read Lis' marriage proposal and subsequent wedding vows to MJ — I feel privileged to be publishing his beautiful, touching words, and I can think of no better way to honor MJ than to feature the work of someone who loves him so deeply.

MJ was the kind of person who would take time from his hectic schedule to make sure you're okay. He was one of the first trans people I knew, and when I came out, he talked with me for hours and hours about my fears, my hopes, my dreams. And when I chose to get sober, he supported me on my journey. The impact he had on my life was more significant than he would ever know. I can't help but think that, if he hadn't passed, his work would be in this anthology as a contributor, and I wouldn't be solemnly dedicating this book to him. Time is a funny thing and, in a big way, MJ's death motivated me to finish TransFocus and push myself to get the work done.

MJ's legacy continues, now and forever, as we take up his task of bettering the lives of our beautiful and vulnerable community. He spent his life advocating for the disenfranchised, doing work with the Community AIDS Network/Akron Pride Initiative (CANAPI), Equality Ohio, Fusion Magazine, Trans Lifeline, and worked as Communications Coordinator of the Ohio Environmental Council. He also successfully petitioned Kent, Ohio, to ban conversion therapy of LGBTQIA+ minors.

Back in 2017, when I first came out as trans, I was terrified. I posted something on Facebook announcing my reality and quickly deleted it, but MJ saw it and reached out to me to see how I was doing. I wasn't at all okay, even though I said I was, but he talked to me for hours as I processed my abrupt and disruptive coming-out experience. We hadn't spoken in years, but he held space for me as I talked through my shock. From that day, I've held a special place in my heart for MJ.

MJ was a force of nature. He was there for our community in a way that I admired more than words can say, and his passing at just 29 years old has left me shocked and numb. By the time this book comes out, he will have been 30. He leaves behind a wonderful husband, Lis, and a stepson, as well as his loving parents and family, and so so so many fellow trans folks, chosen family, and people who walked alongside him in recovery. His favorite hat, emblazoned with "HATE" with the "E" crossed out, is emblematic of who MJ was. Ever passionate about his dedication to love and equality, he was also really fucking funny. Everything he did, every issue he championed, was undertaken with love, grace, and good humor.

MJ was a fighter from the day I met him. He overcame addiction and became a beacon of hope and light for me and so many others in a time of immense isolation. MJ was such a powerful person, and energy cannot be created or destroyed. His power, strength, and giving spirit will *always* be part of our community.

MJ is gone far too soon; but I am trying to reflect on the power that he held and often lent to others in the wake of his passing. That taking up his causes feels like such an insurmountable task is testimony to how very hard he worked to better others' lives in the LGBTQIA+ community.

For those reasons and more, TransFocus is dedicated to his legacy.

You will always be a part of my heart, MJ Eckhouse.

You are a gift to everyone you touched with your love.

HIC SVNT DRACONES

– ON CONTENT NOTICES –
HERE BE DRAGONS

Here be dragons; or, in the original Latin, hic sunt dracones. In some of the earliest drawn maps of the world, this phrase was placed to represent dangerous or unexplored territory. As you explore the pages of this book, you will stumble across the occasional content notice, which looks like this:

Content Notice: Transphobia

Where necessary, we have placed content notices to warn you of sensitive topics. We take triggers very seriously and respect those with PTSD, so we have placed specific content warnings on subjects like suicide, gun violence, and slurs. However, this page is to serve as a general notice for the whole book and covers those subjects we did not specifically place content notices for, given their prevelance within these pages and in the interest of avoiding undue repetition. Within these pages you will find anger, descriptions of transphobia, abuse, unaccepting parents, and other material that is potentially triggering. Invalidation is something all trans people face in one way or another, and if you are in a triggered state, we firmly recommend that you reserve time for reading this book when you are in a healthy and grounded headspace.

PART ONE

ESSAYS AND EXPERIENCES

ELLIOT DRAZNIN

RONI SHAPIRA

LEVI THROWER

CHARLIE CHOWDHRY

DR. NATALIA Z. PH.D

ZOEY SANFORD

ALEX ADAMS

LYS MORTON

EZEKIEL K.

JENNY SANSOM

REN THOMAS

MADELEINE VOLTIN

EM KEEVAN

BRANOK RYLAND FULLER

CASSIOPEIA VIOLET DRAKE

MILES MAYES

RORI PORTER

- Elliot Draznin -

TUMTUM

I'm Jewish and grew up going to a reform synagogue in Fairfax, Virginia. I had my b'nai mitzvah and was very involved in the shul until I graduated high school and moved to Cincinnati, Ohio, for college. At the University of Cincinnati, I'm still very involved in the Jewish community. I go to Hillel (the Jewish youth group recognized internationally on campuses) and hold positions on the student board. I also was a founding member of the Jewish sorority on campus, Sigma Alpha Epsilon Pi (SAEPi), and I now hold the presidency of the sorority, making myself the first openly trans president of a Greek Life organization. Between Fairfax and Cincinnati, very little changed in my Jewish identity. There was a different major change in my life that makes Cincinnati different from Fairfax; I came out as nonbinary.

I searched for acceptance in my Jewish communities regarding my transness. One of the employees at Hillel was a trans man and he pushed for things at Hillel like gender neutral bathrooms. He created a queer Hillel birthright trip. He truly showed me what I needed, that my Judaism and my queerness could be intertwined if I wanted them to be.

Terms

There is something really amazing about Judaism that has a small following in Queer Jewish culture. Judaism recognizes six distinct gender identities. I don't know where I first found the Jewish culture's terms for transgender people, but I knew I had found my cultural and spiritual identity as soon as I did.

There are varying acceptance levels of these terms. Some trans Jews absolutely hate these terms because they focus on genitalia and sex rather than identity. I found comfort in knowing my Judaism created a world for me with the term tumtum. I think it's still imperative to focus and point out the focus on genitalia and how it can exclude people.

The four gender-variant identities recognized in the ancient texts of the Babylonian Talmud are as follows:

An androgynos (אנדרוגינוס) is "a person who has both "male" and "female" sexual characteristics."

A tumtum (טומטום) is "a person whose sexual characteristics are indeterminate or obscured."

An ay'lonit (איילונית) is "a person who is identified as "female" at birth but develops "male" characteristics at puberty and is infertile."

A saris (סריס) is "a person who is identified as "male" at birth but develops "female" characteristics as puberty and/or is lacking male genitalia."

Meaning Behind the Terms & the Focus on Genitalia

One possible reason for the focus modern Talmud scholars explore, is that the appearance of these sex-based genders is directly related to the Greek study of the body (which they were influenced by). The Talmud in which these genders emerge was written during a time when Greeks were starting to medically examine and analyze the human body. There was no rabbinic equivalent to the Greek's study, so these sexual classifications are how they chose to study. They viewed trans bodies as a staple of the existing medical system, and futhermore did not see a separation between the cisgender and transgender bodies in the creation of terms and rabbinic rules surrounding them.

The problem with a focus on genitalia is that, in a modern context, it fundamentally excludes trans people that do not undergo the "full" medical transition. Those who are comfortable with their body as born, and social identity, were effectively left out of these classifications. Many trans people now are actively choosing to not medically transition, and that does not negate their transness. The Jewish identities seem to ignore that possibility, which poses a problem for modern applicability and practicality.

The advantage of using language that is only associated with sexual characteristics is the clarity that such names can provide. There is no room for erasure in these texts because they are so explicit. While they do not include the full spectrum of what modern experience knows to be trans, they make it impossible for rabbinic study to conclude there is not a place for us in Judaism. That, of course, does not stop some people from excluding the study of gender in Judaism, but it inherently cannot be separated.

While the identities listed in the Talmud are based solely on genitalia and do not recognize personal expression and identity, in a modern context, they are applicable and comparable to terms more widely used. Terms such as intersex can be affiliated with "androgynos," because it is based on the characteristic of ambiguous genitalia. "Tumtum," similarly, is easily applied to agender and other nonbinary identities. The term "saris" can be affiliated with trans women, because it recognizes someone who develops as a woman but was not born with those sexual characteristics. "Ay'lonit" resembles trans men, because it sees a person who is born with female characteristics but later develops male characteristics.

There is not a perfect fit, especially between trans men and trans women.

"The semiotics of body surfaces produces other different and seemingly more ambiguous gender possibilities, the androgynos or person with both primary sexual organs, and the tumtum as one with neither, at least not recognizably... The latter is mostly treated as a not-yet sexed person, as somebody whose sexual organs may eventually appear or be uncovered surgically. Meanwhile [they are] regarded as somebody in a genderwise doubtful legal status, the concern being that [they] may yet turn out to be a man, but as yet uncircumcised. The figure of the androgynos, however, is understood to be clearly doubly-sexed and to remain such."

(Charlotte Elisheva Fonrobert, Jewish Women's Archive)

The idea that tumtum is seen as someone who is yet to be identified makes me tremendously uncomfortable, but that is the beauty of Judaism - you can question why it was written like that and find ways to apply texts written thousands of years ago to the modern-day. There is a culture embedded in the religion to question the rules and authority and analyze how those rules and teachings can be applied in any and every situation. Judaism does not preclude me from asking why they would potentially force a tumtum to reveal their genitalia instead of accepting the unknown and allowing them to function within the greater society.

Application to Modern Context

Each of these sex-based genders has prescribed roles by the Talmud because, after studying the body, there had to be designations based on the roles men and women had at that time. Rules about who Androgynos and Tumtum are allowed to marry differ, for example. Androgynos is only allowed to marry a woman, because their supposed 'penis' makes them more alike to men, and therefore if they married a man, it would have been against Jewish law. Tumtum are allowed to marry anyone, and the marriage is considered valid. But the fundamental question of Judaism is, "how do we interpret those laws now?"

"Interestingly, while a TumTum is obliged to hear the shofar and may even blow it like other males, he may only blow the shofar for himself and not for other TumTumim. Unlike the Androgynos who is allowed to fulfill religious duties for others, the TumTum is allowed to fulfill only his own religious duties and may not help others fulfill their own (Rosh Hashanah, 29a). As Rashi indicates, this is due to the blower potentially being a female who would not be obligated to perform the mitzvah, while the listener could be a male who would be obligated to listen. ...which all females are exempt from performing and thus cannot help others perform a duty they are not required to do."

(Melvin Marsh, Sojourn)

The quote by Melvin Marsh on the previous page means that, because Tumtum are unable to be confirmed male or female, they are not allowed to do religious tasks that women aren't required to do; Women are not allowed to help others fulfill religious duties they themselves are not required to complete. In the example above, they speak of the shofar, but there are other tasks that men are required to complete that women are not. While reform and conservative movements are moving further and further away from the idea that men and women have differences in responsibilities, it's a good starting point to figure out what the expectations could possibly be.

The Impact in the Jewish Community

Popularizing these terms in the reform Jewish community allows more people to form a deeper understanding of their religion and how their religion can best reflect their gender identity. They allow people to question a focus on genitalia and comment on modern terms and how those may or may not fit in. The study of a deeper gender in Judaism allows for people to ask how they are supposed to be Jewish as their full selves and find ways that work for them. Finding Tumtum for me was a gift because I knew that I had a way to fit into my community as a trans person and still be Jewish. Allowing that for others is the goal of modern Judaism and is fundamental for its strength as a religion in the future.

Citations:

https://www.sefaria.org/sheets/37225?lang=bi (biblical texts and translation in english)

https://jwa.org/encyclopedia/article/gender-identity-in-halakhic-discourse

http://www.transtorah.org/PDFs/Classical_Jewish_Terms_for_Gender_Diversity.pdf

- Roni Shapira -

15 EXPERIENCES
OF A TRANS SOLDIER

1 ············ You make a choice to go to the army, and your queer friends don't understand; they say you're going to suffer, that there's no room for people like you in that place. You make a choice and realize you're going to have to be in the closet. You haven't been in the closet for a few years now, and suddenly, this option seems absurd.

2 ············ The paperwork doesn't acknowledge you, but dude, you exist. You wish you could draw a square right between the male and female option and mark it there, but the world isn't there yet. You check the "female" option and feel guilty for lying.

3 ············ You aren't used to people seeing you as a cisgender straight woman. You try to convince yourself it doesn't matter, but you can't shake away the feeling of a spy undercover, holding back a secret. It helps to think of it as a game, an anthropological experience.

4 ············ You decide to come out half a year into your army service, first to one friend alone. You're so scared that it'll ruin something, but later that day, she changes clothes in front of you, and you're so relieved that nothing has changed. Don't you see, love? You can do it.

5   Your officemate likes scrolling through Instagram and commenting about girls' bodies. He says that one is so ugly, "she's probably trans." You become so angry, and suddenly you wonder if you'll ever be able to come out to him and if the office space will ever feel like it belongs to you too.

6   You shave your head, going for a classic military guy haircut, and suddenly, people are confused. They ask you if you want to be a guy, and you are so happy that they can see a little bit more of who you are.

7   You do guard duty, and people refer to you as "he." They apologize, but you wish they wouldn't; the dysphoria feels a little less potent once others see it as well.

8   You come out, again and again, and again. You become better at explaining, drawing spectrums, and showing that vast space where you thrive. All of your close friends on base eventually know, and they're okay with it in a way that you could have never expected.

9   They joke that you're gender phobic, that you're not bound by any military law that specifies that it's for men and women. There's so much warmth, and you realize that the military is not only what people say it is.

10   You walk up to that guy in your office and tell him you've been with more girls than him and that trans people are, in fact, people; quite a lot of them are gorgeous, and he's missing out. You tell him he probably knows some trans people, but when he claims he does not, you find the courage to tell him that, yes, he most certainly does. He's shocked and upset but a week later asks to see a picture of your girlfriend.

11   Your commander doesn't understand when you come out, but she is more than willing to learn, which matters more than anything.

12   You roll your eyes when another soldier announces to you that you can't possibly be queer because you're too funny. "Queer people are always aggressive social justice warriors." You're tempted to show him trans social justice memes so he can learn that it's absolutely possible to be both.

13   You begin to speak up. You mention trans rights wherever you possibly can. You try to force it, try to make your surroundings see it's not a dirty word, that trans people are genuinely everywhere. Everyone associates you with the LGBTQ+ struggle, asking questions whenever anything in the news happens. In a way, you're "more trans" in the army than you ever were in the civilian world.

14 You finish your army service, and you're sad, sadder than you ever thought you'd be about it. You can look back with incredible fondness. And you wish you could scream at President Trump, explain that trans people can do military service, that you deserve equality.

15 After your service, when your queer friends meet your army friends, they get along marvelously. You realize that you also underestimated people. Transphobia is a monster we must defeat, but sometimes, just sometimes, people are pretty amazing.

- Levi Thrower -

GIRLS DON'T PLAY BASEBALL

In retrospect, I knew I was transgender at the tender age of seven. My father was in charge of coaching my younger brother's little league team, and, always wanting to be "one of the boys," I had my heart set on playing ball as well. I practiced with my brother every day, hitting, pitching, and catching. Being a natural athlete, it wasn't long before I felt good enough to play with the other kids.

My father, brother, and I played at the park as they began to throw the ball back and forth. Eager to show my father all that I had learned in the past few weeks, I eagerly asked them to throw me the ball. My father held the ball in his fist, glaring down at me.

"Girls don't play baseball," He sneered.

I recoiled.

"But why not? I wanted to try out for the team and play with Jordan."

"Girls don't play baseball!" He exclaimed, shaking his head in disgust.

I didn't cry like I wanted to; dejected, I walked away to play by myself.

That day, I was first introduced to my father's backward views on sex and gender. He believed women should be treated differently from men, as evidenced by his behavior. Instead of baseball, I got put into dance, something I excelled at and would end up coming in handy as I did musical theater in Junior High and High School. In retrospect, I think that's why I liked musical theater so much; I could pretend to be someone else.

But still, I always wanted to play ball.

I remember my first day of dance class; I was forced to wear a leotard, tights, and a frilly tulle tutu, bows and all. And it was pink. Brilliantly, glaringly, femininely pink. I fought it, throwing a righteous fit with my mother, begging her to let me leave the tutu off, but my father insisted I wear it. I ended up wearing the tutu and tore it off as soon as my feet hit the hardwood dance floor.

My transness manifested itself again in Junior High. I was obsessed with a certain tie-wearing, pop-punk singer with a song about sk8er bois. I admired her a lot and wanted to be just like her. I wore a tie every day in seventh grade and even convinced my parents to let me wear one on school picture day. Dad rationalized it as a punky fashion sense and had no idea of the gender dysphoria that fueled that choice. I decided that I could best emulate her by also wearing that striped tie daily with my school uniform. For that entire year, I woke up a little bit early each morning to have my father put my tie in a neat knot for me. He never questioned if I was gay or trans, as I had convinced him otherwise.

When I was seventeen, I began to explore my sexuality. This consisted mostly of getting intoxicated with my friends and experimenting with my girlfriends. My younger brother caught wind of this and tattled to my elder sister. I told her that I was bisexual, and after looking at me in pure disgust and contempt, she made me promise that I only liked girls and didn't want to "be a boy". I lied and promised her that I wasn't a boy, just... queer. For years following, she bullied me and constantly attempted to get my brother to mock me for my sexuality and queerness.

Upon graduation, I was accepted into college in Los Angeles and could not leave San Diego fast enough. I had to get out of my hometown. I had big dreams of carving out a better life for myself and took this opportunity to truly find myself. It was around this time that an acquaintance from high school came out as trans. He and I became quite close, and he found a mentor in a slightly older trans guy who took him under his wing. Even then, I vehemently denied being trans myself; I was just open-minded in my eyes, and didn't judge others for their gender identity. But the cracks in my egg were forming on the surface, and it was only a matter of time before my trans identity burst out of my shell.

The final instance of my transness appearing before I came out was when I went in for a haircut at my father's behest. He offered to pay for it because he thought it would help me find a job as I was unemployed at the time and had little luck in my job search. On a whim, I had the stylist sheer off most of my long locks, and I was extremely happy with the results. When my dad returned to the salon to pay for it, he became incensed and verbally berated the hairstylist for cutting my hair so short, as if he had done the cut without my consent. I was embarrassed, of course, and quickly ushered my dad out of the salon before he could get even more aggressive and had the police called on him.

I never forgot the day I was denied the right to play with the rest of the little boys; that day is seared in my memory forever. I finally came out as trans at 25 but, looking back, the signs were always there. I wanted to be "one of the boys" because I was a boy all along. Now at 31, I try my best to nurture and care for my inner child daily. I also see a therapist once a week, which helps give me the tools I need to better my mental health. I definitely have some trauma from all that I've been through in coming to terms with who I am. I'm forever a work in progress, but I can honestly say I've never been happier.

RACISM IS A PUBLIC HEALTH CRISIS

TRANSPHOBIA KILLS

29

- Charlie Chowdhry -

HOW WRITING HELPED ME
COME TO TERMS WITH MY GENDER IDENTITY

When I was first starting to write my book, I had a choice to make: do I write in first person or third person? I'd mostly done first person stuff before this point (save for the odd short story for school in which I had to write in different styles). Did I want to challenge myself or stick to a style with which I knew I would feel comfortable? I ultimately decided to stick with the first person narrative.

Then I had the idea of making a different character narrate each chapter. This would give the personal touch that first person adds to the story while having the third person's general overall perspective. I was rather proud of myself for that idea.

I had a couple of stock characters in mind. The story is set in a small Scottish high school (a detail that gives the story its title), so the narrators are all sixteen or seventeen years old. I had Frank, the incredibly chaotic and hilarious pansexual disaster. I had Charlotte, the uptight but fiercely protective mum friend. Then I had Olly, a painfully shy boy who is slowly learning how to trust others.

The other two seemed pretty believable by themselves; Frank's personality tracks logically from the backstory I came up with, while Charlotte's narration and descriptions in the book are detailed enough to render her into a 3D character. I had trouble with Olly, though. No matter how many different backstories I tried, I could write nothing that could adequately explain how he ended up so reserved and fearful of others. I struggled to explain why he was scared of anyone other than his two best friends, and I furthermore couldn't justify the strained but still loving relationship he has with his mother. Then, it hit me; Olly is trans, but I didn't realize it when I was first creating his character.

I knew I wanted my book to be diverse, but I wasn't sure how I felt narrating as a trans character when my own gender identity was, at that time, unclear. I had been see-sawing between 'genderfluid' and 'trans' for the months leading up to the start of my book project and felt it would have been irresponsible to narrate a trans character with a gender identity different from my own. Because I was so uncertain of my own gender identity, I was terrified of being misleading, particularly to a person unfamiliar with the trans experience. At one point or another, I decided, "fuck it, it probably won't get published anyway," and I just started to write. To face my apprehension head-on, I made Olly the narrator of the first chapter of the book.

The book starts off with a surreal sequence in which Olly is trapped in a hallway reminiscent of a hospital's while being pursued by grotesque figures. In a feat of 16-year old genius, I made the dream mean something in accordance to a 'dream meanings' website I came across on search, and the main features of the dream represent everything Olly is going through at that present moment. If you're curious, look for a hospital setting and being chased in a dream individually and thread the two together.

I realized later, reading over the chapters narrated by Olly, that I was projecting an, albeit shyer, version of myself onto Olly. And, in a funny way, Olly was being projected back onto me. As I lead Olly through his troubles, helping him face his fears and becoming more confident, I realized that I was doing the very same for myself. Olly became less isolated by allowing his friends to help him, and I, in turn, did the same.

There's a silly scene in which Olly's friends pretend they're on "Queer Eye" and give Olly a makeover (featuring an argument over who gets to be Jonathan Van Ness), and that marks a turning point for Olly's mentality. He realizes that his friends aren't reluctantly accepting that he's no longer presenting as a girl, as Olly had first thought – rather, they've flung themselves headfirst into loving and accepting him as the young man he truly is. When I found the group of friends I'm currently a part of, I experienced the same feeling of a burden lifted from my mind. I had nothing to prove to these beautiful people, just as Olly had nothing to prove to his friends.

I often tell my friends that when I'm writing, sometimes the characters write themselves. I'm sure other writers will experience a similar thing – a character will do something different than what you planned, and somehow it fits better than what you intended anyway. I felt that profoundly when I was writing Olly. It was apparent because I was writing in the first person. The thing that struck me was that we still went through many of the same things despite me and Olly being very different people.

Writing increased my empathy; I had to get into people's heads utterly opposite to myself to write effectively. As a result, my personality became healthier. I realized through my different characters that I am not unique or better because I'm different.

The most important thing that happened to me because of my writing was that I realized that I am not doomed to darkness and rejection because I'm transgender.

Suffering does not define transgender people. Some of us may have to face being outed, crippling dysphoria, hatred, and rejection throughout our lives, but just like any good story, our lives, too, have happy moments. We dream of being writers, actors, scientists, musicians, parents, painters, doctors, and dancers. We pretend we're on "Queer Eye" with our friends and laugh until our ribs hurt. We are braver than the most courageous knights and wiser than the most enlightened scholars. We love with our whole hearts so much that we feel we could burst.

I hope that if future readers of my book take one thing away, it's that Olly is not a tragic figure haunted by his life before his transition and constantly plagued with suffering. Instead, I hope they see that Olly is a teenager with loads of potential. All of the kids in the book, and even the horrible ones, have the opportunity to grow; it's just a matter of whether or not they choose to take the chance. I hope that I don't come across as a bit odd for saying that I'm proud of Olly for everything he achieves in the book, but I genuinely feel a sense of pride while rereading what he does and how he succeeds. Olly does that; I did that; trans people all over the world did and continue to do that. They blossomed and flourished despite the adversity.

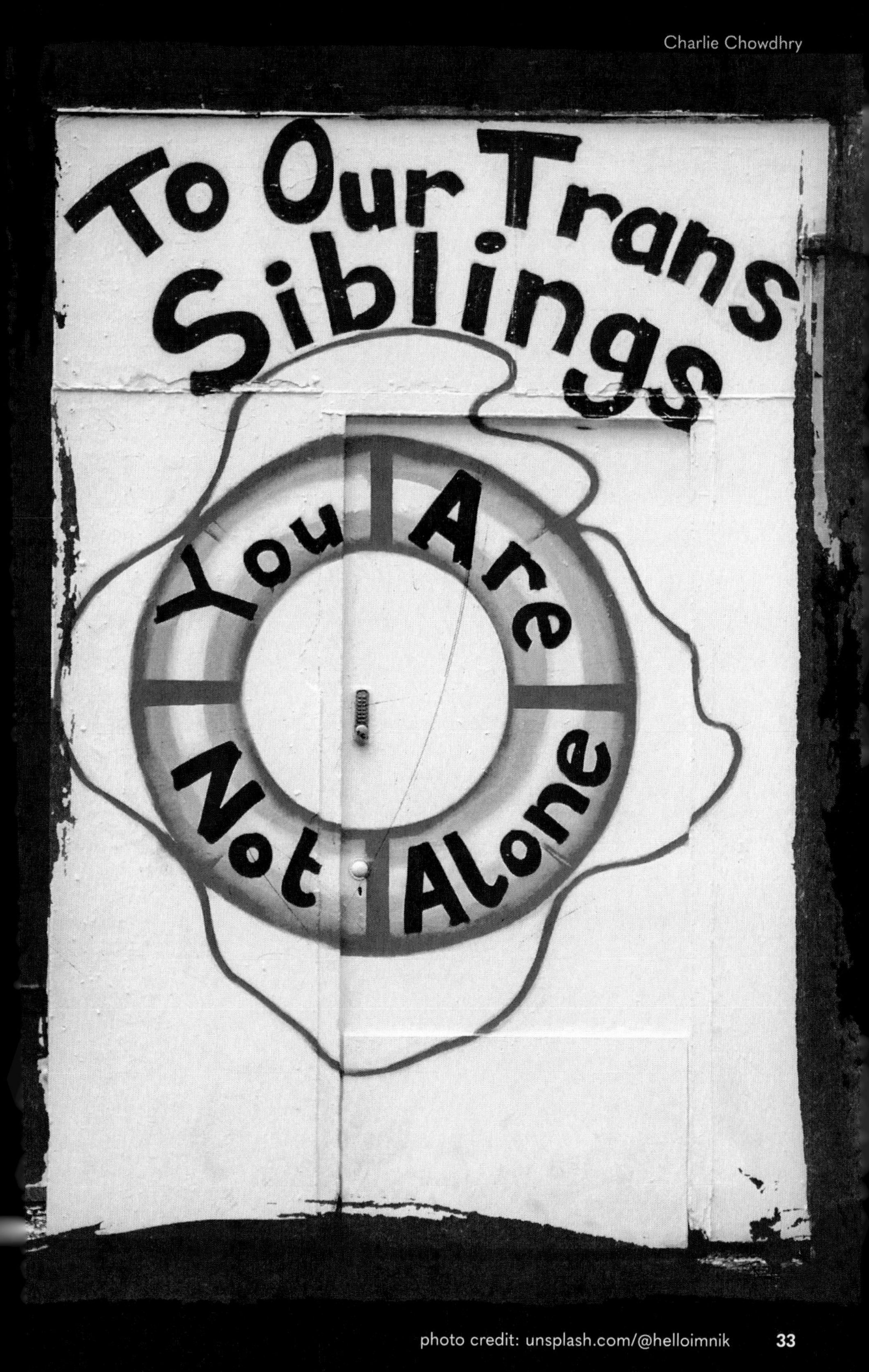

photo credit: unsplash.com/@helloimnik

- TransFocus Editors -

WHAT IS GENDER DYSPHORIA?

Content Notice: Addiction; Mention of Ideation, Self-Mutilation

Dysphoria is a word that you will see repeated a lot through this book's text because of how many trans people experience it. The simplest definition is that dysphoria is a strong feeling of incongruence and discomfort with one's assigned gender. The American Psychiatric Association defines dysphoria as "psychological distress that results from an incongruence between one's sex assigned at birth and one's gender identity." In reality, a straightforward definition of dysphoria is harder to pin down.

Each trans person who experiences it defines dysphoria differently. For some, it may be discomfort and anxiety that stems from their bodies not aligning with how they perceive themselves. Topics that often come up in trans circles are bodily dysphoria, which can be specific to genitalia, breasts, chest, face, hips, or other parts of the body with features that can strongly align with a particular sex or gender.

For instance, many trans men experience chest dysphoria and bind their breasts to form a more masculine appearance to the chest, and, likewise, many trans women wear fillers in their bras. Many trans women also tuck their genitals or wear tucking panties to smooth out the pubic region, and many trans men place what are called packers, which most commonly come in the form of silicon phalluses, in their underwear to create the appearance of a pubic bulge.

Nonbinary people can also experience dysphoria in any direction, with those assigned female at birth (AFAB) often binding their chests or packing as well. Many nonbinary people assigned male at birth (AMAB) similarly tuck their genitals and pad their bras like many trans women. Conversely, many trans people do not experience dysphoria but rather experience euphoria when presenting as their actual genders. Furthermore, many trans men and AFAB nonbinary folks experience dysphoria when they have their period or abdominal cramps. Trans women and AMAB nonbinary folks, conversely, can experience dysphoria due to their inability to carry a child.

In the absence of dysphoria, there is a heated (and frequently myopic) debate in the trans community regarding whether or not those folks are truly transgender. This debate pits those with gender dysphoria against those without, and effectively defines folks dysphoria as "transier than thou." This attitude is called transmedicalism and it is, to be blunt, a gross form of gatekeeping other peoples' trans identities.

Many without dysphoria question whether they are trans enough due to these attitudes, a common concern enflamed by trans people who do believe that you have to desire medical transition to be trans. But, the fact is, being trans is more than just dysphoria. Being trans is merely a state of being that means we do not align with our genders assigned at birth. Dysphoria often accompanies that state of being, but it is by no means a prerequisite for being or identifying as trans. Anybody who insists otherwise is woefully misguided and pits their dysphoric pain against others whose pain is nonexistent or less acute. The trans experience is not defined by pain. The trans experience is defined by being trans.

Gender Dysphoria is an expansive issue and generally means that one experiences discomfort with some combination of our secondary sex characteristics, deadnames, defunct pronouns, or being socialized in a manner inconsistent with our gender identity, but not experiencing dysphoria in this way is not the be-all end-all of being trans. Yes, it can certainly refer to our bodies, but it can also refer to the discomfort we experience when wearing clothes that do not fit our gender expression or when being forced into gendered activities, or divided arbitrarily along gender lines. Many trans people express their first encounter with dysphoria as when they entered school and were made to line up with either the boys or girls, then being "corrected" for choosing the "wrong" line in that common scenario. Many, if not most, trans people are forced to wear the clothes most commonly associated with their gender assigned at birth for years before identifying their transness, and end up feeling a tremendous sense of relief when they can finally wear the clothing of their choosing.

Dysphoria can similarly refer to the feeling of moving through the world as visibly trans, and can be induced by being misgendered, deadnamed, or even stared at or attacked in public for appearing as we are. When this occurs, the dysphoria that we experience is due to being treated in a way that strongly differs from how we see and experience ourselves, or generally being mistreated for being trans.

Similar to many binary trans people, many nonbinary folks experience dysphoria when made to choose between male and female activities. In grade school, many nonbinary children experience extreme discomfort when having to line up behind boys or girls despite feeling like neither (or both), and, like binary trans folks, are often told they are wrong when getting into one line or the other. Having to choose at all can be a dysphoric experience for many and highlights just how overlooked nonbinary people are in our culture. The erasure of nonbinaryness is pervasive and insidious and, as one author in this book says, "leaves one wondering which box (between male and female) [they'll] have to tick today."

Dysphoria is an extraordinarily complicated subject. It's a diverse and varied experience, and no two trans people experience dysphoria in exactly the same way. What causes dysphoria to one may not cause dysphoria to another. Not all trans people hate their breasts or chests, and not all trans people hate their genitals, regardless of whether they're binary or nonbinary trans. Not all trans people want surgery or hormone replacement therapy, just as not all trans people identify with "being born in the wrong body." We are a diverse, expansive, and beautiful community, and we share as much in common with each other as any marginalized group. The one thing that truly unites us under the trans umbrella is that each one of us experiences gender in a different way than we were expected to through a predominately cisgender culture's lens.

With all of that said, most trans people do experience dysphoria in one way or another, and in varying degrees of severity. Dysphoria for one person might incite suicidal ideation, or even the desire to self-mutilate, but for another might be a sense of extreme discomfort that they have no drive to act upon. For those who experience dysphoria on the severe end, many will be driven to medically transition, which can take the form of surgery upon the genital region, top surgery in the form of mastectomy, breast reduction surgery, or breast augmentation/implants, facial feminization or masculinization surgeries, body contouring, facial electrolysis, bodily hair transplants, vocal training, or other procedures one may take toward acheiving their transition goals. For most who do undergo medical transition, their dysphoria is alleviated or at least mitigated by medical intervention.

Perhaps the most common procedure most trans people undertake is hormone replacement therapy (HRT), which for transmasculine and AFAB nonbinary people involves replacement of estrogen by use of testosterone shots, dermal patches, or dermally-applied gels, and for transfeminine and AMAB nonbinary people involves suppression of testosterone and introduction of estrogens by means of estrogen shots, dermal patches, dermally-applied gels, progresterone, as well as antiandrogens like spironolactone. Even so, not all trans people wish to undergo HRT, either for personal or medical reasons, or because they do not wish to experience the side effect that hormone therapy causes.

However, some trans people experience lessened dysphoria by dressing in a manner consistent with their gender identity, socially transitioning, or changing their name and pronouns, and ultimately find that they do not want or require medical intervention. There is truly no singular path toward alleviating dysphoria, and every path under the trans umbrella is valid.

So really, there is no clean and easy definition here. Dysphoria is whatever an individual trans person says it is or is not for them personally, and while a great many of us experience dysphoria, not all of us do; it by no means defines or exemplifies what it means to be a human being experiencing and living life as a trans person. Dysphoria is merely a symptom of gender incongruence that many trans people experience, and is simply the diagnosis that accompanies trans-affirming medical intervention when it is covered through health insurance. Which is to say, it is a utility—not a box into which a trans person must be shoved for validation.

- Dr. Natalia Z. PhD & Zoey Sanford -

UNPACKING DYSPHORIA

- WITH DR. Z. PH.D. -

Dr. Z Ph.D. is a clinical psychologist based out of Los Engles known for her no-BS approach to trans healthcare and advocacy. The following discussion was facilitated by Zoey Sanford, a trans woman based out of Los Angeles and one of the founding members of TransKind Los Angeles. In this chat, we discuss attitudes around gender dysphoria and how the medical system often fails trans people in accessing the most basic gender-affirming care.

Zoey: Thank you for joining us today. I wanted to start this discussion by getting a little bit of background from you. I know you focus solely on transgender care. What made you decide to make that the focus of your career?

Dr. Z: I've always had this kind of intensity to fight for the underdog, even from when I was a child. This inner drive led me to work with individuals who are largely marginalized in the community, and it was 14 years ago when I had my first trans-identified client while seeking my master practicum. That got me passionate and excited about working with this community. Especially with the combination of my passion and background, it felt like a perfect fit.

Zoey: Got it, 14 years ago. So you've really seen the community change and evolve so much from a time when it was a lot more about being stealth and hiding in plain sight, to now where things are way more open and accepting, and we have people living their truths and being far more visible.

Dr. Z: Yeah, and what's interesting is I started off in Portland, Oregon, and migrated to the Los Angeles area about six to seven years ago, so I've also been exposed to different kinds of demographics and different areas of the gender-diverse communities. It's been fascinating to witness various shifts in other areas of the country.

Zoey: What would you say some of those differences might be?

Dr. Z: I think the differences are pretty subtle. Both Portland and Los Angeles are relatively liberal in providing equal levels of access to both medical and psychological services to the gender-diverse community. Probably the main difference would be how inclusive or exclusive a community is, and I would say, Los Angeles, in my experience, has to be a broader and much bigger community than Portland.

Zoey: Interesting. Considering that both are very liberal-leaning and way more open and progressive on views, I find it interesting that there is much of a difference. How have you seen the medical community change and evolve around your time since you've started helping the trans community?

Dr. Z: I would say the medical community has really taken off and probably hit what I would call a tipping point in the last two years. I think for the past 20-30 years, you've had doctors who worked with the gender-diverse community, but it wasn't until about two years ago when you started seeing big, major institutions providing access to gender-affirming care. For example, in Los Angeles, we have Cedars Sinai and UCLA hospitals shifting toward informed gender-affirming care. Now we're seeing the big shift and movement toward providing much more medical access to the community.

Zoey: Right. Kaiser's trying to be at the forefront in SoCal and NorCal as a provider to offer gender-affirming surgeries for all different types - transmasc, transfemme, nonbinary. They are doing so many great things, and it's wonderful seeing the scope of trans healthcare change and evolve. How has it changed and evolved for you, specifically as a psychologist?

Dr. Z: It has evolved quite a bit because I see far more care providers who provide psychological services to the gender-diverse community. My challenge with mental health providers providing access is that people are still not educated enough in this field, and that's personally an issue I have with mental health professionals in general; whether you provide to the gender diverse community or any other, not specializing in these areas is unfortunately common. I think that creates many problems for the gender-diverse community when you have somebody who says they're an LGBT-Friendly therapist who is not specialized, and patients spend six months to a year of getting inadequate therapy before finally being referred to hormones. And I think, unfortunately, that prolongs the suffering of people living with gender dysphoria.

Zoey: Yeah, I experienced something like that as well. My gender dysphoria became really intense and dark for me, and it became almost a thing of life or death. I just found the first person in insurance whose profile said "gender issues" in West Hollywood, which is an LGBTQ mecca for those who don't know, and he'd never had a trans patient before. So he was learning as we went along, just as I was learning, and it was interesting because I did like that he was able to help with other things I was experiencing. Issues of gender identity, gender dysphoria, and gender euphoria are things that do require a specialty to treat. Fortunately, I got into the Los Angeles LGBT Center, which helped me get paired up with someone who only handles trans clients, and that was a big help. So yeah, I do agree with that.

Rori: I think most trans people who have sought mental health treatment have some kind of experience getting into therapy with someone who just wasn't all that prepared to deal with a trans client, or a care provider who wasn't as well versed in trans care as stated on their website. "Handles LGBT issues" is often something that gets tacked onto someone's list, even if it's not entirely true. My first experience getting into therapy was with someone who didn't understand what nonbinary or trans was in any specific way even though she listed it on her website, and that was something I found to be highly frustrating at $200 an hour, particularly when I was uninsured and paying out of pocket. I was trying to find a specialist who could help me navigate what I needed to do and found myself in a room with someone I had to do a lot of emotional labor with.

Dr. Z: It is an issue of absolutely not having specialists in mental healthcare. In my opinion, gender dysphoria is a medical condition, not a psychological condition, however often it is treated as such. Now, the symptoms people have over gender dysphoria or incongruence they are physically experiencing are certainly psychological in nature - depression, anxiety, suicidality, hopelessness, etc. However, the condition itself is medical, so the biggest challenge is people not having access to medical care because once you take care of the medical part, the symptoms tend to go away or subside. So while seeing a therapist is of great importance and can be very helpful for many, I don't think it's necessary for all gender-diverse people. It's gatekeeping, in other words, and it becomes a huge issue.

While sometimes, seeing a specialist can also be a challenge because specialists, like me, don't take insurance, and, as a psychologist, I charge the rate of psychologists, so I'm unfortunately not accessible to everybody. But I think it's essential to put the information out there. Getting on hormones in California, for example, requires a therapist letter, as well as to initiate any kind of surgical intervention. So I encourage people in very real ways to contact people who specialize because all of us who specialize are always very open to sharing that information freely.

So while you may not always be able to see us, we share that information, refer you to the right people, educate you, and don't have to see us for six months to a year if you do need hormones. This is the biggest impediment of the trans or gender diverse community that we put all of these kinds of roadblocks in place. And that all starts way back from when we had gender dysphoria categorized as "gender identity disorder" in the DSM, so when you look at it, you see the difference, right? Gender identity disorder, which sheds light on it as a psychological issue, versus Gender Dysphoria, which focuses more on symptomology.

Rori: Right. Something that reminds me of is that we're finding that a lot of what we're seeking is not well populated with information when we access these services. You mentioned that your pricing can be inaccessible for many people, but something you do that most other psychologists do not is maintaining your social presence and a blog through which you deliver information to people at no cost to which we otherwise wouldn't have access.

In fact, through your blog, I learned about the dangers of Spironolactone, which is an antiandrogen/testosterone-suppressant that doctors commonly prescribe to trans women and other AMAB trans folks. Your blog enabled me to carry some of that knowledge, research the topic further, and then bring that information to my doctor, who honestly was relatively uneducated about the dangers of spiro and some of the more recent studies on the drug. I think that's where informal care like yours, which provides a free service and hosts an informational blog, is something that the trans community has limited access to but is extremely valuable when we can find it.

Dr. Z: I appreciate that, but I think we're going back to ethics, right? Ethics in all professions, and for me, are such that if I am accessible to particular populations, but I am inaccessible to another segment of the population, I must ask myself how I can still provide value to the community. I think that is ethically important for all of us, whether you're a medical health provider, mental health practitioner, or anybody else serving the gender-diverse community. That is exactly how I tend to do it with my blog, YouTube channels, and newsletters. But I think one of the best that I can ever offer to the trans community, which is one of the biggest impediments for them, is to do free letter writeups for any gender-related surgery.

I think that's one of the biggest blocks and provides quite a challenge. I get people for those evaluation letters who say they see someone like a gender therapist but cannot provide letters. I find that incredibly frustrating. But also, it's an issue of mental health providers who've not taken crucial steps in educating themselves. At the very minimum, they need to write these letters, but all providers should provide that at a minimum. So part of that code of ethics for me is helping other medical providers write letters, and I provide templates and answer questions to help make my colleagues more aware and competent in trans care.

Zoey: I know of so many trans folks who have their doctor or therapist write a letter, and then get denied by insurance because it didn't properly state everything. You wrote me a letter for FFS (facial feminization surgery), which my insurance had as an exclusive, but they ended up approving it. I don't know if that's because I had letters from you and my doctor. However, yours went into the nuts and bolts of why this is why the diagnosis is official and necessary. I think it would undoubtedly be beneficial for other psychologists to have that template because it seems to be what is needed for these insurances that make the easy denial when the critical info isn't there.

Dr. Z: I'm all for sharing resources, and I'll consult with my colleagues for free, and I won't charge them, with the stipulation that they become competent working for this community. The reality and challenges are that people don't often reach out. I experienced this firsthand when I had someone looking for help to understand the letter writing process, and I offered to share the template and support them in the process, but they took the template and never followed up. This is just a reality that exists today, unfortunately, and hopefully, the more we talk about this issue and take it to the forefront, people will realize that there is a problem, and we can take tangible steps toward solutions.

Zoey: However ethically questionable, I do get why the insurance companies want to deny us. They want to deny everything possible because the more stuff they approve, the less profitable we are to them. So they look for any reason they can to deny, and that's why when they read your letters, there's no way they can look at it and deny the necessity of care. You write letters in great detail, for which I'm eternally grateful. You're out there, helping other providers get educated—you and Dr. Will Powers out of Michigan.

Ultimately, we have to be our own best advocates; especially when you're in an area like Rori mentioned, when dealing with a doctor whose never been with a trans client before, to know these are the steps we need to take, these are the risks, these are the problems. In California, we are lucky to have providers operating under informed consent, and in some places, you can get same-day hormone therapy. What other ways do you see how the psychology side of trans care can change for the better?

Dr. Z: From the medical community, I would personally like to see more endocrinologists be knowledgeable about hormone treatment, who do their footwork in understanding, and start moving away from this arcane prescriptive model of spiro and estradiol, and start exploring other options that are out there. Same with surgeons - I want to see more surgeons specializing in transgender care who go and get adequate training and are, more importantly, transparent about how much work or how little work they have done to work with trans individuals. I would love to see that very much. There's nothing wrong with starting out. When I started, I made mistakes with pronouns and understanding the unique needs of gender-diverse clients, and I'm still educating myself constantly because things are always evolving and changing. As I am specializing only in this, I see it as my responsibility to continually educate myself. But there are people, like Aiden Olsen Kennedy of the L.A. Gender Center, who, by the way, also does letter writing and is incredibly knowledgeable. So we are out there, we exist, and we are always open to share and communicate.

Recently I had a firefighter supervisor email me and say, "I have someone in my workforce who is transitioning from female to male, and I just wanted to get a basic understanding so I can serve them the best I can." And I just consulted with them today, and I just thought, how great this person who is making an effort to look up a gender specialist, reach out, and set up a phone call. We had a great discussion. Imagine how much better informed that person is today to help that person transitioning in the workplace.

I think that's a very basic step that all of us can take, and it's not just medical providers. Employers need to educate themselves and parents, siblings, friends, extended family members, and teachers—anybody who has a trans person in their life, really. Which is to say, all of us.

Zoey: That's the key that it all comes down to—education. There's so much diversity in the community, and I've learned a lot as a binary trans woman. But I love being around the community and learning so much more. I've gotten pronouns wrong too, but it's learning and growing and changing as you know more.

Rori: To that point, Los Angeles is indeed a trans hub; this is kind of the place for us— the city to move to and get proper care and procedures that maybe aren't being done correctly in other areas or perhaps aren't accessible at all. Los Angeles is this shining beacon of the accessibility of these amazing services juxtaposed against the extreme inaccessibility of services from where many of us came. I was raised in the midwest and never saw myself moving to a major city until it became vital for me to get out of Ohio to find a place where I could safely transition and be myself. Los Angeles was that for me. I think there's something to be said for the fact that, in seeking internal and external congruence, many of us find ourselves living in abject poverty. So, some of this access comes alongside inaccessibility for many people. Even being adjacent to proper trans care is better for the majority of us than living in those communities where we get spotty care can't get any trans-affirming care at all. So, I want to thank you, Dr. Z, for the access you provide and the information you give out free of charge.

I also want to round back to the L.A. Gender Center, which has been a significant resource to my life since beginning my transition-related care. They are currently helping me fill out my paperwork for my legal name change, which is more difficult and complicated than I ever imagined it would be. It's just kind of a bittersweet note to say yes, these services are exceptional, and the access to care I've had since moving here is comparatively stellar, but I'm also watching my friends back home who can't seek any of these medically necessary procedures and services. I guess what I'm getting to is that there can be a kind of survivor's guilt in having this much access, which I want to be looking it as, "Everybody deserves this level of care, and thank God I have it." Well. It's complicated.

Dr. Z: Even though L.A. is very progressive in many ways, in other ways, it's not so progressive. In the medical community, we have plastic surgeons who are like old dinosaurs who do the same old same old, and then we have some who are doing great work and advancing the field. But even though it's still very progressive, it's also not.

To this day, I have people contacting me for therapy, and I have to clarify that I realize it's not therapy they're seeking; they wanted permission for hormones. There are a bulk of people who are unaware that you don't technically need a letter from a therapist to start hormones, and that's a big problem. This information is somehow not fully accessible, and there are people in other parts of the country who couldn't get any help whatsoever.

The biggest issue here is not so much access to psychological care, which, again, is very important, but let's note that once people start medically transitioning and their body starts to become congruent with how they identify, what happens? People stop seeking psychological services. I see this time and time again. Most if not all of my clients who have reached physical congruence no longer see me and no longer need to unless something specific is going on in their lives. Other than that, all of their symptoms of gender dysphoria tend to go away or become very manageable and minimal.

So, the issue is that dysphoria is a medical condition, and it needs to be recognized as such because the gatekeeping of services is becoming a bit injudicious, to be honest. So, for example, when people come to me, many are already on hormones, so they've been on hormones for one or two years, and now they need a letter for FFS/FMS, any kind of bottom surgery, and here's the foolish part: These people have already been diagnosed with gender dysphoria through their medical doctor, who has prescribed them hormones. To put someone on hormones, you have to place a medical diagnosis, so you already carry a diagnosis, but now need to have a psychological office confirm, even though you have a medical diagnosis. What is unfortunately happening is that we need to verify that you're not "delusional," which is a horrible practice.

This would be like if you went to a doctor to get a medical diagnosis of cancer, and then they say, "before we give you full surgical treatment for your cancer, first go to a psychologist to confirm that you truly do have cancer." So this is the silliness and gatekeeping in the system that I think is a problem. I think that gender dysphoria needs to be in the DSM, but it also needs to be much more recognized that it's not a psychological issue; we are only dealing with its symptomology. People should not have to come to my office for evaluation; they should have autonomy over their body, and it's medical doctors who should be making decisions about surgical necessity, sending out any letters, and they should be referring people to surgeries in the same way that they refer people to therapy treatment.

Zoey: I think that would be a great help to the community because for one surgery, I had to get a set of letters, and for the subsequent surgery, another, and then another set of letters for the next. My insurance has these from the previous surgeries; why do they need to make me jump through hoops again? They gatekeep and put up roadblocks for us to give up and say "well, I guess it's just not meant to be." But then you sit there and live in that dysphoria and just get stuck in that mental health loop, when they know that it helps most dysphoric people with their dysphoria. Not all, of course, because there can be some issues with dysphoria and dysmorphia persisting after gender-affirming care, but I can tell you that I've had I feel so much better and congruent with my body with each surgery I've had. Every time, I need to take the next step now, and I have to jump through all these hoops, all this yellow tape, and as you said, it's a medical issue. Why couldn't just my doctor say this? Why did I need you, my doctor, AND a therapist to confirm that I'm trans and have dysphoria? Hopefully, it will be a thing that happens less and less over time, as more insurance plans come on board and more and more procedures are covered.

In time, they should see how much less we're paying in mental healthcare when dysphoria is properly treated. Thousands of hours of therapy vs. a medical procedure are bound to be comparable in cost. The chances are that what surgery costs vs. multiple 72-hour 51/50 holds in a mental facility are also comparable. That's where I was as a teenager because I didn't have ways of handling this. Insurance companies have to make a choice between preventative care that treats symptoms and medical care that treats the root causes of dysphoria. So yeah, it will be interesting to see how this changes and evolves over time.

Dr. Z: The medical and psychological barriers are a big problem. I can understand the doctor sending someone to my office when it's questionable that they can consent to surgical procedures, such as when that person is distraught. But, even then, this one of the biggest issues, and I agree with you Zoey, 100%. Before any kind of surgical intervention, you have to already be in some kind of medical system receiving treatment. Most gender-affirming care should fall under the scope of care of that medical treatment as a requirement, and there should be absolutely no need to get another letter each time you need a gender-affirming surgery.

It just becomes so very frustrating, redundant, and an unnecessary expense, both in terms of finances and time spent, and it just doesn't serve anybody and exhausts the systems we currently have in place. I'm one of the few psychologists I know in Los Angeles who provides letters like this; as with bottom surgery, one of the letters has to come from a Ph.D., which becomes a problem. I see about 5-7 people a week.

Right now, I can afford to give away the time, but soon I will not be able to give away 5-7 hours a week to write letters. I'll still be doing letters for the rest of my career, but it saddens and frustrates me that people need them.

Rori: You know, that's interesting because, in the trans groups at the L.A. LGBT Center, there's recently been a bit of constricting of those appointments, going from weekly down to biweekly. The facilitators are the only people at the center doing trans letter writing. In the lack of access and people we have on the ground doing this work, we see other services taken away or limited because letter writing is so important and mandatory to get these things done. It's messing with other services we access.

And now letter-writing is taking such a large amount of your time that you have to consider doing less of it. It's a shame for our community that these letters are as necessary as they are when, like you were saying, it's just gatekeeping and another barrier to care, when as adults, we should be able to consent to anything we want.

Cis people don't have quite the same issues as getting surgical procedures done as trans people. Nobody gatekeeps cis women when they want facial surgery or breast augmentation or body contouring or fillers. Nobody gatekeeps cis men when they want a more angular jawline or, body masculinization or ab/pectoral implants. But when trans people wish to have these procedures as a means of saving us from the often extreme emotional distress that dysphoria causes, the medical community is suddenly concerned for our mental health and questions our agency and autonomy to consent to gender-affirming medical care. It's exasperating how infantilizing these practices are.

Dr. Z: Right, it comes back to insurance. I believe we should have autonomy over our bodies, but it comes down to what is cosmetic and not cosmetic. I very much like for medical doctors to make that decision. If you're on hormones or not but are seeing a medical provider overseeing your care, and if you fall in the gender dysphoria category, those medical providers should be able to make that referral, and that should be enough.

You shouldn't have to be jumping through all these hoops that cis people put in place. It's completely unnecessary, and it's a waste of my personal time, and it's a waste of patients' time. All of this prolongs dysphoria, and time is suffering. People who live with gender dysphoria are struggling, and a lot of times, a simple surgery can incredibly alleviate a lot of the symptoms. It's ridiculous that we're preventing people from getting essential medical procedures, and I hope that one day it'll go away, but who knows. It's just one of those silly bureaucratic things.

Ultimately, it's about marginalized communities becoming nonmarginalized, and I think there is a real fear of the world being overtaken by gender diversity, however ridiculous as that sounds.

Zoey: I know you have a list of surgeons on your website that you feel are qualified, and that's another resource because many people don't know where to start their search. I started digging into all of this mid-2000s. It's helpful to find professional thoughts from someone like you who works with us and sees the good and the bad in different surgeons, so I appreciate you putting that out there for people as another free resource.

Dr. Z: Yeah, I think it's absolutely important, and the gender-diverse community has vetted everybody that I have on my resource page. In fact, I had to remove one of the surgeons recently because I kept hearing terrible things from people. We need more resource pages like mine because it's primarily focused on California, and while I try to update it, we need more regional resources like this, about who is a gender doctor, or at least gender-friendly.

Using the WPath.org organization, you can search by provider. It's an option where you can look up a provider in your area, which is very, very helpful because chances are if someone has a listing on WPath, and they're paying that membership fee, and chances are they are in one way or another invested in working with the gender diverse community and not enough people know about that resource.

Zoey: As far as WPath goes, do you feel they are doing anything wrong that you think should change, or do you think they're doing things pretty right, or as best they can with the knowledge at hand? In the community, we often acknowledge that most trans people have a love-hate relationship with WPath, given some of their more arbitrary guidelines for trans-affirming care and how that's led to some gatekeeping by medical professionals.

Dr. Z: It's hard to say what standards of care they will put in there. Honestly, I don't get involved or pay much attention to WPath, partially because they don't dictate standards of care. They provide guidelines, like needing to be on hormones for a year, but none of these are set in stone. People are different, their transitions look very different, and no case is alike. For that reason, I don't do much aside from supporting them with my membership, but I cannot say that they are substantial to me and my practice. Personally, what's most important to me is staying as informed as I can about who is discovering something new, especially about medical services offered to the community, and especially about doctors offering new procedures, like Heidi Wittenberg.

Zoey: Going off Heidi Wittenberg, it's impressive that she's also working on surgeries for nonbinary people, gender non-conforming, and genital surgeries for that too, and I'm glad that things are evolving and people are providing those things for the community.

Dr. Z: Ultimately, information is power. It's important to push forward and to hopefully get gender dysphoria to be a medicalized condition and take it out of the therapy office so the therapist can focus on the symptoms of dysphoria. And hopefully we can get there. I really do think gatekeeping has been one of the biggest impediments that still exists to this day in many parts of the country. Even in Los Angeles, Blue Cross Blue Shield pretty much the only insurance I know of that will request two letters for top surgery even though guidelines only require one. A lot of people don't know this, and it's unfortunate, but I can't tell you how many individuals, especially trans-identified guys who would contact me, get a letter from me and have surgeries scheduled only to have it canceled because Blue Cross Blue Shield tells them they now need a second letter for that procedure, and it's just ridiculous. Insurance companies are starting to create their own specific criteria, and that's extremely sad. Insurance companies can go as far as requesting photos of patients to see if they really need masculinization or feminization, and that's a dangerous kind of gatekeeping.

Rori: That's interesting. I just recently got off of Blue Shield insurance because I couldn't get anywhere and had arguments with them because they were not covering electrolysis, but they would cover laser. I kept telling them that one of the procedures that they would cover required electrolysis, not laser hair removal. So electrolysis is what I needed, but they just wouldn't cover it, so I fought with them for a year before putting my hands up and accepting that I had given them $600 a month for no trans-specific care, and now I'm with MediCal which is excellent, but my experience with that particular insurance was horrendous.

Dr. Z: Yeah. That falls back into letter writing, right? There have been times when insurance will deny procedures for people, and I will end up writing letters citing research that shows that not only is denying my client's right to access care a direct approval of psychological suffering, they are also putting the client under duress. Sometimes you have to go back and throw all of this medicalized jargon at insurance companies and their position shifts. I have some authority by having a doctorate degree, and I'm able to leverage this with many insurance companies, which affords me a privilege that enables me to push back.

Zoey: Going to Rori's point, I think that these insurance companies want to get us frustrated, so we give up because it saves them a lot of money. As you said, it causes a lot of duress and stress and makes everything harder for us. They don't want to do the preventative procedures to stop worse things that can happen down the line. I'm hopeful about what that you're doing. Hopefully, in time it'll become easier to access the medical care we need. So thank you very much.

Dr. Z: Hmm. The pleasure is all mine. I actually don't understand when people thank me for waking up and doing what I love to do, grateful and excited to do it. I don't think I'll ever quite understand when people thank me for doing what I consider necessary.

Rori: Well, I will instead say thank you for joining us because you joining us for this chat has been amazing. Part of why I wanted you involved in TransFocus is to give our audience hope that there are people out there who are taking care of us. So thanking you is not to say, "Well, it's time to pat the cis person who's helping us on the back," but more to say: Thank you, because you are doing work that other people aren't, and that shouldn't be rare, but it is. And that what you're doing for our community is highly appreciated.

Zoey: Very much so.

Dr. Z: I really appreciate that. I'll keep doing it until the day I drop dead or retire.

Zoey: Hopefully you'll retire first.

Dr. Z: No, no, I'm here, and my mission is to provide as many gender-confirming letters to people as I can.

Rori: Your website is DrZPHD.com. Is there anywhere else we should direct our readers?

Dr. Z: Everything is there. My website has all of the information they need, access to all of the blog posts, access to my resource page, and there's also a list of books. I just started writing a blog for family and partners. There are many really great research blogs for families, parents, and especially those dealing with trans children, understanding gender dysphoria, and recognizing it in your child. So it's all on my website, and again, everybody reading this, don't hesitate to reach out.

Zoey: Thanks again for joining us, Dr. Z!

- Alex Adams -

DISCOVERING ME

Growing up, I never felt like other girls who enjoyed dresses and make-up. Sure I played with dolls with my sister, but I grew bored of them quickly. There was also the disconnect from being female; it was like everyone was playing a trick on me by switching male and female before my birth. As a child, I truly believed this. I fully felt I was born a male, but everyone was pulling a cruel joke on me by making me think I was the wrong gender. As I grew up, I would try to accept the body into which I was born. However, every time I looked at myself, the disconnect I felt from my body grew more assertive. It simply wasn't mine, but I didn't know I could change my outsides to match my inside. Nobody told me that was an option. Then, like the opening of floodgates, I learned about transgender folks. At first, I did not know this was what I was. The more I learned about trans issues and how others found out they were transgender, the more I started to question myself and who I was as a person. Was I a male or something else? For a while, I did not care what gender people referred to me as. I wouldn't correct them if they thought I was a man from behind, even if my body from the front and name screamed that I was female.

In January 2019, I started to question my gender more deeply. I reached out to friends who were also trans men to ask how they figured out they were trans. After their advice and thinking long and hard about it, I concluded that I am a man and subsequently wanted to be called Alex. I was finally happy to know who I am, and I was ready to tell others.

The Call to Mother: It had been two days since I finally figured out I was a man, the knowledge of my truth weighing on my shoulders. I had told my partner and close friends, knowing that I wanted to be public; I wanted out of my closet. However, there was one person I wanted to tell before I came out to everybody else: my mother. I felt I owed her that. I planned to wait until I next saw her in person, but I knew that would be a while, and I wanted her to know before my mother-in-law came over later that day. So I had a choice to make – keep it hidden, or call my mother to tell her the news. My nerves had me shaking before I even pressed the call button. Would she be mad?

Would she hate me? I wasn't sure why I was so nervous, as she would always say; "As long as you're not hurting anyone, do what you want." Even with my mother's words in mind, the butterflies still fluttered in my stomach. With a deep breath inward, I pressed the call button, held the phone to my ear, and listened as the phone rang.

No answer.

I let out a deep breath I hadn't realized I'd been holding in. I never did like phone calls, even without the added stress of coming out as transgender. I quickly sent her a text asking her to call me back and impatiently watched my screen for the inevitable reply. A minute went by without an answer, and I tried again, wanting so badly to tell her the news of my discovery—this time using Facebook voice messenger.

She answered this time.

After greeting me with her usual 'What's up?' I replied.

"I have something important to tell you."

"What is it?" She asked. Her voice was laced with worry. I wondered if she thought I was hurt or in some sort of trouble.

"What would you say if I told you I was trans?" I asked, again holding my breath in anticipation. For the split second before she answered, I feared the worst.

"What's that? Is that where you want a change sex?"

I confirmed and went into a few more details, asking her in more concrete terms exactly how she felt about me now being her son.

"I don't know; what brought this on?" She asked. I quickly explained how I have never been feminine growing up, and I reintroduce myself as Alex. I ended the call by telling her she can tell others and that I love her – something I hardly do with blood relatives. With that finally out of the way, I went on with telling more people about myself, so they could know that I am no longer Antoinette and I would now be living life as the man I was always meant to be.

My name is Alex

- TransFocus Editors -

WHAT IS DEADNAMING?

Deadnaming is when, despite knowing a trans person's chosen name, their old or "dead" name is used. While not all trans people undergo a name change, many do, and it is of the utmost importance to respect and use their new name. Choosing a name is an essential step in the coming out process for many trans folks, and it can be jarring to have one use a name that we consider to be "dead."

Some trans folks rather dislike the term "deadname" because of the assumed implication that we are metaphorically killing our pre-transition selves. The reality is that "deadname" does not necessarily refer to the trans person symbolically dying and being rebirthed, but specifically to their name being effectively retired. The word "deadname" is used because it has a strong impact and drives home the importance of not using a trans person's old name. Deadnaming can cause severe emotional distress and dysphoria to the trans person in question, and the harshness of the word is a means of driving the point home. That said, some trans people absolutely *do* identify with their past, depressed, self-hating self metaphorically "dying" and being rebirthed as their true trans-affirmed selves. Ultimately, whether a trans person identifies with the term "deadname" is hugely up to the individual. Some people prefer the term "mis-named" or "birth-named" as an alternative to avoid the connotation with metaphorical death and rebirth.

It is an unfortunate truth that many cis people struggle to adapt to using trans peoples' new and affirmed names. Every trans person who changes their name experiences deadnaming with varying degrees of frequency and severity. Some of our families flat out refuse to use our names, citing things like, "But you're my baby, and I'll always think of you as *deadname*." Sometimes, our friends or relatives, particularly elders, try their best but frequently slip up due to lapses in memory.

It is an unfortunate reality that our families and friends who knew us before coming out and will never forget our deadnames, however much we wish they would, and adapting to a new name takes time and effort. But, with effort, practice, patience, and care, there will come a time when cis folks will see their loved one as whatever name they've chosen. The keyword there is "effort." When someone flat-out fails to commit to the effort required to switching to someones new name and consistently deadnames a trans loved one due to negligence, it is frustrating and often painful to experience.

Messing up and using a deadname is, at first, entirely understandable, but it *always* requires correction. As trans folks, we understand that our families and friends knew us as a different name for most of our lives, and switching to our real name isn't easy for most people. We can be patient, but only to a certain degree. A conscious effort must take place. When we're deadnamed, it's likely that the person who does so has not been practicing with our new name and pronouns.

Every time we're referred to by others, use our real names. Folks should correct themselves even when we're not around. Practice is the only way folks will get it right and not make the mistake of deadnaming us to our faces. No human is perfect, and trans people understand that. What you shouldn't do if you accidentally use a deadname is apologize so profusely that you prolong the moment. Trans folks generally want to move past being deadnamed as quickly as possible. Stretching out the duration of an apology is almost worse than receiving no apology at all. Here's a prime example of what we very much don't want to hear:

> *"Oh my gosh, I called you Rebecca. I'm so sorry, Jasper, I just... it's so hard! I can never remember your new name! I just always knew you as Rebecca, so it's difficult for me to change. Can't teach an old dog new tricks, you know? Ha. I'm sorry though. I won't call you Rebecca ever again. I mean, I'll probably slip up and still call you Rebecca sometimes, but I'm trying. You okay, Rebecca? I mean, Jasper?"*

This example is not much of an exaggeration. Using our deadname further in an apology may sound backward (and it most definitely is), but it's all too common. This sort of apology exhibits a misunderstanding of how jarring and dysphoria-inducing being deadnamed can be. If cis people understood the severity of dysphoria that many trans people face when confronted with their deadname, they'd make more of an effort not to cause that dysphoria in the first place. Refusal to adapt is often because cis people do not understand how bad dysphoria can get, or from a straightforward and sincere lack of concern for being the cause of that emotional distress.

Most cis people do not want to cause that distress, however, and when dysphoria is explained properly to an ally they tend to work hard to never put a trans person through that unnecessary anguish, particularly when we're dealing with everything else the world throws at us as trans people. Something that all allies have to get comfortable with is being corrected upon a slip-up, and not getting defensive when they do.

Ultimately, not using our deadnames is a matter of basic respect. Whether intentional or not, using our birth or given name is not okay. Use our real names -- the names we've chosen for ourselves. Honestly, if folks can refer to Reginald Kenneth Dwight as "Elton John," or Peter Gene Hernandez as "Bruno Mars," or Stefani Joanne Angelina Germanotta as "Lady Gaga," they can certainly call their trans friends and families by the names they choose. Many people deadname trans people not merely because they'd rather use our birth names, but often because they are transphobic and wish to hurt us.

Whatever the intent, deadnaming is not okay.

Deadnaming is also a common practice in media. Wherever you read stories about trans pioneer Marsha P. Johnson, you are also likely to see her deadname attached, which often happens to trans folks who have transitioned within the public eye. In nearly all instances of when the media covers a trans person's murder, at least one source uses their deadname. It's a monumental disrespect of the deceased to do this.

Call us by our *real* names—the names we've chosen.

Our deadnames are gone and dead.

Hello! my name is Awesome

- Lys Morton -

NO PRIVILEGE IN PASSING

Content Notice: Use of the "T-Slur"

Mexico was the safest I felt in a long time. Seniõr, padre, and amigo greeted me with every interaction. It was a new feeling of gender euphoria that followed me right onto the plane when the security officer scanned over my passport, dead name, and "F" marker plain as day, then looked at me and said, "Safe travels, sir."

I almost felt cisgender, almost forgot that I was trans.

The sharp slap back to reality was as crisp as the fall air that hung over Vancouver's Horseshoe Bay ferry terminal. I was on my last leg home, practically dragging my lower extremities along as I bartered with myself about when I could nap once I hit the dorms.

Laundry washed, dried, and folded first.

Laundry washed and dried first.

Laundry removed from the suitcase and placed in my hamper first.

I was still shaving off steps from this monumental task as I sat down in the foot passenger waiting area, oblivious to the other passengers waiting for boarding. Until...

"Is that the video of the tranny?"

Dry ice doesn't freeze as fast as I did at that moment, fingers poised over a half-finished message to my aunt. I sat stock still, shocked by the slur.

"Fucking hell, the way it was dancing," a young man laughed cruelly.

A group of boys sat on the other side of the room, phones out, comparing notes from a show they had been to that weekend. They gathered around one phone in particular, the owner grinning with pride as he showed the video to his friends.

"You think it realized how weird it looked?"

I knew that whoever they were most likely referring to was not likely directed at me; I wasn't dancing anywhere. Still, it didn't stop all too familiar words from creeping up.

Nothing more than tits and a beard.

As they laughed, I felt myself shrink into my seat, trying to make sure I remained invisible. And then I was hit with a sudden realization.

Was I pretending to be a cisgender boy, or a butch female? What, exactly, was I hiding as? Dysphoria had me convinced that everyone within a mile radius knew I wasn't a "real boy", but experience slowly taught me that I passed for cis far more often than I didn't. And so I sat there, grappling with the concept of safety versus authenticity.

Passing is a constant topic of debate in the trans community; the term referring to someone being able to "pass" as a cisgender individual. In media, it is often touted as the ultimate goal for trans individuals, but for many, it is unattainable. Multiple factors play into this, ranging from cost, health, access to good surgeons, general support in what can be a long healing process, or in nonbinary folks for whom passing simply doesn't always apply.

A common phrase in the community is, "testosterone is one hell of a drug," spoken in either a tone of impressed wonder or utter disdain. The hormone has lasting changes to the body and easily overruns estrogen's effects. For transmasculine individuals, this turns into a somewhat rapid change as "Puberty 2.0" rolls through like a stampede. Voices crack, faces square out, hair sprouts pretty much... uh... everywhere, and one becomes worried they might eat the entire contents of their fridge in one sitting as hunger doubles in intensity. For transfeminine individuals, testosterone's masculinizing effects have usually already taken place, and they're pitted against the hormone as they start their transition journies. It leads to numerous more surgeries than transmasculine folks, and poses a constant battle against appearances that are deemed masculine, with a rather higher risk of being "clocked."

Tracy was someone who was clocked frequently. She was 42 when she was able to come out as trans and start hormone replacement therapy (HRT). Due to her age and wear-and-tear on the body that came from the construction work she did from age seventeen, just about all gender-affirmation surgeries were off the table. Genetics had either blessed her or cursed her, depending on how she felt that day, with the very definition of a five o'clock shadow spreading across her face daily. At 6'2", she was tall when barefoot. Nonetheless, Tracy would stop you dead on the street to show off her new heels. And that day, as we wandered off Prince's Island Park in downtown Calgary and walked to Bow river, she was rocking six-inch silver glitter pumps.

It was the middle of summer, and I had just partaken in my first pride since coming out as trans. I was the awkward kid with a couple of pronoun pins stuck to my chest, and miniature trans and queer pride flags shoved in the back of my hat. I wandered the event with a sense of awe, timidly walking up to booths and asking questions, still trying to suss out where I fit within the community. Where did the agender transmasculine pal who was still trying to decide upon HRT and where they fit along the binary belong in this massive parade of rainbows?

Amidst the various booths selling flags, pins, and memorabilia was one dedicated to a project called, "Living Without Disguises," dedicated to give a voice to the community, helping queer individuals tell their stories. Standing there, giving quite the spiel about the traversing the dating scene in Calgary as a middle aged trans woman, was Tracy.

"Maybe it's a bad stereotype, but I thought cowboys would have some decent manners to them. I'm not asking for you to pay for a lobster dinner in the middle of the prairies, but maybe asking about my lady parts should be left for the third date."

It was the promise of writing something that had me stepping up to the booth, intending to snag a pamphlet and scurry off. Instead, I was caught in Tracy's gaze as she turned to rope me into the conversation.

"I just hope you younger boys have some better manners to you. I'm no cougar, but there are little girls on this island right now who are in for a world of hurt."

Youu never know until in that situation, but one freezes when a woman a whole foot and a half taller than you draped in more boas than are probably healthy for the June heat of Calgary stares down at you with a kind but critical look. My spot-on impression of a deer-in-the-headlights gave Tracy time to give me a once over and notice the toonie-sized "they/them" pronoun pin emblazoned on my hat, and the dime sized "he/him" one that half-covered by it.

"You going to be breaking any girls' hearts?"
There isn't exactly an answer you can give with confidence when faced with such an out-of-the-blue question. I stuttered about, unsure of what the proper response should be.

Tracy seemed endeared to me. "Aren't you just the sweetest? What's your name, sweetie?"

My tongue stumbled over my name back then, muscle memory trying to beat my brain to the punchline, and I mumbled out, "...uuhhh... Lys." Tracy weaseled out some more information from me, leaning her tall frame against the table as she smiled and nodded along with me while I gave a ragged SparkNotes of my current coming-out story. I told her of how I was confident that "girl" was not anywhere close to what I was, but "boy" didn't feel quite right either. I told her further of how this was kind of my first pride parade since coming out, and with that confession, Tracy's eyes lit up.

There's a cardinal rule iin the queer community: When you find a fledgling queer, a gayby, or a transby, you protect that child, dammit; you shower them with compliments; you answer whatever random question falls out of their mouths and, if you're a Canadian queer, you invite them to Tim Horton's for a donut and coffee. "We should go for Timmies," said Tracy warmly, "I'm just dying for an Ice Cap in this heat, aren't you?"

I was so swept up in the big and bold entity that was Tracy that I was already following half a step behind her before I had fully processed the question. But that's the magic of pride; strangers connecting like friends for one glorious day in the summer sun simply because we could see each other and, perhaps moreover, be seen.

You could feel that magic depleting the moment you crossed one of the bridges that connected Princes Island Park to the Calgary city core. The laughter and music were quickly lost to streams of endless traffic and quickened paces of those around us heading to their various destinations. Many shot Tracy a look as she strolled on past, but she hardly noticed with her eyes forward and head held high, as I half jogged beside her long strides like a puppy trying to keep up to the pace of their owner.

We came to a stop at an intersection a couple of blocks away from Prince's Island Park, and I was trying to map out where the nearest Tim Hortons was to us, when a man rolled up to the intersection and rolled down his window.

"Gentlemen," he sneered, glaring at Tracy as she kept her eyes focused on the pedestrian sign across the street. The man chuckled nastily before glancing at me, and the sneer hastily faltered. I copied Tracy's strategy, counting down with the traffic light as he looked me up and down, frustration and confusion mixing on his face.

The light finally turned after what felt like an eon, little white LEDs illuminating a walking figure, and Tracy strolled off with me in tow as if she didn't have a care in the world. I returned to the near jogging pace I had to take when walking with her, fighting to keep myself from looking back.

"He's right," Tracy said out of the blue, and I looked up at her in confusion. "You're quite a handsome gentleman."

It felt odd, the spark of triumph formed from an insult. As if claiming the obvious transphobia as a win for me did less damage to the lady now escorting me into the blessedly air-conditioned coffee shop. I wrestled with the conflict as we stood in line, trying to focus on Tracy as she chatted about a small boutique shop that was a few blocks away and always carried women's clothes in larger sizes; a small privilege that had never occurred to me before.

I faced a number of moments like that during the first year of my transition, straddling the middle ground of looking both male and female; a gender oddity that had many people doing a rude double-take. For most, they simply stumbled around my pronouns and titles.

"Hello ma'am... uh, sir."

"He was... she was here first."

"Mister. Sorry, miss."

"Miss. Sorry, Mister."

For many trans and gender non-conforming individuals who are non-binary, there's a sense of triumph here, in the life of "either or," or "neither nor." Playing back and forth with that middle ground, reveling in the contrast they presented. Many of the folks I knew who are agender were happy for people to flop back and forth with the binary. For me, however, it was an added stressor.

Every flip-flop had me waiting for the age-old name of "sheman." Every stumble had me braced for them to settle on "her." As much as I embraced the change testosterone was starting to bring forth, I struggled with the middle ground I was currently sitting in. Each social interaction now came with a giant wheel divided up with alternating "him" and "her," and I was learning to dread the spin of that wheel.

It was during that time two things started to became clear: Like the man in the car that day downtown, people were quick to assume that I was a trans woman, and the transphobia with which I was dealt stemmed from that line of thought. People were quick to call me a man, declare I had a penis, and that I was only playing dress-up. Considering that I was still dressing in masculine clothes, that last claim never made a lick of sense to me. This queer had no dresses to speak of, and the last time I'd worn make-up was in my grade ten production of Les Misérables. High school drama class, the epitome of playing dress-up.

I distinctly remember one woman who engaged with me in the comments of a CTV Calgary Facebook post. It was the annual debate about whether certain crosswalks around Calgary should be painted with the rainbow flag for Pride Week. People were always quick to demand that the money go to the homeless. They insisted that it was unethical for the LGBTQIA+ community to shove themselves down everyone else's throat, masking their bigotry with a concern for the homeless that they only seemed to have once per year when the queers took over the city. Would we not think of the poor children this would ruin?

I quietly pointed out that the money had been raised by the Queer-Straight Alliance club at a school near the crosswalk, and they had been able to paint the crosswalk themselves so no tax money had gone into the project. A few minutes later, the following message popped in my inbox. "You're never going to be a real woman; don't you get that? You're a man. Get over yourself, you fucking perverted freak."

If only she knew just how close her words were to the chorus that had been playing out in my head for years.

The other thing that was becoming clear was that, when the wheel landed on the other option, when someone declared me male, a small part of me lit up with a feeling I had no words for yet.

And it was growing every day. Euphoria.

Costco is always a sensory nightmare. Add in the tension of trying to navigate the cart after dad as he strolled to this and that corner of the store, and I was on a hair trigger.

"We need milk?" Dad asked.

We were a family of five with a father who was raised on a dairy farm; we were always in need of milk. I gave a small nod in response and hauled the back end of the cart over so it was pointed toward the dairy freezer. Dad pressed on, and I shuffled after him giving an apologetic smile to a mom with four kids crammed into her cart as I accidentally cut her off in my haste. If looks could kill, bodies would be strewn around Costco.

We were an aisle away from the cooler when dad turned around and breezed past back to the freezers behind me. "Hold on; we need bacon."

That I couldn't argue with Dairy-Farm-Dad there, but I gritted my teeth as I wrangled the cart around and tried to maneuver it around a sample table. He was standing halfway down the aisle, eyes scanning the various packages when I rolled up.

Dad looked pressed.

"You see any that your mom can eat?" He asked, scratching his head.

Allergies to sulfates will cut out many things from your diet, and there were only two brands of bacon mom could eat. Neither of them could be seen in the cooler in front of me, and I shook my head in response this time.

"Are you sure?"

If looks could kill, I was about to be charged with patricide.

Dad shrugged and turned to head back down the way we'd come. By the time I had the damned cart turned around once again, he was engaged in conversation with a couple I didn't recognize.

"We don't see you at Calgary Curling anymore." She was a middle-aged lady, iron straight blonde hair, and she was barely taller than me. Her husband was six foot something with a whisper of grey here and there in a beard I was eyeing up heavily.

"I'm down at ARC now," dad replied. "They're a little better at getting me a sheet for the team."

The couple both nodded, then the lady glanced at me. "This is your son?"

Her smile was warm, and there was no threat to her tone. Nevertheless, I was met with a clash of excitement at the "not female" gendering of me, followed by panic at what dad's response might be. The most recent fight between us had been about my transition and was less than 24 hours old, so I braced for a stronger reaction than what that question might usually spark.

"This is my..." he started. Then the sentence faltered, and he shot a look at me out of the corner of his eye. "This is Lys. My eldest daughter."

I barely remember shaking the hands of the couple we met that day, their stuttering apologies for the "mistake". I can't even recall their names. I was too overwhelmed by the complexity of emotion crammed into such a simple statement.

Ever since coming out, ever since claiming Lys as my name, he had refused to even acknowledge it. For him to introduce me as Lys, unprompted, was a triumph. And yet, it clashed with the assertion that I'm a girl. I wanted to both hug him in thanks and slug him in frustration. A simple sentence felt as if he was trying to take the self I was finally getting to define and give it back to "her". That damned expectation I had spent so long trying to force myself to achieve. It's a moment I cling to. One of a handful since coming out where dad seemed to budge ever the slightest towards acceptance of the journey I was on.

There's a final argument in the debate of "passing." The idea that the term implies one is passing for their gender. To say that I am passing is to imply that I am pretending to be male, that this is all dress-up. Oddly enough, these accusations can come from inside and outside the community. The transmisogyny is coming from inside the house, so-to-speak.

I will never be cisgender. There are characteristics of life as a trans male that are wholly unique in comparison. Some will argue that to pass completely is to deny these aspects; to deny an aspect of who you are in order to strengthen another—a duality to contest with. As much as I would like to be just an average guy, I cannot spend my life chasing that. It is an unattainable goal that leaves many trans individuals chasing after false hopes and half-promised surgeries, leaving us hating who we are now in favor of an ideal that might never come.

On the other end, passing puts one at risk of ending up in a crowd that can be hostile when if they clock us; in the presence of those who think trans people aren't worth respect and are easy to spot.

"Hey buddy!"

The voice made me jump, gripping tight to my phone as I looked up at the boys still crowded around their phones. The proud owner of the one containing the video was smiling warmly at me, waving his phone at me.

"Want to see this? It's fucking hilarious."

Sometimes camouflage can backfire on you.

- TransFocus Editors -

WHAT IS PASSING?

Content Notice: Mention of violence against trans women of color

For many trans people, passing (or cis-assuming privilege) is seen as a golden standard. That is to say, passing as a cisgender person rather than being seen as a person transitioning from "one gender to the other." Effectively, it means to become not visibly trans. The term was first used similarly by Black American communities to describe light-skinned Black people who could pass for white or non-Black. In both circumstances, passing implies stealth and safety in a society where appearing as you are can be dangerous.

From a binary, cisgender perspective, passing might seem like the ultimate goal of the trans experience. Going from male to female, female to male, innie to outie, or outie to in, as they say. Passing and the desire to pass is a specific slice of the trans experience that is valid and to be respected, but it is not something that all trans people identify with or strive to achieve by any means, nor does it define the trans experience. In many ways, passing is such a focus in many people's lives because, in its absence, trans visibility can be dangerous. Passing is sometimes referred to as "cis-assuming privilege" because there is often a great privilege and safety in being able to be seen as "not trans."

Nevertheless, for many of us, passing is not even an option or possibility within our grasp, no matter how much we may desire it. Some of us, whether by choice or otherwise, will always walk this earth visibly trans.

But what about nonbinary people? What does passing mean when one's identity does not align with the prescribed gender binary? Passing can be a deep and complicated subject for those who fall somewhere in-between or outside the binary and is by no means a mandatory desire one must have to be "properly trans." A person can be a binary trans man or woman who appreciates their androgyny, femininity, or masculinity. Folks can also be nonbinary and wish to pass in a typically binary way.

Passing is an authentic and valid part of many trans individual's experiences that some make a goal of and others do not. For many, particularly nonbinary trans people, passing simply does not apply, and the term can be rankling when it comes up as often as it does in trans circles. Frankly, passing comes up more or less constantly in gender-diverse spaces, to the point of some forums actually having to ban user posts questioning if they pass or not. Many online trans communities can become flooded with selfies attached to the words, *"Do I pass?"* Moreover, the answer can be super awkward when it's, *"No, but why should that matter?"*

Many of us would be happier if we could put the desire to pass behind us, in the bucket of cis nonsense that we choose to ignore. There is a practically endless list of highly problematic cis norms and perspectives we must choose to ignore in order to be happy exactly the way we are without the influence of cissexism, heterosexism, homophobia, and transphobia guiding us. That is not to say that those who wish to pass are invalid; quite the opposite. Rather, the problem is the implicit expectation that trans people make a concerted effort to pass in order to be considered valid in their trans identity. Passing simply shouldn't be a requirement trans people must acheive to be respected by cis people. We should not have to change *anything* about ourselves for people to respect our chosen names and pronouns. Furthermore, we should not have to undergo surgery to be seen as the genders we genuinely are.

More to the point: is there privilege in passing? Well, it's a complicated "yes and no." As Lys points out spectacularly in his piece *"There's No Privilege in Passing,"* passing does not erase the emotional impact of being trans in a transphobic culture. The misperception of there being no trans people around can even invite people to share their transphobia with us more readily. There is often physical safety, if not emotional safety, in passing. However, even trans folks who generally pass risk being clocked by transphobes who can become irate when they feel as though they've been "tricked" by our existence. Even trans people who experience cis-assuming privilege can be visibly trans if one knows what to look for, and the safety of passing can quickly devolve into a highly unsafe situation, such as the one Lys found himself in and describes in his story. These situations can be jarring, triggering, and downright terrifying, and while it would certainly be worse for someone who doesn't pass, oppression isn't a contest and trauma is trauma.

Many trans women of color have been murdered because a cisgender heterosexual man found her attractive before discovering that she was trans. In the last several years, we have seen a steady increase in violent crime committed against trans women of color, especially Black trans women. At least forty-four trans people were killed in 2020, making it the worst year on record for trans violence since organizations like the Human Rights Campaign (HRC) started counting. It is worth noting that, while forty-four may not sound like a huge number, it is merely the tip of the iceberg. Most trans people are disrespected upon the event of their deaths and are misgendered and deadnamed more often than not, on top of the trans community being especially small compared to other LGBTQIA+ populations. Since 2013, at least two-hundred trans people have been victims of violent hate crimes that cut their lives tragically short.

A factor in the under-reporting of violence against trans people is that most transgender victims of violent crime are misreported, with many trans women identified as "John Doe" by bigoted members of law enforcement until their friends or family sets the record straight. This makes keeping a comprehensive list difficult, if not impossible. A fair number of cases also go unreported because it is unclear if the murder occurs because of transphobia or other factors. This sum also doesn't include trans people who die by suicide due to bullying and social ostracization, which would greatly increase the numbers of trans people who die in any given year because nearly half of all trans people attempt suicide at some point in their lives. Unfortunately, 2021 is on par to surpass 2020 in reported instances of fatal violence against trans people, disproportionately impacting trans women of color. The convergence of transphobia, transmisogyny, racism, sexism, homophobia, biphobia, and the American free access to guns all play a significant role in these killings.

An HRC report on trans violence in 2020 states that most of these victims were murdered by acquaintances, romantic or sexual partners, and strangers. It is worth noting that, in the general population, being murdered by a stranger is excessively rare. This is all to say that not passing as cisgender is extremely dangerous for many trans folks. Getting romantically involved with cis men is dangerous. Walking in public or commuting while visibly trans is dangerous. Moreover, men who sleep with trans women frequently choose to murder their trans romantic partner rather than publicly admit their attraction toward trans bodies.

Especially in the United States, we live in a dystopian culture of violence, leaving trans women of color most at risk, with some statistics stating that the life expectancy of a Black trans woman is just thirty-five years old. Let that sink in.

So you see, the need to pass, while earnestly desired by many trans people, is largely due to the lack of safety that many of us experience as a result of rampant transphobia in our culture. We are not even necessarily safe in our own homes, lest we invite someone in who sees our transness as an assault on his heterosexuality and fragile masculinity. We are not safe on public transportation, lest an angry cis man decide that our presence assaults his cis male sensibilities. We are targeted by the TSA, the police, and often find ourselves struggling to remain employed and housed, further putting our community's most marginalized members at risk of violent crime.

At its crux, passing is an unjust requirement for respect placed upon a vulnerable and unprivileged community by a sick society that fails to appreciate the beauty of trans bodies. Passing is a privilege, a burden, and a fundamentally cissexist concept, and, indeed, sometimes camouflage can backfire on you.

Citations:

https://www.hrc.org/resources/violence-against-the-trans-and-gender-non-conforming-community-in-2020

https://www.cbsnews.com/news/transgender-community-fatal-violence-spike/

https://www.them.us/story/anti-trans-homicides-increased-300-percent-2021

- Ezekiel K. -

B'TZELEM ELOHIM
OUR DUTY OF ACCEPTANCE

As LGBTQ people and people of other marginalized communities, acceptance is something we fear we fall short of. Every day, people amongst our ranks are murdered or dying from policies that leave us vulnerable and persecuted by the fires of hatred committed by those who continue to oppress us.

It is a form of reconciliation, then, to look at the concept of b'tzelem Elohim; the notion that we are all created in the image of G-d. How can we be, though, when we have no visual concept of Elohim? Genesis tells us about the creation of the world — the skies, the waters, and the trees — but commentaries such as those by Gunther Plaut show that the creation of mankind was carried out with much more consideration. The fundamental blocks of humanity are complex, so how can we all be so different from one another yet still share in this image?

We can look at the rather unique intellectual complexity of humanity; our thoughts and emotions, where many of us share in awe our place in the earth and the whole of existence. Our capacity for compassion and acts of justice — not for reward, but simply because there is an intrinsic aspect to us as human beings that stand up for those around us principally because it is the right thing to do — is a manifestation of the ways in which we are shaped in this image. And it is how these displays of mercy, love, and compassion trespasses beyond our physical or psychological fences, like our gender identity, our skin color, whom we find ourselves attracted to, that shows us that, at the core of our beings, we are sharing in one image Because of our awareness of our existence and creation, we are able to realize our moral potential.

"Above all demarcations of races and nations, castes and classes, oppressors ad servants, givers and recipients, above all delineations even of gifts and talents stands one certainty: Man. Whoever bears this image is created and called to be a revelation of human dignity."

- Leo Baeck, The Essence of Judaism

Like a jigsaw puzzle, from one piece, you cannot see the whole picture. Humanity and, indeed, all living species upon this earth are symbiotic and sharing one ecosystem. To quote a rather incredible movie, The Prince of Egypt, it is much as Jethro says to Moses around the campus. "You must look at your life through Heaven's eyes." We cannot see how beautifully we fit together to form an image in the likeness of G-d, and we must always bear in mind the lens upon which we first interpret the idea of an "image" is that of human — of physicality and visuality. It is our actions that define us.

Transgender people are b'tzelem Elohim. It is our spirit that is of our identities. Ourselves are inside of us, and the physical casing we find ourselves in does not define us. That we as human beings can understand these nuances and comprehend through evaluation, education, and interaction with others is a blessing upon all of us. It is indicative of our unique place in the world, and this is a place that cannot be stripped from us—our belonging. Our right and blessing to exist is paramount and everlasting, no matter the prejudices we face. It is a central truth we must do all we can to never lose sight of — and, in that regard, to remind one another in our community of in times of darkness.

There is much more to be said, such that can fill volumes with words upon pages. But if there is anything to take away, it is this:

As Jews, it is our duty to pursue social justice, to pursue love, and to fight for the rights of our siblings and others on matters which may not affect us in the immediate but may leave others downtrodden. For those who have distanced themselves from the faith due to the ignorance and hatred of others, I hope this has provided some reconciliation that you may peace once more, should that be your pursuit. For non-Jews and those who do not believe, let this show you that we can work together, and even in the interest of philosophy, we have a wealth of beauty and interpretation that spurs us to fight alongside you despite our differences. Just as Jethro, a Midian priest, accepted Moses the Hebrew as his son, we too must accept each other and join arms by one another's sides.

B'tzelem Elohim.

Barukh atah Adonai Eloheinu melekh ha'olam dayan ha'emet.

TIKKUN OLAM

REPAIRING THE WORLD

- Jenny Sansom. -

THE NOT-SO-GOLDEN CORRAL

Content Notice: Transphobia; Guns

This is the story of how my friends and I almost got shot.

I am a lesbian trans woman from a small rural hee-haw town in the middle of a hick state. That being said, as one can imagine, any sort of trans-related healthcare is anything but standard. Even more complicated is finding somewhere my insurance will even cover because they think that sort of stuff is "all elective and cosmetic."

Micah, a trans man, knows just how hard it is to find a doctor. He sent me a message one day telling me how he found an endocrinologist who would actually take my insurance plan. After the first couple of visits, my doctor could no longer take my insurance and has been nice enough to cover my appointments pro-bono to this day. I digress. The doctor is located out of state in neighboring Ohio, which brings us to the road trip that nearly saw my friends and me riddled with bullets across state lines.

So my friend Micah, my high school sweetheart and fiancé, Kelly, and my childhood friend Bobby all decided to make the trip with me. My friend Micah drove us up there, and to be honest, I think he was more excited for my first appointment than I was. That's not to say I wasn't excited; I could barely contain myself and was a complex swirl of anxiety, fear, and unbridled joy. The trip was an arduous three-hour drive. Even so, the journey itself was excellent and would leave behind a trail of stories and laughs for years to come. We even got somewhat intense with one another as we crossed into the buckeye state, with the laughs passing into a deep and introspective conversation.

We joked around, playing pranks on one another, such as sticking fries up Bobby's nose as he slept. Micah and I sang along to a slew of Against Me! songs as the band was actually how we kind of met, and we both adore the lead singer, Laura Jane Grace. We once got to meet the band at one of their concerts, but that's a story for another time; I just want to brag to a captive audience of fellow trans folks who recognize the significance.

Once we arrived at the office, we left Bobby asleep in the car, and Micah hyped me up as we made our way inside. The doctor was charming, and we joked around for a bit to break the ice. She listened to all of my concerns and answered the questions I had for her. When she set me up with my first prescription for hormones, I must admit I cried a little. When it came time to walk back to that car, prescription in hand, I had to hold myself together to avoid drawing attention in unfamiliar territory. When we got back to Micah's car, I could contain myself no longer and felt such an immense weight lifted from my heart. I suddenly began to sob uncontrollably, terrifying everyone in the car, including myself. I mean, the whole ugly cry. Big, fat tears streamed down my face. As the name "ugly crying" implies, it was not one of my prettier moments. A very bewildered Bobby attempted to console me, as he didn't expect such a burst of emotions. Such an emotional display was very uncharacteristic for me, and even caught Kelly off-guard. She was so moved by my emotion that she insisted we celebrate the momentous occasion with dinner at the buffet-style restaurant known as The Golden Corral. We had passed it on the way to the doctor's office, and we were all famished from the long trip.

A few minutes passed, though it felt like an hour stretched by, as we were all ravenous and eager to celebrate. We entered the family-friendly restaurant, and delicious smells wafted over us when we opened the glass front doors. We basked in pleasant sights and smells, taking in the ambiance of the tantalizing buffet. After piling up several plates of American fare, we were having a great time keeping to ourselves as we celebrated my important milestone. Well, rather, we had been, right up until I noticed a middle-aged man following closely behind when I got my food from the salad bar. He was the typical hick. He wore a discolored blue baseball cap, a plain (but disgustingly stained) white teeshirt, dirty blue jeans that looked to be a couple of washes away from falling to threads, and mud-caked steel-toed work boots. He also had a large bowie knife holstered to his belt by a leather sheath, pulling the "unkempt country boy" outfit together. I had been out two years prior, so I was rather used to the kind of looks he was shooting my way. I met his hostile gaze with a sweet smile and walked away briskly, trying to not give him a second thought. Usually, given my tall, strong frame and the fact that I wasn't bothered by their glares ended up being well enough to deter most assholes, but this old man was different.

He continued to stare me down but refused to do anything else, and I could sense that he was trying to goad me into making the first move. I could practically feel him seething at the fact that I refused to do anything. My friends and fiancé watched what was transpiring and grew increasingly uneasy, but I shrugged it off like I always did. I told them to not freak out, as it was a common occurrence, and we didn't exactly have the home-field advantage. It was best to just let the good ol' boy stare until he strained his eyes; no sense in causing a fuss. Strangely, I supposed I could understand why he was so angry. Given his narrow views, our table must have looked like a small pride parade, what with Bobby being a cisgender gay man, my cisgender lesbian fiancé, Kelly, and Micah plus myself representing the T.

He looked over at us several more times, but eventually stopped since we refused to acknowledge his existence any further. Still, I could almost feel the white-hot anger radiating from across the room. With a groan of anticipation, I realized that I had to use the restroom. At the time, I had never before had any issues using public restrooms but felt it would be safest if I brought Kelly along. I went to the women's room as any woman such as myself would do with her fiancé, and, fortunately, it was completely empty, exactly how I like it.

I was in the stall for no more than a few minutes noticing the chipped paint, trying to get my mind off of the angry old man. I knew he wasn't worth my time to even think about, but something about his menacing energy was getting under my skin. Then, as I was about to wrap up my business, I jumped as I heard a muffled voice through the stall. It was undoubtedly the woman who was sitting with that menacing old man. She was nearly shouting at her children, demanding for them to get into the restroom. I assumed that she wanted them to pee before leaving the restaurant or something, but one of the little girls spoke up. "I don't have to go, though!" I listened intently as the woman physically shoved the girls into the restroom before running out. That was when my fiancé, who was standing watch for me by washing her hands, saw an employee of the Golden Corral enter the restroom. The employee looked around the toilets, puzzled, before leaving without a word. The woman then entered the restroom, angrily pulling the girls out by their wrists, one of them crying out, pleading with the woman to let go of her tiny arm.

A little bit shaken and confused, we made our way back to the table. Bobby told us how he watched the lady approach an employee and very loudly shout about there being a man in the women's restroom with her innocent little girls. The thought of her trying to paint me up like some sort of predator made me feel sick to my stomach, and since we were almost finished eating anyway, we grabbed our belongings and left.

Fortunately, at The Golden Corral, you pay before you eat, so we didn't have to belabor our stay and were able to get the hell out of there.

Micah sat in his car for a minute, fumbling around with his cellphone, trying to find the song "True Trans Soul Rebel." by Against Me! playing so he could blast Laura's angelic vocals as we drove off. It was as if it were our war song, good tunes for a battle won. Sadly, his phone wasn't cooperating, and we scrapped the idea.

We began to drive off, and the way that The Golden Corral was set up was that you had to drive past the entrance to leave, and that was when we saw him. The old hick man was glaring daggers at us, his face flushed scarlet from either over-indulging on salty buffet food, rage, or some combination therein. His arms crossed as he tried his damnedest to be intimidating. My friend Bobby decided to give the man the finger as he was just sick of him. That was when old man hick ran over to his shitty rusty robin-egg-blue truck, and I saw the glint of his steel handgun as he tucked it into the waistband of his tattered jeans. Huffing and puffing, he gave chase, running after us as we were stuck at a red light at the entrance that was just down the hill from the restaurant.

He pulled what looked to be a .357 revolver out from his waistband and pointed it at us like it was a problem solver, just as the light changed to green. Micah slammed his foot down on the gas pedal, our tires leaving behind a black streak on the gray road as we merged into traffic, never to see the angry man again. Needless to say, that was the last time any of us will ever go to a Golden Corral.

It just goes to show you never know how petty someone is and how willing they might be to shoot you. Please be careful out there. One wrong move, and I might not be alive today to tell the tale.

- Ren Thomas. -

WEDDING DAY

This moment had been months in the making, and I was terrified. I had spent hours in the department store with my partner feeling extraordinarily uncomfortable, fighting off panic attacks for this day. I had only one option. My sister was getting married, and I was simply not going to wear a dress. I encountered some difficulties as I looked for the suit jacket and pants, as I have short arms, short legs and wide hips. Most places don't stock the sizes I would need, but somehow I found all the pieces, one by one. I was only missing two things: a tie and a dress shirt. My mom surprised me with the shirt; when I was home from college, she pulled it out, and I was so happy that she'd thought of me and searched for it. It was a millennial pink, a super comfortable, cotton-blended dream. Then in the mirror, I saw it: three letters that made me cry fat tears on the spot. Embroidered on the sleeve was R-E-N. My chosen name. My REAL name.

The day before we left for the wedding, I realized I didn't have a tie that matched. The only one I had was a blue striped number that would've clashed something horrific. My dad, very calmly, took me into the closet and helped me pick out a tie from his own collection that matched. I joked that all of his ties looked as if they had just arrived from the 1980s, but that was only to hide how wide I was smiling on the inside.

Mom didn't want me to wear all of the pieces together until the wedding. I'm notoriously clumsy, so something would've definitely happened, and then there would've been a problem. Once the day came, as I got dressed in the bathroom, I prepared myself for the worst.

I prepared to look in the mirror and see my seven-year-old self, wearing one of my dad's old t-shirts to bed, drowning in ill-fitting men's clothing. I prepared to look and see nothing more than a little kid playing dress-up.

But then I looked.

There were no illusions of the past, no intrusive dysphoric thoughts, nothing. For a few seconds in my head, it was nothing but silence and awe.

Then in the smallest voice, part of me whispered a solemn, "Wow."

In the mirror, I saw nothing but myself. I saw myself in the truest, purest form ever. I'd never felt so elated over my appearance. Euphoric. It was me. *Me.*

Ren.

- TransFocus Editors -

MICROAGGRESSIONS TO AVOID

Content Notice: Transphobic Language

A microaggression is an indirect, subtle, and often unintended slight against a marginalized community. Microaggressive phrases or statements can seem innocuous but can also be incredibly demeaning, insulting, and damaging. Sometimes, microaggressions can also be intentional, as in the case of trans exclusionists calling trans women "dude" or "guy," with those wielding such gendered greetings as a weapon while hiding behind the perceived colloquial gender neutrality of those words.

There are some common microaggressions said of the trans community that, more often than not, are a side effect of ignorance more than they are utilized with malicious intent. We are here to teach what words and phrases not to say concerning the trans community.

"Born a boy/girl" or "biologically male/female."

Nearly every trans person has heard this. While some trans people do personally use such language to describe their experience, when uttered by a cisgender person, it can come off as demeaning and reductive. "Born a boy/girl" implies that we *become* trans later in life, and this language minimizes the reality of our identities. The fact is that trans people are born trans; we merely come out and express our true genders after we have been assigned the wrong gender at birth.

Bringing up our biological sex is also invasive and ultimately unimportant because it tends to focus far too heavily upon our genitals and secondary sex characteristics. Regardless of our biology, we are humans. Biology is frequently weaponized against the trans community because many cis people cannot wrap their heads around the fact that, regardless of our transition goals, sex and gender are social constructs. A trans woman who has a penis has a female penis. A trans man who has a vagina has a male vagina. A nonbinary person with any configuration of genitalia has nonbinary genitals. So, statements like "well, you are biologically male/female regardless of your identity" illustrate plainly just how fixated cis people can be on our bodies. Ultimately, our anatomy is the business of nobody except ourselves, our sexual partners if we are allosexual (non-asexual), and that of our medical professionals who need to make sure our bodies are healthy. In short, we are more than the sum of our parts.

"Wow! You pass so well! I would never have known that you used to be a boy/girl!"

Whether a cis person realizes it or not, a statement like this comments on how well we "pass" as cisgender and is not a compliment. Similar to questions regarding our sexual biology, a statement such as this focuses too heavily on how we presented before making moves toward transitioning. It also illustrates a misunderstanding of the reality that we were *always* trans and were always the gender we present as now regardless of how we presented in the past. One does not become trans; it is a part of us that we discover and come to embrace.

"Have you had / Do you plan to have 'the surgery?'"

What surgery? There are a lot of them! Questions like this are another example of a mindset that focuses too heavily upon our bodies. Whether we intend to have surgery to alter our bodies is a personal choice and is not something we necessarily want to discuss with cis people. The question ultimately boils down to, "So, what is in your pants?" because cis people tend to associate "the surgery" with surgical alterations to the genitals. Asking any person about their body is invasive. Cis folks would do well to avoid this line of questioning altogether.

"You are so attractive... for a trans person!"

This... is also not a compliment. When one reads between the lines, what this is saying is, "Gosh, trans people are usually so ugly, but you look pretty good!" The surprise from cis people that some trans people are conventionally attractive places too much focus on our looks and rather than the content of our character.

"You are my first trans friend / you are the first trans person I have met!"

That may be the case, but it is very likely not. Not all trans people are out and visible, and just because none of a cis person's friends or family have come out does not mean they are not suffering in silence. Many trans people come out later in life, primarily due to repression stemming from a violently transphobic society, and most of us do not want to hear that we are someone's token trans friend or relation. Statements like this tend to place an undue burden upon trans folks to educate those who are meeting an out trans person for the first time and, especially early in our transitions, we are often ill-equipped to be perceived by our cis loved ones as a monolith for the trans experience. Furthermore, it can be incredibly isolating to be told over and over that you are the only trans person someone knows, and it puts a lot of pressure upon the trans person in question to leave a good impression on their cisgender friends and family of what it means to be trans and uphold an image as "one of the good ones."

"It is sad that you are transitioning; you are so attractive as a boy/girl."

How attractive we are is hugely unrelated to our transness. Most people transition because of a deep feeling of incongruence with their gender assigned at birth, while others transition because they experience euphoria when presenting as their authentic selves. Focusing so heavily on our looks absolutely misses the point. We have to live our truths, even if that means that we will no longer be "conventionally attractive" as a gender that causes us discomfort and pain.

"Did you transition because you thought you were an ugly girl?"

Some cis folks may be surprised at this question, but many trans men, transmasc individuals, and AFAB nonbinary folks have heard things like this. It may sound like an overly rude line of questioning, and it certainly is, but it happens all too often. The fact is, trans people are usually not transitioning because they have a desire to become attractive; we transition because we have to be true to ourselves.

"If you want to be treated like a girl, you need to shave."

Many trans women and AMAB nonbinary folks who refuse to shave (whether their faces, legs, underarms, etc.) are met with attitudes like this. Our culture associates hairlessness with femininity, while body hair is simply a natural part of being a human, whether man, woman, nonbinary, or otherwise. Some women can grow facial hair, whether it is because they are trans or because of polycystic ovary syndrome. Enforcing cultural norms upon trans people and refusing to respect our identities until we obey is, to be blunt, entirely fucked up. Nobody questions a cis woman's womanhood when she makes a choice to not shave her legs or arms. Allow trans people that same level of autonomy.

"Why can't you just be a femme man/butch woman?"

Simply put, many trans folks cannot do that because it is not who we are. We do not choose our gender identities, and expecting a trans woman or nonbinary AMAB person to pretend to be a feminine man or a trans man or nonbinary AFAB person to be a masculine woman, is akin to asking a cis gay man why he cannot try being straight.

For that matter, gender expression does not equal gender identity. Not all trans women are feminine, not all trans men are masculine, and not all nonbinary people are androgynous. The cis-heteronormative expectation that trans people align their gender expression with binary concepts of gender entirely misses the point of what it means to be trans.

"Well, you understand what it is like to be a man/woman, right?"

This assumption is interesting because it implies, for those who have lived in the closet, that trans people live out a cis-normative experience of gender before coming out. The fact is, in many ways, trans people experience gender fundamentally differently than cis people, so while a trans woman might have experienced some semblance of male privilege before coming out, she never experienced privilege in the same way as a cis man OR a cis woman. Most trans folks have never known what it is like to be cisgender and could not know what that experience is like because we were trans and therefore never experienced cis privilege. This is much the same in how gay, lesbian, and bi/pan people cannot know what it is like to be straight, as the gay/lesbian/bi/pan closeted experience is fundamentally different from the straight experience. What trans people experience before coming out is what it is like to be a closeted trans person. There is ultimately a stark difference between the closeted trans experience and the cis experience.

"But you were socialized as a man/woman!"

Trans women are rarely socialized as men, and trans men are rarely socialized as women. Nonbinary people are also rarely socialized as their genders assigned at birth. We are, in most cases, socialized as trans. Many of us are robbed of our childhoods and are forced into gendered boxes that do not fit us to suit the comfort of others. To say that we are socialized as the genders we were assigned at birth is to ignore that the trans experience is remarkably different from the cis experience. Many of us face conversion and are on the receiving end of intense bigotry because of our femininity, masculinity, or androgyny. This is something that cisgender heterosexual people never experience.

"But how do you have sex?"

Oh, we find a way. It's also nobody's damned business.

"Oh, you're trans? Are you *sure*?"

Of course we're sure. Otherwise, we wouldn't likely be coming out. Before coming out, most trans people wrestle greatly with their identities, so it's not like we figured it out the day before telling people. It's a process that typically culminates in the coming out experience and is not typically a big revelation that we fill people in on immediately.

"What is your *real* name?"

Our real name is whatever the hell we say it is. Our deadnames may be our names given at birth, but they are not our "real names." Our chosen names are our real names, and what we used to be called is ultimately none of anybody's business unless we voluntarily choose to disclose that information. If a trans person trusts a cis person with their deadname, the cis person in question should never use it or disclose it to anybody else without expressed permission and should honor that knowledge with privacy.

"When did you realize you wanted to be a boy/girl?"

While this question seems innocuous on the surface, it implies a few things: First, that we're not actually a boy/girl or man/woman, and that we weren't always our gender. Furthermore, questions like this are often asked to gauge whether or not we're "really trans," as many people buy into the narrative that if you don't come out at age three that you're not a genuine trans person. The reality is more complicated than that for many, with most trans people coming to realize that they're trans later in life. For that matter, the question mirrors what medical professionals ask us to verify our transness, which results in a lot of gatekeeping. Because of that, the question can be a bit rankling. This question also poorly applies to nonbinary people, many of whom didn't know they were nonbinary until they learned of words that described their experience. A more apt question might be, "when do you know you were different?"

- TransFocus Editors -

COMMON MACROAGGRESSIONS

Content Notice: Transphobic Language

A macroaggression, unlike a microaggression, is a direct, malicious, and usually intentional slight against a marginalized person or community. Macroaggressive statements are generally pretty obvious and are designed to knock the wind out of the recipient. Where a microaggression is typically subtle in nature, a macroaggression is overtly bigoted and hateful in nature. The aggressor is usually intending to harm or demean the person or marginalized group in question, and can result in several emotional, social, or physical harm.

"You will never be a wo/man, or You will always be ___ to me."

A statement like this is designed specifically to undermine a trans person's identity and autonomy, with no room for hairsplitting or room for interpretation. It immediately puts the trans person in question on the defensive and forces them into the position of having to justify their right to be accepted as their true gender. It is a short, undercutting declaration that invites one to explain how and why trans people are valid. An aggressor can use six words to invalidate the trans experience, while it takes a trans person or ally far more to tackle this level of bigotry. It is intended to devalue a trans person's reality and force them to justify their identity and cite modern science and psychology in the process. Ultimately, arguing with a proclamation like "you will never be a woman/man," is typically pointless, as it illustrates that the person who said it isn't willing to listen and has already made their mind up on the matter in spite of the bevy of knowledge the modern age carries on the nature of gender and sexual identity as a social construct.

"I don't want a man using the women's restroom."

This is another statement that, from the jump, illustrates that the aggressor doesn't see trans people as valid in their gender identities and will always center themselves and their comfort over that of trans people. To counter such a macroaggression involves a lengthy explanation of why trans women are women, and how they are unsafe using mens' restrooms. "I don't want a man in the women's restroom," is immediately invalidating of trans women's identities and directly pits trans women's safety over cis women's and men's comfort. Funny enough, these folks also don't want transitioned trans men in the women's restroom. The focus is almost always on trans women.

"Men shouldn't be allowed in women's sports."

Again, statements like this immediately invalidate trans women as the women they are, asserting that they are men infiltrating women's sports. Statements like this are typically followed by articles about a handful of trans women who have placed highly in women's sporting events, citing their apparent "superior strength" as to why they succeed. Trans women who participate in women's sports and don't place highly are largely ignored, however, and it is the few who are athletically gifted who get singled out not merely because they are winning, but because they are winning and trans. It's an important distinction to make. Furthermore, it is difficult to argue with people who think trans women are men and have equal strength to cis men because it assumes a couple of things. First, that all women are inherently less athletic than all men, and that trans women retain all of the muscle mass from before they started transitioning. It is also worth noting that these bigots take no issue with trans men participating in sports with cis men, but do take issue with trans men competing against cis women only when the trans men in question win. The issue ultimately is not with trans people participating in correctly gendered sporting events, but rather with trans people who excel in athletics and beat cis people.

"If you have a period, you're a woman. A *Womb*an."

This kind of language is common among "trans exclusionary radical feminists," or TERF, hate groups. In stark contrast to actual feminist theory, which seeks to stop painting people with a uterus as brood mares, TERFs demonstrably think of women as walking wombs. That some cis women don't have wombs or a period is often glossed over, because if transphobes reflected upon their own logic for even a second they would see that they are directly enforcing misogyny, not dismantling it. Not only does such a statement explicitly exclude trans women, it forcibly labels trans men as women, thereby denying trans folks their right to self-determination. Furthermore, TERFs typically ignore the reality of nonbinary people, insisting that they are caught up in "trans activist ideology." To be entirely honest, there is simply no way to combat a TERF. They are in a hate cult, and the only way out of a cult is to choose to leave it.

"I can't call you he/they/she, that's ridiculous."

When someone refuses to use a trans person's pronouns, they are effectively saying that their comfort and perception are more important than that of the trans person in question. It is of the utmost disrespect to refuse to use the right pronouns for someone, especially if they have repeatedly stated that it harms them. Making a mistake can constitute a microaggression, but repeated refusal to use the correct pronouns constitutes a macroaggression.

"So, what's in your pants?"

It should go without saying, but asking a trans person about their genitals is grossly invasive, but it happens all too often. Cis people would never dream of asking another cis person about what's in their pants but somehow feel it's fair game to ask of a trans person. However, it's not just invasive; it's also hugely disrespectful and betrays a metric tonne of implied bigotry and transphobia.

"I don't want you around my kids."

Many LGBTQIA+ people have heard this upon coming out, and it's typically predicated upon queer people being sexual predators, which flies in the face of actual statistics showing that the majority of predators are cis/het white men. Furthermore, trans women are far more likely than almost any other demographic to experience violent assault, and the lie that children and cis women are at risk of trans people committing a crime against them sits solidly under the list of transphobic myths perpetuated by TERFs.

"Oh, you didn't know? _____ is trans."

Coming out on someone's behalf is a gross invasion of privacy, and given the damage it can cause, it constitutes a macroaggression. Trans people are often very cautious and selective about whom they come out to, and coming out on someone's behalf is not only invasive but can also issue a direct risk to their personal safety. If a trans person comes out to you, or any LGBTQIA+ person for that matter, consider it a secret until you either know that they're comfortable with you sharing that knowledge, or until you know that the other people in their life are already aware of their trans identity.

"Sex is Real!"

When a TERF says, "Sex is Real," what they are saying is, "Only my outdated perception of biological sex as it relates to gender is real." Such a blunt statement leaves no room for the existence of trans people. It's also a gaslighting tactic because, to the average reader, "Sex is Real" is a fairly innocuous statement. How could anybody disagree with that? *Of course* sex is real. It effectively implies that trans people think sex isn't real, and those three little words force trans people to explain our position on gender identity as it pertains to sex. It's yet another means of putting trans people on the defensive while allowing the TERFs to appear calm and collected while leaving the trans community perturbed. In the following pages, TransFocus's editor, Rori Porter, dissects this statement, its intention, and its ramifications in full detail.

- Rori Porter -

SEX IS REAL
AS ARE NONBINARY GENITALS

Some cisgender folks might think trans people don't think sex is real. After all, the Trans-Exclusionary Radical Feminist (TERF)/"Gender Critical" call to arms, after having grown tired of shouting *"this is not a drill,"* is "Sex is real!" So, trans people must think sex is... fake? Imaginary? An illusion? When trans people have sex, *we just merge our sad trans lachrymal essences together?*

No, no, we must just think sex is fake, right?

This is the implication that Joanne Karen Rowling laid against trans folks when making unfortunate history in December 2019 when she tweeted out in support of self-professed "gender critical feminist" and infamous TERF/Twitter Troll Maya Forstater. Many other TERFs use similar statements to effectively make trans people look ridiculous when we get upset with these gaslighting tactics. *"Of course, sex is real,"* thinks your average cis person on the fence about trans rights. *"Why would you fire a (cisgender) woman for saying something so simple and true?"*

To jump straight into the point, TERFs say "Sex is Real" for the same reason why competing brands add stickers like "Gluten-Free!" to a bottle of water to imply that competing brands must filter their spring water through a grain mill. For that matter, Forstater's work contract was not renewed because she was *harassing* trans people in the workplace and online, not at all because she uttered the words, "sex is real." This gross oversimplification of the case against Forstater is straightforward gaslighting of the situation in favor of a Twitter-friendly quip.

I have never heard a trans person insist that sex isn't real, and most of my close friends are in the community. In fact, we very much realize that sex is real because many of us are uncomfortable with our secondary sex characteristics. Ultimately, transgender people are, very often, acutely aware of sex. TERFs simply don't understand sex, binary sex, nonbinary sex, the incredible complexity of chromosomes as they apply to gender. TERFs are just angry, cisgender, mostly-white women on the internet, not biologists by any stretch of the imagination. Most of them back up their bigotry with debunked studies and widely repudiated scientists. Besides that fact, many trans people don't even have genital dysphoria, which is rather the point — nonbinary people are valid, and genitals simply aren't that important outside of the context of having sex or receiving professional medical care. I cannot begin to imagine why my parts should matter so much to someone like JK Rowling, but they apparently do.

And that, in a nutshell, is the entire point to be made: Sex is real, but all people are more than the sum of their parts.

Cisgender people tend to agree with this right up until such a concept applies to a transgender person because they still want to judge people on their gender or sex assigned at birth. But a cis man who has an accident that sees his penis amputated is not less of a man, and anybody who feels that way would be quickly labeled a massive jerk by even your most staunch TERF. A cis woman who has her uterus or breasts removed due to cancer is similarly not less of a woman. TERFs will almost always agree with these points. But when it comes to trans people, the things we do to heal our bodies are considered, at best, smoke and mirrors to hide our origins or, at worst, a tactical takedown and dilution of cis womanhood and an afront on fragile white cis feminism.

Queers didn't dilute anybody's marriage, however, and we trans folks certainly won't dilute anybody's gender identity... unless their cisgender identity was a fragile facade hiding their transness in the first place. What we see here, and what is fabulously on display in Rowling's 4,000-word essay justifying her radicalization that can be read on her website, is that cis people are *so uncomfortable* with trans people challenging the status quo that they lash out at us. Rowling even seems to think that if transition-related care were more readily available when she was younger, she might have made the honest mistake of transitioning to male to avoid the patriarchy, which is utterly bizarre in the context of informed consent and from the trans perspective. But, of course, as a cis woman, Rowling cannot possibly know what it's like to be trans, and nobody transitions solely to "escape the patriarchy." For that matter, trans men, women, and nonbinary trans folks are autonomous creatures, which is somehow hard for TERFs to grasp.

If Rowling had earnestly made the mistake of transitioning to male, that would be her own mistake to make and would have literally nothing to do with the millions of trans people who require trans-affirming care and never regret their choices.

For that matter, she makes it seem as though transitioning is easy, though it's decidedly not. I've been out for several years now and I'm still going back and forth with my insurance to cover my gender-affirming care, so I don't know how Rowling got it into her head that medically transitioning is like flipping a switch and taking a leisurely stroll into the surgery wing of a hospital for a restful body swap. But no... even if it's an easy enough choice to make, medically transitioning itself is fucking *hard*, as any trans person who is undergoing gender affirmation surgeries can certainly attest to.

We often see TERFs attacking trans folks online with vicious bigotry and cruel words designed to undercut our personhood in an attempt to force us back into the closet for their comfort. Rowling does not truly care for trans children, as she actively opposes their right to access trans-affirming healthcare. But moreover, this fake concern for trans peoples' wellbeing post-transition is just gross, particularly given that Rowling is just making our lives more frustrating by thinking her voice needs to be heard over that of trans folks. She has literally nothing to be oppressed about; she's a massively wealthy cisgender white woman. Rowling found this one thing that people would rally on her side over, allowing her to appear to be the victim in a situation in which she is the abuser. But *look*, she made trans people mad and then had to hide in her mansion! What a victimized martyr she is. What *bigots* those trans people are for calling her out on her bigotry. Poor rich white lady :(

Will someone *please* think of the white cis/het mega-millionaires?

Ultimately, transphobic cis people cannot conceive of trans people who are of sound enough mind to make informed choices about their bodies. Instead, they believe our gender identities are little more than side effects of mental illness or childhood abuse. The insidious part of this is that TERFs gaslight and attack trans people who are living with mental illness, and by doing so greatly exacerbate those illnesses. Moreover, it's true that many trans people were or are abused in their lives because of their transness, and using the reality of that abuse to invalidate our identities further is fucking evil.

Rowling has added unfortunate credibility and respectability to the TERF argument by turning herself into a martyr for "gender-critical" feminists by "sacrificing" her pristine reputation as a neoliberal icon. If someone as metered and well-thought-out as Rowling is anti-trans, then it must be an ideology that makes sense, right? After all, the woman taught us to triumph over evil and fight for what we believe in! *Incidentally,* Rowling also taught me how to do the same; I just never expected her to turn into one of my community's villains. If you'd have told me ten years ago that I'd be denouncing Rowling in this way now, I'd have called you delusional. Who could have ever predicted that the creator of Hermione and Dumbledore would become more akin to Professor Umbridge?

It ultimately all comes down to respectability politics, which is why TERFs operate on throwaway phrases like "Sex is Real." As evidenced by the thousands of articles regarding Rowling's shift towards transphobic feminism, these tactics put the trans community on the defensive in a *big* way. I've seen trans folks, particularly those who are young or living with mental illness, lashing out in understandable, if inappropriate, ways that, unfortunately, get thrown back in all of our faces as though we are a monolith. TERFs take advantage of the fact that our culture is still massively transphobic, and when we lash out at them for abusing us, the incident gets used to demonize the whole of our community further.

This is similar to how cases of sexual assault in which a trans or other LGBTQIA+ person perpetrated the crime are used to demonize all of us. The same handful of domestic cases get thrown around by TERFs to justify the idea that trans women are inclined toward assault, and such instances are used as evidence that we don't deserve the right to utilize the bathrooms that align with our genders. Unsurprisingly, there is no correlation between being trans and being violent or a sexual predator. That correlation is, also unsurprisingly, most substantial for white, heterosexual, cisgender men, who are more likely to murder trans women than trans folks are to hurt anybody. As a community, we are largely sensitive and passive, except where society has hardened us to the realities of our transphobic world. We shouldn't have to harden ourselves to a world that treats us as deviants and freaks, but that is the world we live in. We should be allowed to be ourselves in peace and remain sensitive, but transphobes make that increasingly difficult.

Hell, I have been verbally assaulted in every kind of restroom I've entered — male, female, and even single-stall—and yet, TERFs are thinking we oppress *them* by trying to safely pee in a gas station toilet as if that's the very height of our evening. As a trans woman in her thirties who doesn't "pass," I am unfortunately used to this treatment. The fact is, trans people are disproportionately survivors of violence and sexual assault, not the perpetrators. The idea that anybody other than white, cis/het men are responsible for the statistical and functional majority of sexual assaults is racist, homophobic, and transphobic.

And that's another point here, right? Whenever bigots want to tear marginalized people down and demonize those they want to eradicate, they over-sexualize us because doing so both draws negative attention to us and sees us kept at arm's length. It makes people fear us. This has happened with people of color, particularly Black American men, as well as lesbians, gay people, and bi/pansexuals. Bigots use this tactic because sex is taboo in much of the West, and even supposedly sex-positive TERFs use the sexualization of trans people as another weapon in their toolbelt of bigotry to turn people to their side.

Whenever bigoted white women want to demonize a population, they lob accusations of rape and assault at them, regardless of whether or not it's true, and will use a sparse few cases to pretend as though there's a trend. Too many people have been murdered because of cisgender, white women's fragility. Throughout history, earnest, white lady tears have been a weapon against the disenfranchised, and how TERFs treat trans people is no exception.

Furthermore, Hollywood has played a *huge* role in the demonization of transness and trans people. JK Rowling and other TERFs, however much they groom others, were likewise groomed into seeding their own transphobia by a culture that loves to paint us as villains and finds it easy to convince people of that lie. Look no further than Norman Bates, Buffalo Bill, and Angela Baker.

For more on the role of trans representation in media, flip to page 220.

Trans folks don't enjoy being put on the defensive by a millionaire who shifts from benevolent to malevolent based on your flavor of marginalized. We don't like having to explain that sex is a sensitive subject for many of us and that this focus is designed to trigger and get us to react. And it *sucks* having to explain to cis people who still support Rowling that this is all a gaslighting technique designed to anger and get us to lash out. TERFs *want* us angry so they can play respectability politics and turn more cis people to their side by appealing to fragile cis/het-sensibilities inclined toward tone-policing. I don't want to be told by anybody else that Rowling is a good person. Yes, she has helped children in cages, advocated for anti-poverty, funded multiple-sclerosis research, and made huge donations to worthwhile charities. Yes, Rowling has done good things, but she is, at her core, *not* a good person; she has made hurting the trans community the broad focus of her last few years, when she could have just shut her mega-millionaire mouth and kept being a prolific philanthropist *quietly,* without the vocal transphobia.

JK Rowling is trying to groom the children and young adults she raised with her books into radicalizing into a TERF cult. I also believe that Rowling realized how many of her fans were trans and decided to do something about it in a way that would not only gain her new fans but get more people to join her on the wrong side of history. I am sure that Rowling feels she is doing the right thing, but so have Christians who have made demonizing gays the cornerstone of their sermons and fundraising efforts for decades.

That I have to write this entire essay to combat Rowling's three little words will be used by some to discredit my argument, rather than highlight the clever technique Rowling has deployed upon a community that doesn't need her ignorance right now or ever. The point is not to prove TERFs wrong, or convince anybody that trans rights are human rights. You and I know that, otherwise this book wouldn't likely be in your hands. Rather, I am here to say that our sex parts are nobody else's goddamn business.

Sex is real—as are nonbinary genitals. Now, people need to stop focusing so much on our genitalia, *it's fucking weird*.

And I think I can say with some authority... *Fuck you*, Rowling.

- Madeleine Voltin -

THE JOURNEY

Figuring out oneself is like a journey; it takes courage, strength, wit, and knowledge. Along that journey, you will run into obstacles, the occurrences that try and block your path. You will also learn heartbreak and pain. If you persevere, you can reach the end of the journey, your destination, your ultimate realization. Realizing who you have been all along being the destination of that journey.

Being transgender is part of my identity and has been a part of my life for many years. I was born Madison on August 24, 1993, to two parents. I was born too early and had to be taken to the NICU for many months. If you ask my parents, they would tell you that I was a miracle child. I was their little boy.

That would eventually change 20 years later.

Being a young child and knowing that you are different from others is a confusing experience. I would ask for Barbies for Christmas and wear dresses when playing with my cousins. I would call myself a girl. This confused my parents. They had gone to a doctor and had asked what to do. Back in the 90s, transgender was not well known, especially in the area of Texas I had grew up in. The doctor told them that I might be gay later in life and that there was nothing wrong with me and nothing they could do about it. Even though I had the relative freedom to express myself, I was only allowed to do so freely behind closed doors.

As a teenager, I started to develop a sense of my sexuality. Beforehand, I had never had a little crush on some girl in my class. I had lots of girlfriends, but they were girl friends and nothing more. I already knew I was different. I was girly, and I didn't like what the boys liked to do. I had to hide that from everyone with whom I went to school. During that time, my parents had divorced, and I was living most of the time with my mother. We had moved to the countryside where my mother had grown up. That meant that I went to school in the country too. It was difficult in middle school. Boys always talked about how they liked girls and talked about heterosexual sex. Of course, I tried to blend in and lied about liking the same thing. I was already bullied for my weight and being too feminine, so I tried to make things easier on myself. Other kids would call me "gay," often and I would deny it. A few years later, I would realize that I could not hide my sexuality anymore.

High school was entirely different from middle school. I was not spending all my time in class with the same fifteen students; I now had sixty students in my class. This environment wasn't ideal, to say the least, but it was much better than the one in which I had grown accustomed. At the age of fifteen, I came out as bisexual to my parents after an unsuccessful relationship with my best girlfriends. It would be a few months later before I would come out as gay. I knew I was attracted to men, both sexually and romantically, but I didn't have the words to express my gender identity properly. I desperately wanted a relationship and would do anything to get one. Whether that meant unsafely going to dating apps designed for adult men or secretly talking to the boys who wanted me to be their secret gay sexual experience in school. At that time, I was not sure of my gender. I knew I was more than just feminine, but "transgender" was a word that had not been entered into my vocabulary or understanding just yet.

College was an important time in terms of my self-discovery. I was in my first relationship with a man a few months before college, and we had decided to try and work with a long-distance relationship. I also was finally in a campus Gay-Straight Alliance. That GSA would eventually help me realize that I was transgender. I spent a year and a half identified as a gay, cisgender man with a feminine personality. After my break up a few months after I started college, I had that time to stop and really think about who I was. I knew I liked men, that was clear, but certain parts of myself just didn't feel right. I didn't want to be touched in certain erogenous areas and didn't know why. It would be a year and a half after I started college that I would come to realize that I was, in fact, a transgender person.

A year and a half after I had started college, I was questioning myself after I had been going to the gay club in a neighboring town dressed in full drag. One night I posted a picture of myself and my friends, not knowing that my family would see that picture as well. That night, my mother called me and told me that what I was doing was against what God had envisioned for me.

I was shocked because I didn't know what she meant by that. That accusation would eventually help guide me to realize who I was.

One day in 2014, I had gone to the library with my friend to work on an assignment that was due for one of the classes I was taking that semester. I had spoken to my friend at the time about how I was confused about my gender. I already tried to find a label to fit myself: genderqueer, genderfluid, transsexual... would those suit me? I decided to research how I felt and one thing was clear: I felt something was wrong with my body. I already knew I was not comfortable in my skin. I never paid much attention to my lower half, and I always imagined myself with feminine curves. Then the word "transgender" appeared on the computer screen. I looked through different articles and watched several documentaries. Finally, I felt that I had a word to describe how I had been feeling for all those years, searching in the dark. After that, I decided I would do whatever it took to make my goals come to fruition.

There was one person in my life who made me feel like I could never come out, but his death signaled my pathway to living my truth. My mother married my old stepfather when I was in middle school. He was very nice to my brother and me at first, and would take us places and pay for what we wanted. It felt right to give my mother away to him when they decided to get married, but after a few years his attitude drastically changed. He would put me down any chance he could get and would argue with me constantly. He never came to support me at any extracurricular activities while I was in high school or college. The man who had once been a good stepfather turned into a drunk, angry, mentally abusive man who would target me for my sexuality and gender expression. After his death, I finally felt relief. That feels horrible to say about the person who paid off my mother's home and was a father figure to my younger brother, but I would never have decided to come out as transgender if he hadn't died. I suppose, sometimes, the truth is horrible.

In November 2014, I decided that I would come out to my mother as trans. I made the plan with a friend and we traveled to spend the Thanksgiving holiday with my parents back home. I remember feeling a pit in my stomach. My mother had already expressed displeasure at me questioning my gender, so I was unsure if she would accept me. I already knew that she was accepting of my sexuality and had been for a few years, but trans was a whole different ballpark.

I drew in a quick breath and went into my mother's bedroom. I told her that I did not feel right in my body and thought I might be transgender. She was not at all surprised, but neither did she bring up the subject again while I was on break. Although it was hard to realize how difficult my mother found it to understand at the time, she would eventually become my greatest supporter and cheerleader.

In March 2015, I got to see an endocrinologist to start hormone replacement therapy. I drove with my friend to downtown Houston, Texas on a rainy day. It was more than a little nerve-wracking to be seen by a doctor who would determine whether or not I would receive the medication to help me with my journey. In came the doctor, wearing cowboy boots and scrubs. Oh boy. I told him about how I felt I was born in the wrong body and wanted to start my transition. I truly thought he wasn't going to prescribe any medication to me because I was under the age of 21 but, to my relief, I got my first prescription for estrogen and spironolactone that day.

On March 13, 2015, I would finally start on hormone replacement therapy, and a little blue pill became part of my daily routine.

It has been almost six years since I came out. A lot of things have happened since that day. I started dating again in 2015, and I met the person who I would eventually come to live with in Austin, TX. We moved in together a few years after that. I graduated from college in 2016, as Madeleine legally on paper after receiving my legal name change back in 2015, and then changed my gender marker in 2017. Lastly, in June 2019, I had gender confirmation surgery: the end of my journey to womanhood.

I do not know where life will take me, but I do know one thing: I am loved for who I am, transgender and all. My advice to parents is to support your child through their journey of discovery. When your child tells you that they are questioning themselves, hug them tight and be their greatest supporters. Figuring out oneself is a journey. It took me a while to realize mine, but I would not change a damned thing about it.

- TransFocus Editors -

WHAT IS MISGENDERING?

Misgendering is, whether intentional or not, the incorrect gendering of a trans person, typically by using the pronouns associated with their assigned gender at birth (AGAB). Misgendering can cause extreme emotional distress to the trans person on the receiving end of it and constitutes a microaggression, but it can be a macroaggression when repeated, malicious and intentional. When left uncorrected, it can result in a trans person distancing themselves from the cis person or people (or, occasionally, even fellow trans people) who exhibit this form of disrespect.

Repeated intentional misgendering is a hostile act that often seeks to undermine a trans person's true identity, disregarding their right to be seen and regarded as their authentic gender. In some US states, such as California, this can be illegal, depending on the setting, and often constitutes harassment on the basis of gender identity. For many trans people, our pronouns are extremely important to us, and asking for people to change the pronouns they use for us is often an essential step in affirming who we are in this world.

To give an example, misgendering would be calling a trans woman a guy or a man, or addressing her/them with "he/him/his" pronouns, despite her requesting to be referred to as a "girl/woman" or with "she/her/her's" pronouns. Conversely, referring to a trans man as a woman or girl or with "she/her/her's) pronouns despite asking for "he/him/his" and other masculine identifiers are also forms of misgendering. Similarly, repeatedly referring to someone as "they/their" when they have requested binary pronouns can also constitute misgendering.

There are subtle forms of misgendering as well, such as referring to a trans woman as "buddy," which is a typically masculinized word. Referring to a trans woman as a "dude" is also a form of misgendering, despite the word coming to widespread use more neutrally in recent years. The fact is, many transphobes intentionally use traditionally gendered language like this to misgender trans women and transfemmes, hiding behind colloquial gender neutrality to justify it in what ultimately equates to gaslighting. No matter how comfortable most cis women and men are with being called "hey guys," in a group, it can be an uncomfortable, vaguely invalidating experience for trans women and nonbinary folks.

Conversely, standard greetings like "hey gals/girls/ladies" are rarely used in a neutral sense because our language and what is considered neutral or "default" is fundamentally influenced by the patriarchy. The fact that words and greetings like "hey guys" and "dude" are now considered neutral is furthermore exploited by transphobes, particularly "Trans Exclusionary Radical Feminists" (TERFs), who search for valid reasons to invalidate trans identity and the use of gender-affirming pronouns. As mentioned above, TERFs use that fact to gaslight any trans person who tells them that these words constitute misgendering and hurt them. The simple fact is that if someone tells you they don't like "hey guys" or other masculine greetings used in a neutral manner, you should respect their wishes. Combating or debating them on the cultural perception that historically masculine greetings are now neutral is simply disrespectful. We *know* that's how they're used, and trans people are allowed to push back at the patriarchy making masculine greetings neutral without doing the same to feminine greetings. For instance, your average group of cis/het men won't take kindly to being called "gals," but the rest of us are expected to be okay with being called "guys." It's a double-standard that is absolutely worth criticizing and correcting when it makes trans folks uncomfortable.

On a related note, the most respectful thing you can do is always use a gender-neutral greeting for any person or group. One of the favorites of many trans folks is the greeting "hey y'all," given the *delicious* irony of pulling a trans-friendly greeting out of the notoriously queer/transphobic American south. We can also recommend "Good morning/afternoon/evening, Fellow Humans," "Greetings, Compatriots," "Hi, Folks," or "Hello, Theydies and Gentlethems!" And while those may not sound natural to everyone, your trans friends and family will thank you for the efforts toward inclusivity in how you address groups of mixed-gender people.

Back on the topic of singular misgendering, nonbinary people and other trans folks who use "they/their" pronouns or neopronouns like "xe/xir / ze/zir" are also frequently, if not *always*, misgendered, and it is only within the last few years that pronouns perceived as plural have been respected in the singular. However, many are misgendered with either set of binary pronouns regardless of their gender assigned at birth. Of course, many are misgendered with the pronouns associated with their AGAB. Still, those who appear neither masculine nor feminine often confuse cisgender people, resulting in a hasty flip-flopping of incorrect binary pronouns. Our most uncomplicated advice to any cis person reading this that we can provide is to refer to all people as "they/their" until you know for sure which pronouns they use.

There is a frequent debate about the validity of the neutral "they" due to a scholarly misunderstanding that "they" is inherently and solely plural in nature. The fact is, "they" was used as a singular pronoun *long* before it became regarded as plural. According to the Oxford English Dictionary, the plural "they" can be historically traced back to 1375, where it appeared in the medieval romance *William and the Werewolf*. In that text, an unnamed person whom the author didn't want to give away the gender of is referred to as "they." It was only in the 18th century that linguists began to warn against use of the plural "they," citing that it was an improper use of a plural pronoun taking the place of a singular pronoun, which ignored the universal reality of the word "you," which can refer to a single person or multiple people and has become rather unremarkable.

Nowadays, the singular "they" is increasingly respected and understood as proper English in the accommodation and accepted reality of nonbinary people. Any scholarly rejection of the singular "they" is staunchly placed in ignorance and a false piety regarding the English language's perceived infallability and inflexibility. The fact is, language constantly changes to accommodate the current age, and there will never be any one "correct" way to utilize, write, and speak the English language. Any curmudgeons who have a problem with that sit firmly on the wrong side of history, *lest they start speaketh in a mann'r liketh this to prithee* long-dead white men like Shakespeare, who, somewhat ironically, invented a vast quantity of his own words.

Another gross form of misgendering is when the pronoun "it" is used for anybody who doesn't wish to be addressed that way. In most cases, "it" refers to an inanimate object and is typically only used to refer to a person as a means of dehumanizing them. Of course, a small percentage of trans people do use that pronoun as a reclamation of a pronoun commonly used to harm us, and that is to be respected, but, for the most part, trans people do not wish to be called "it," ever.

What it ultimately comes down to is that misgendering in any form is disrespectful, regardless of the justification for it. To keep the trans people you love in your life, you must accommodate their pronouns and work hard to change the pronouns you once used for them to the correct ones.

It's all about basic respect.

- Em Keevan -

WHEN I WALK ALONE
I AM AFRAID

When I walk alone, I am afraid... that I am small and the world is big... that if attacked, hit, battered, or worse, the world wouldn't even stop to notice or give a damn. I am afraid people will see me as easy pickings and choose me as their next target.

Being out and proud adds to the anxiety of living in a world where it's not okay to be anything but white, cisgender, and straight. Statistically, the odds seem negligible, sure, but I still feel my throat squeezing shut as I fight to remind myself it's really not, that I can still breathe.

Heart pounding against my ribcage as breaths catch in my throat, I know no one can see the struggle within, but I find myself wishing, wondering, what if they could? Then maybe they'd see the panic is justified. Counting seconds, moments, minutes, footsteps, I keep a steady pace from point A to point B. This fear comes from within, and I race against my own heart, but I have to remind myself that it also comes from the world we live in.

Gasping for breath only when I'm safe, safe inside, behind many locked doors; safe only until the next time I have to venture back outside. Fears consume me. They shouldn't, I know this, but I feel powerless to control the spiral, the fear, and I pray to pass no other people today, to walk truly alone, unwatched, free from their gazes, free from their judgments.

I try not to watch the news because it's unnerving and saturated with people just like me dying with nary a thought or a trace, dying only to be misgendered in death, disrespected and forgotten by all but their own who are left behind to set the record straight. I ask, why isn't anyone doing anything to stop it? But I already know the answer: we are second-class citizens.

I can feel it when going outside; I feel it whenever I leave the comfort of my safe space. Safe inside where I may be trapped, but at least I am free. But am I really free if freedom only extends within a locked room wherein I know nothing can hurt me?

Statistics, statistics, statistics. I know the odds are slim, but still, I want to hide inside. Until there is change, I know I'll always live in fear, just like we all live in fear because we're gay, lesbian, bisexual, queer, trans, and all the other letters in our LGBTQIA+ alphabet soup. All because we're different from the majority, because we refuse to hide who we are, hide like society wants, begs, and demands us to.

My fears consume me.

I write not just because I can but because I hope I can make a difference. Maybe one day, there will be a time when people read what I've written and truly understand that they are not alone in this cold, scary, violent, taunting world.

You are not alone, no matter what this society may tell you.

Pouring my heart and soul into the words, choosing to prove I don't want to feel this way, that maybe I don't have to feel this way, and hoping that perhaps it'll help someone see they don't have to feel this way either.

Statistics, statistics, statistics. Yes, the odds are slim to none, but I nevertheless spew out all the words I can before my time is up, before my fears become a reality, because I know what could happen and that every day could be my last each and every time I leave my home.

My fears consume me.

I pray I won't have to pass by anybody today.

- Em Keevan -

I THOUGHT IT WOULD BE EASY

When I sat down at the computer, I thought it'd be easy. Write about your experiences being under the trans umbrella. Easy. But there's so much I've done and been, and it feels like nothing has changed. I haven't spoken to my mother in over a month, not since she threw a hissy-fit on social media when I asked to be respected. I guess I can write about that, since that's the freshest and most confusing and the most aggravating. Sure, I could have handled it differently, but I'm not sure I wanted to. All I wanted was respect.

My new year's resolution was to respect myself and not let others disrespect me. I usually think resolutions like that are silly because people hardly ever follow through with them, but I needed this. I came out to everyone I knew on social media last July. I'd discovered that I was nonbinary during the previous two semesters, but had to wait until I was out of my parents' home to come out officially. All of my friends, my brother knew and my partner Seth knew, but my parents and extended relatives? That was what I dreaded the most. My parents are very religious, and I already knew they weren't going to take me coming out well. I wasn't close to either of them, and the more my mother tried to force a relationship, the more I hated her. And I hated that I was afraid to be around her, as she was unpredictable and terrifying. She'd get angry over nothing and scream and yell and threaten to punish my brother and me with no electronics or no friends or whatever. Then she'd come back a while later acting as if nothing was wrong and typically tried to buy us off with ice cream or a movie.

Moving into an off-campus apartment with my partner Seth and two other roommates was a breath of fresh air, one that I desperately needed. Once I was out of the toxic environment I grew up in, I knew I had to come out. I couldn't stand being misgendered all the time. And, of course, it was partially my fault. How could I be angry if they didn't know better? But I couldn't stand it anymore; I needed to be free. I needed to be me. So I finally did it. I made a post and told everyone that I used they/them and was nonbinary. Female-coded language was off-limits.

Friends who already knew gave me encouragement. My family said nothing.

In the following months, it was as if nothing had changed. My parents still aggressively referred to me as "she." My mother refused to let me shop outside the "women's" clothing section when she'd offer a peace offering of shopping to get clothes that I would like. All my extended family refused to acknowledge that I wasn't a girl. It was as if nothing I said mattered. I made more posts, reminding people.

I made charts; I made pictures; I made slides. They weren't listening. And it was crushing me. I thought I'd be safe and free once I came out, but I only felt more afraid and alone. So after a lot of deliberation, I decided on another coming-out post, putting my foot down this time. It wasn't necessarily out of malice, I think. I just wanted people to at least TRY or ACKNOWLEDGE that they weren't respecting me. So I knew I had to give an ultimatum. That's the only way people ever respond to change.

It went like this: "My 'New Year Resolution' is to be a better self-advocate. That said, EFFECTIVE JANUARY 1, 2019, I will no longer tolerate being misgendered. I use they/them pronouns. She/her will no longer be accepted. If you don't 'believe' in using they/them, he/him is allowed *despite not being my preferred pronouns*. She/her pronouns and female-coded language will not be tolerated! Failure to do so will result in an end to all communication, regardless of relation or how long we've known each other. Thank you."

Now sure, there was probably a better way to word it, but I just needed to get it out. I commented that there's a difference between accidentally slipping up and not trying whatsoever. I had to get rid of the people who weren't trying, for the sake of my sanity and mental health. The first comment was encouraging; my friend Sandy, who is ten years my senior and whose children I used to babysit, praised me for coming out. She and I had talked before about it, but I hadn't come out to her. But after Sandy's encouraging comment came nasty ones from people who I had considered family. First, my aunt. She said that I "can't teach an old dog new tricks." I had suspected my aunt would be hesitant to accept me as anything other than a girl based on how she'd ignored my requests to cut my hair shorter (she was also my hairdresser up till this instance) and only would cut my hair "feminine ways." Sandy and my friend Glynn jumped to my defense and told her to be respectful. I unfriended my aunt, as I'd promised, and knew I had to follow through. Two of my aunt's three children sent me private messages saying that they apologized for their mother's behavior and they were sorry some people were too bigoted to respect me.

Then came my mother.

She said I was a bully, demanded an apology, and declared that she and my father raised me better than that; that I had to be nice or else. She said she was "trying to respect the choice I made" and that saying I wouldn't tolerate being misgendered was disrespectful, and I should just let it happen and say nothing.

I finally snapped. After years of my mother manipulating me, I couldn't stand it anymore. Numerous friends jumped to my defense. People who knew my mother, people who didn't, all came together gloriously to defend me. I knew what I had to do. I unfriended my mother. I didn't want to, but I also didn't want to deal with her anymore.

I cried—a lot. Crying's a pretty day-to-day thing for me since I'm a hodge-podge of emotions swirling inside of me, and being neurodivergent didn't help much, but this was different. I'd done something I spent my entire life avoiding and hiding from: I finally stood up for myself.

Many things have happened in my life that I wish I could take back, and all of them were based around not standing up for myself, for my autonomy, my agency, for my ability to say no, for my inability to do things neurotypically expected of me. And I'd finally done it. And I cried. I felt terrible, and the only thing I wanted to do was go back in time and stop myself from making the post. That's how I typically handle confrontation; not do it, or if I do, backpeddle and pretend it never happened.

After a day or two, however, I began to feel better about my decision. It was truly like a weight was off my chest. Sure, there was plenty of stuff I still had to deal with, like school, professors, and the family who refused to comment or say anything, but I felt better for having held my ground.

Like everyone, I just want respect. I deserve respect. I just want to be myself, and I deserve to feel good in my skin. If I can do that, I can do *anything*.

I just wish it wasn't so hard.

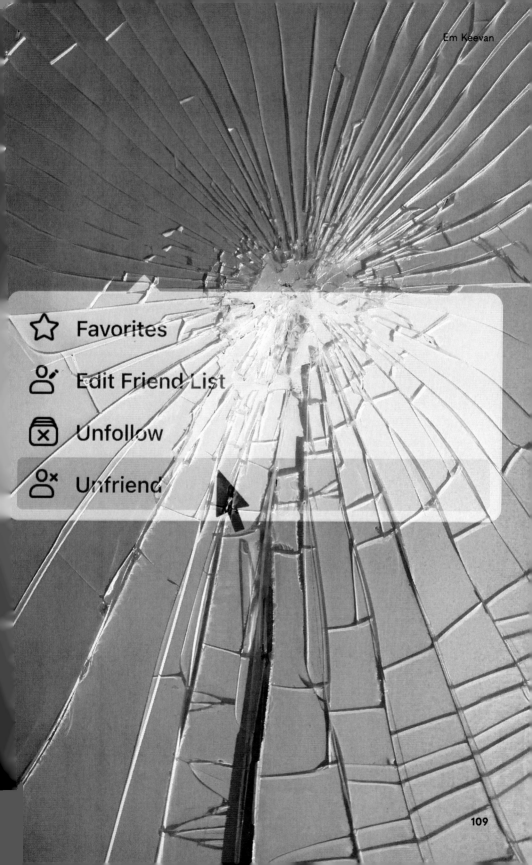

Em Keevan

☆ Favorites

  Edit Friend List

☒ Unfollow

Unfriend

- TransFocus Editors -

WHAT IS TRANS DAY OF REMEMBRANCE & TRANS DAY OF VISIBILITY?

"Those who cannot remember the past are doomed to repeat it."

- George Santayana

On the 20th of each November, we hold Transgender Day of Remembrance (TDoR), concluding Trans Awareness Week, which runs from the 13th to the 19th. This annual observance honors the memory of those lost throughout the year to violence, hate crimes, and suicide. It was started by trans activist Gwendolyn Ann Smith in 1999 to honor Rita Hester, a Black trans woman murdered in 1998 in Allston, Massachusetts, and TDoR has been held every year since and has spread across the globe.

TDoR is a solemn occasion during which we take time to reflect and mourn those we've lost. We highlight these losses because, all too often, the loss of trans lives is largely ignored by the media. We draw attention to these untimely deaths because violence against the trans community, especially Black and Latinx trans women, is far too common and is a plague upon our communities. We take this time to express love, community growth, and defiance in the face of great intolerance and hatred.

Across the world, trans people and our allies gather to read the names of those who have lost their lives. Candlelight vigils are a common occurrence that accompany these readings, as are church services, marches, food drives, poetry readings, discussion forums, art shows, visual memorials, diversity trainings, and screenings of films and documentaries like "Pay It No Mind - The Life and Times of Marsha P. Johnson" and Netflix's "Disclosure."

We have seen a steep rise in violence against trans people of color in recent years, making TDoV especially important, especially as the world remains largely indifferent to crimes against the trans community. Trans people are frequently victims of police violence in addition to partner violence and violent transphobic attacks. Increasingly, TDoR is honored in schools across the world, educating students, teachers, administrators, and parents about trans issues and the reality of what it means to be trans in a transphobic world, and serves to open cis peoples' eyes to issues that they frequently overlook and ignore.

In 2020, US President-Elect Joe Biden made history by being the first US president to draw attention to TDoV, stating that the murders of Black and Brown transgender women are intolerable. Biden concluded his post with a simple message: "To transgender and gender-nonconforming people across America and around the world: from the moment I am sworn in as president, know that my administration will see you, listen to you, and fight for not only your safety but also the dignity and justice you have been denied." Biden made good on that promise by bringing on Pennsylvania Health Secretary Rachel Levine to be his assistant secretary of health. While TransFocus does not endorse any politician or political candidate, we do wish to acknowlege this groundbreaking and historical occurence of TDOV being observed by a sitting president.

Conversely, Trans Day of Visibility (TDoV) is when we take time to celebrate the trans community. Across the world, trans people post declarations of pride, self-love, and self-actualization. We are more visible today than ever before in history and more and more trans people use TDoV to come out and make their truth known to their loved ones.

The day was founded by trans activist and Executive Director of Transgender Michigan, Rachel Crandall, in 2009 to help amend a lack of recognition of trans people. By this point, TDoR had been held for ten years, but we had few opportunities as a community to celebrate the lives we lead. In a way, it felt as though trans people weren't loved or celebrated until we died, and TDoV sought to reconcile that oversight.

On TDoV, we raise awareness and increase trans visibility largely by posting to social media and talking about our lives and what it means to be trans, as well as the struggles we face in the workplace, in housing, in seeking affirming healthcare, in our family dynamics, and when we come out to a transphobic world. We celebrate our accomplishments, successes, and triumphs as trans people living in a cis-centric culture. We furthermore take the time to speak on the importance of trans representation in government, media, music, education, science, and the arts.

While we celebrate our accomplishments on TDoV, we also recognize that there is much work yet to be done. In 2021, thirty-three US states have introduced at least 117 anti-trans bills that seek to undermine the few rights that trans people have, and that number will surely increase by the time this book goes to print. Most of these bills directly impact our most vulnerable transgender youth and their right to gender-affirming healthcare, with one bill in Alabama making it a federal offense for physicians, psychiatrists, therapists, nurse practitioners and other healthcare providers to dispense transition-related care, and even goes as far as forcing adults to out trans children to their parents. We are also seeing ID restrictions, curriculum bans, and bills seeking to ban trans people from participating in organized sports consistent with their gender identity, even though trans people exhibit no undue advantage in athletics on the basis of being trans and assertions to the contrary have been widely debunked.

With these attacks on our community, Trans Day of Visibility and Trans Day of Remembrance are of the utmost importance. We proclaim who we are, celebrate our community, and honor those who have left us because who we are is important, our lives and safety are deserving of focus, and our community is actively under attack.

Some day, we may not need trans days of visibility and remembrance, but today is not that day. For now, we need TDoV and TDoR, and will continue to observe both annually until they are made obsolete by virtue of trans people being safe, cherished, celebrated, loved, and respected across the globe.

not he
not she
just me

- Branok Ryland Fuller -

A DAY IN THE LIFE

Xe smiled as they looked in the mirror.

Hir outfit was a great choice and felt very neutral.

The day wore on, and the smile faded a bit more each time xe heard xemself referred to as ma'am or their pleas just to call them a guy were ignored. They worked for such a progressive company, but it felt impolite to correct the customers on anything but drink names or sizes, even more so considering hir location. Each day the burden grew heavier, but they still went out of hir way to make people happy. Xe always checked the spelling of their names and related that they understood, as xe had an unusual name xemself. "Oh? What is it?" and when xe answered, the person would always mishear or say how pretty it was. This was the problem, though.

They weren't pretty. Or at least, they didn't want to be. Xe wanted to be called handsome like the other guys with whom they worked. In many cases, xe fit the box for a nonbinary person. They had hair dyed in odd colors, piercings, masculine haircuts, compressed hir breasts as much as xe safely could, their clothing was always a mix of masculine and feminine, they used the most masculine mannerisms that xe could comfortably adopt, and even occasionally wore makeup.

They hoped for days when xe didn't have to speak to the public so they could avoid being misgendered. Even people xe regularly reminded frequently said the most hurtful words without harmful intentions: she, her, daughter, girl, woman.

After another, long, typical day, xe fell into bed; hoping, once more, that when they woke up, xe would at least be comfortable in their body for once. They cried, hoping to wake up with a flat chest, no curves, and stubble. Xe slipped from the waking nightmare of their life into the peace of unconsciousness, into who xe was without others' expectations. The ease of a life where they would never worry about which box to tick.

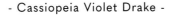

- Cassiopeia Violet Drake -

BLOSSOM

Content Notice: Suicidal Ideation/Attempt

There is a very early memory that I think about a lot nowadays. I am about five years old and lying in my bed at night, about to go to sleep. Before I do, I pray to God. Just one prayer. I say, "God, when I wake up tomorrow, please let me be a girl."

I said that same prayer every night for three years straight.

One day, I stopped because it never happened, and I repressed those feelings of wanting to be a girl.

I also remember consciously and subconsciously referring to myself as a girl during this time. Every time I did so with my parents, they told me I was wrong and confused and "corrected" me. It made me feel like something was wrong with me, so I stopped talking to them about it.

I acted rather feminine my first few years in elementary school, and the kids my age would bully me quite a lot for it. After a while, I started overcompensating with masculine behaviors to make the other kids stop. I hated acting masculine and hiding who I truly was. That, combined with my prayers remaining unanswered, caused me to become depressed, bitter, and miserable when I was only eight years old.

It just didn't get easier.

When puberty hit, my depression skyrocketed. I hated pretty much every facet of what my body was becoming: the deeper voice, the facial and body hair, all of it. I had intense dysphoria regarding it all but didn't have the language to express what I was feeling to anyone adequately. Plus, I was terrified of being bullied again.

I didn't even know of any transgender person until I was 16. When I found out about her, it was like a lightbulb went off in my head. I wasn't alone in my feelings. There were people like me. But then, I swiftly turned the light off. I remembered what had happened the last time I let those feelings loose at the forefront of my mind. I desperately tried repressing them again, but all it succeeded in doing was making me far more depressed and highly suicidal. Those feelings about my gender identity never went away, and, frankly, they never will for anyone who has them.

I graduated high school and felt a brief moment of actual happiness for the first time in my life. It lasted about an hour, then went away.

I spent my college years hiding myself from everyone. I had initially joined an LGBT group on campus but then got too scared to keep going and stopped attending. My suicidal ideation kept getting worse. Somehow, I did graduate college, and that was the second time in my life I felt happiness. Rather like the first, it lasted around an hour, then faded.

During this time, one of my high school friends came out and started transitioning, which was the first time I personally knew of any transgender person.

In November 2016, I got into my first relationship, and my then-girlfriend referred to me as her boyfriend. Rather than feeling joy, I felt so off. That just wasn't right, and I didn't want that in any way.

Within a week, I messaged my friend from high school to understand her experience. We spoke for hours at a time for almost a year about gender identity, what I wanted to look like, act like, be treated like, my memories throughout my life, and many other things. On August 30th, 2017, after over 21 years of confusion, denial, and repression, I finally wholly accepted and knew the answer to what had been bothering me my entire life.

I was, in fact, not a man but a woman. The realization was incredible, and I finally felt like I could progress in life.

But that feeling quickly faded as my fears about how I would be treated by my family, friends, and society as a whole overwhelmed me.

46% of transgender people have, at some point in their lives, tried to commit suicide. On September 5th, 2017, I became one of them. It did not succeed, and for that, I am eternally thankful.

For several reasons, I went back into the closet for 18 months. The most pressing reason was the lack of support and frequent transphobia from my girlfriend. She had threatened to break up with me if I transitioned. I also closeted myself due to the knowledge of what my family thought about transgender people, which wasn't positive in any way. It was an incomparable misery. I knew what and who I was, but I was trying so hard to repress it, and it made my depression the worst it's been in my entire life. It got to the point that I was incapable of feeling any emotion. I tried so hard to be someone I wasn't just to please those close to me, and all it did was cause me to suffer immensely. Early March 2019, I decided that I couldn't go on living like that and decided to transition. My girlfriend broke up with me, which was expected, and then I started the process of transitioning.

I came back out to my friends who supported me. I came out to my family, who were sadly much less than supportive.

I want you all to understand just how crucial support, visibility, and understanding are. I was born in 1996 and didn't transition until 2019. I spent those 23 years of my life lying to myself and everyone around me. My personality was completely fake. Nearly everything I did during that time was not what I actually wanted to do; I only did it because I was too scared and terrified of being targeted. I cannot get that part of my life back. I cannot relive my life as the girl I should have been. I had no girlhood. I had no female adolescence. Everything I learned about how to act, socialize, talk, walk, dress, and the like was not how it was supposed to be.

On July 9th, 2019, I started hormone replacement therapy. I took anti-androgens to block my testosterone and took estrogen and progesterone pills.

I want to put things in perspective here. Between 2010 and July 9th, 2019, I took approximately seventy-five pictures of myself total in the whole of nine years. It makes sense, considering I hated the way I looked.

After a month, I hadn't noticed anything different. I was tired and still depressed and seriously thought about stopping transitioning since I wasn't getting any better. I went to my endocrinologist, who told me that my estrogen levels were half of where they should be and bumped up my dose. I decided to try for one more month to see if anything changed.

I consider that day, August 14th, 2019, as the day I was reborn. Within 24 hours, my depression and hopelessness that had been an overwhelming part of my life were gone entirely. I felt genuine happiness for just the third time in my life. But this time, it didn't go away. I felt relentlessly optimistic about my future living as my authentic self. Since that day, my depression has barely shown up. Every day has been incomparably amazing, and I keep getting happier and better constantly.

I started dating someone genuinely wonderful. They're non-binary, and being with them made me realize that my gender identity is not entirely female. It's primarily female, but there is a not insignificant part of it that is non-binary, which is why I also use they/them pronouns. I am completely confident that no amount of my gender is masculine in any way, however.

I cannot stop smiling now. I still get overwhelmed thinking about just how far I have come in life. I actually get to be me. I get to be Kira.

Many LGBT+ people say that it gets better. When I first heard that almost a decade ago, I didn't believe it. But then it happened to me.

I tried counting the number of pictures I have of myself since that fateful July 9th. I stopped after the 500th one.

Transitioning not only saved my life, it gave me a reason to live. It gave me a reason to love myself.

I will leave you all with a summary of what transitioning did for me: For 23 years of my life, it was a harsh winter, but now, spring has finally come, and I am in full bloom.

- Miles Mayes -

COMING OUT

Hey, I'm Miles. I came out to my dad on October 8th, 2018 when I was sixteen. We had a homecoming dance at school that night, so I wrote him a letter explaining how I was trans and gave it to him so he could process everything by the time I got back home. I didn't really enjoy the dance all that much; I was way too worried about what my dad would say when I got home.

When I did end up going home, he said that if I wanted to live my life as a boy, I could, as long as I waited to do hormone therapy after high school. He's supportive; he just doesn't use my proper pronouns or my real name yet, but I think he'll come around eventually. I'm waiting to talk to my mom before I ask him if he can start using the correct name, because I really want to get it legally changed. Since that night when I gave him the letter, we haven't really talked that much about it, but I have hope that will change after I start transitioning. Once he sees that this is who I am, he'll have to accept me.

My plans after high school have been getting brought up a lot with my boyfriend. I've been dating him for about a year and 7 months now. We've talked a lot about college and what we're planning on doing. He's planning on helping me get on hormone therapy, and we're gonna save up so I can get top surgery. And for the future... someday when we get older and want kids, we're planning on adopting.

My life really hasn't been the best for the last couple of years, but knowing I have something to look forward to after high school is making it all worth it. He's the best boyfriend I could ever ask for. I hope that if you don't have the right person for you yet, you know that you'll find them. They're out there, and when you find them, they're gonna be your number one supporter.

Everyone deserves someone like that in their life.

- TransFocus Editors -

HAVE YOU HAD "THE SURGERY?"

Surgery is an integral part of many trans people's experience, but a question like "Have you had the surgery?" is hugely unnecessary. When cis people ask us this, it's usually about bottom surgery or surgery on our genitalia. Bottom surgery entails any surgery a trans person might have to allieve dysphoria of the genital region, and includes orchiectomy (removal of the testes), penectomy (removal of the penis), vaginoplasty (the creation of a neovagina), vulvoplasty (no-depth vaginoplasty), metoidioplasty (creation of a neophallus using existing genital tissue), vaginectomy (removal of the vagina), and phalloplasty (the creation of a neophallus using skin grafts from the arm or thigh).

These surgeries are often very invasive, and many trans people opt not to undergo bottom surgery due to the extensive and challenging healing involved. Undergoing bottom surgery, perhaps with the exception of orchiectomy, results in a fair amount of downtime and bed rest, so many trans people cannot afford to have bottom surgery because we have to work and are often unable to get the time off necessary to recover completely. Of course, some trans people do not have bottom dysphoria at all and have no desire to alter their genitalia.

In general, it's not okay to ask someone about what's going on in their trousers. Cis people often let their curiosity get the best of them and ask trans people questions that they would never dare ask a fellow cis person. Respect flies out the window when dealing with a trans person, and "have you had the surgery" is a question that one should seldom ask of a trans person. Unless one knows said trans person very well and is positive that they will be comfortable answering such questions, it's best to avoid. It's a good rule to avoid asking anybody about their genitalia in the vast majority of cases.

The great interest in what we have in our pants is a frustrating topic for many trans people. We're just trying to be happy, find secure housing, work comfortably, have our medical expenses covered by insurance, and walk through the world safely. Cis people focusing so heavily on our bodies absolutely misses the point. It's objectifying and is effectively asking us if we're "real" men and women. The fact is, some women have a penis, and some men have a vagina, and it makes them no more or less their gender if they choose to keep the genitals with which they were born. For that matter, a nonbinary person's genitals are nonbinary, regardless of their configuration.

All of that aside, the question betrays a certain level of ignorance from the start; there are many surgeries trans people can choose to undergo aside from altering the genitals. There's top surgery, which can be mastectomy, breast reduction, or breast enhancement. There is also facial feminization and facial masculinization, which contour the facial features to be more feminine or masculine. There is also body contouring, which can seek to masculinize or feminize the body's curves. Some AMAB trans folks might choose to have their trachea shaved to remove the adam's apple, and some AFAB trans folks may decide to have a trachea implant to create one. The surgeries we choose to undergo are as diverse as trans people themselves, and asking "Have you had the surgery?" betrays just how ignorant the person asking the question really is.

If a person is inquisitive about the surgeries trans people may or may not undergo, the best option is to do some personal research on the subject. Trans people are not here to answer every curiosity and question that cis people have, and answering invasive questions can feel particularly burdensome.

Katie Couric infamously asked trans model and former drag star Carmen Carerra during an interview, "Your private parts are different now, aren't they?"

Carerra refused to answer the question, and Couric later asked Laverne Cox about the incident and what she thought of Carerra dodging the question. Cox replied that "the preoccupation with transition and surgery objectifies trans people and then we don't get to really deal with the real, lived experiences."

Couric apologized and called herself an "insensitive bafoon" over the exchange. In a later interview with Time Magazine, Laverne Cox said that she had "never seen someone challenge that narrative on television before." While getting to that result may have been frustrating, it's important to note that things are moving forward, and the discussion is moving away from what's in our pants to the real issues we face every day.

Therein lies why the focus on surgery is so problematic for many trans people. It objectifies us and focuses on our body parts when we're out here dealing with unequal housing and losing our jobs for coming out or speaking up about transphobic harassment. We're disproportionately unhoused and at risk of suicide. We're disproportionately victims of violence, and trans women of color are far too often the victims of murder, often at the hands of their partners. We have far more significant issues to deal with than what we choose to do with our bodies, and cis people and allies should be focusing on those issues, not the configuration of our parts.

- Rori Porter -

AUTISM, MASKING, & TRANS IDENTITY

I've thought long and hard about what I wanted to write for the experiences/ essays portion of TransFocus. As the editor of this project, I've had the opportunity to put some extra time into what I present here, and I think it's essential that I highlight autism in the trans community. A disproportionate number of trans folks and other LGBTQIA+ people are autistic when compared to the general population. While I cannot necessarily shed any light on this phenomenon, I can speak on my own experience and how my autistic and trans identities factor into one another and how I've come to identify myself as an autigender trans girl under the nonbinary umbrella.

Among autistic folks, there is a concept called "masking" by which we compensate or hide as neurotypical(NT) to survive an ableist and neurotypical-centric society. Basically, it's sort of like being in the closet, but rather than a closet itself, masking is often more like having a dry cleaner's carousel of neatly organized costumes and outfits that fit multiple scenarios and situations. We may not realize that we've put on a particular mask at all; we sort of pop into it when a typical situation arises that demands that specific behavioral switch. The simplest way to put this to an NT person is that it's adjacent to putting on your "customer service voice," and simply living there.

This essay is about my experience as an autistic trans woman and what the intersection of these identities has looked like throughout my life. Often, through writing posts like this, I have come to some of my most significant existential realizations. In fact, it was in the writing of a long-since abandoned blog post that I came to understand how much my neurodiversity has impacted my perception and understanding of gender. In my earliest piece published on this website, I spoke briefly of my "binary-ish" gender but didn't get very deep into the concept— mainly because even I didn't quite know what I meant by "binary-ish." I've attempted to write a piece about this several times but never gotten into the meat of the issue, primarily because I'd not yet come to terms with the fact that I am autistic/neurodiverse (ND).

Even NT people can relate to this on some level, as there's a sort of "costuming" demanded of going into a professional office environment, or in having a conversation you have to pretend to be interested in, or in feigning enjoyment of a poorly cooked dinner with the in-laws. However, for ND folks, masking goes beyond the NT understanding of being civil in stressful places. Masking can induce a significant stress response in the autistic brain, with many reporting headaches or even excruciating migraines following an extended camouflaging period. Autistic women are particularly susceptible to over-masking their ND traits and are more likely than autistic men to develop anxiety and depressive disorders as a result. This often directly correlates to misdiagnosis, with autistic women being treated for peripheral symptoms rather than being taught how to live and accept that their brains work differently from those of NT peoples'.

I've learned most acutely from my partner Levi, a Black trans man, that autistic/ND people of color experience masking on a different and often more stressful level from white autistics. Autistic Black folks, for instance, may have to both mask their neurodiverse traits AND code-switch between African American Vernacular English (AAVE) and General American English. Autistic traits and behaviors can result in folks being abused more often than the general population. There are frequently more highly developed masking traits in those communities, which explains why women and people of color receive autism diagnoses less than cisgender white men and boys.

Many factors are involved here, as some people of color with children may be less likely to seek out diagnoses for their kids due to a valid mistrust of potentially racist doctors and healthcare practices. Racism in healthcare is all too common, and the aversion some folks have to doctors examining and diagnosing their children is only to be expected. On the surface, it may seem as though non-Hispanic white boys are more likely to be autistic. Still, it seems far more likely that this is not the case. Other demographics are simply not being appropriately diagnosed or are just as likely not being assessed for autism diagnoses in the first place.

Furthermore, because marginalized people tend to be more adept at masking, whether because of race or gender, our autistic traits go unnoticed or ignored and are therefore diagnosed less often. My experience as a white trans girl is different than my Black trans boyfriend's experience. He had to mask to survive and not be murdered by police; I had to mask to stay employed and keep people from thinking I'm weird.

We are dealing with far different levels of stress behind our masking.

Many undiagnosed autistic adults do not know that they are masking until they are finally identified as autistic, whether clinically or socially. Through my own identification and diagnosis as an autistic person, the extent of my own masking has started coming to light.

A Boys' Club

The perceived phenomenon of young male autism diagnoses is mainly because early studies on the matter were performed almost solely upon young boys and men. Women and girls were largely left out of these studies because their autistic traits were seen as less defined by the male-centered standard. Rather, more often than not, their autistic qualities have been deemed socially acceptable for girls. Basically, a quiet or timid boy shirks social norms more than a girl who is "painfully shy," fails to make eye contact, or develops a special interest in something like cooking or the color pink. These traits are celebrated or reinforced in girls but are seen as inherently aberrant or divergent in boys. In my own case, my autistic traits enforced the idea that I was gay. The fact that autism exhibits differently in boys/men and girls/women is such a recent development. For that reason, autistic women are only now starting to hold space for themselves in autistic community spaces that have historically tended to exclude and over-question women's autistic traits. Furthermore, very few studies have been conducted on how trans/nonbinary people exhibit autistic characteristics versus our cisgender counterparts.

The fact is, marginalized autistic people are more adept at masking than your average cishet white autistic boy because there has been a lot of work done in American culture to accept white ND boys. ND girls, trans folks, and BIPoC have to mask far more to survive a culture that is ableist AND racist AND sexist. As intersectional identities add up, there become more things to mask and more reasons for which to do so, with trans people often hiding both their autistic traits and their true gender identities and the associated gendered (or non-gendered) behaviors.

As more autistic cis women, BIPoC, and trans people address their neurodiversity, we begin to see intersectional feminism inviting us to live our truths in safe spaces. Through meeting fellow autistic trans folks, I've been able to identify how masking has followed me throughout my own life, both keeping me safe and hindering my development as a person.

As a young child, masking was a skill that I did not come by naturally until I hit grade school. I had been homeschooled up to that point, and rather than realize that I was autistic, my parents merely thought that I was an emotionally underdeveloped child. I was born in the summer, and there was the option of putting me into school at age six, nearing seven, or at age seven, closing on eight. They opted for the latter, and despite the extra year homeschooling, when I got into the classroom, I said and did things that were seen as confusing and strange to other children. As such, I had few friends. The adults in my life didn't understand why — I was such a sweet, sensitive, and intelligent kid, so why couldn't I just figure out how to make friends like everyone else? Even nerds like me weren't interested in my friendship. It seemed like it shouldn't be too hard to find another kid in the first grade obsessed with the entire catalog of Animorphs books and Beanie Baby preservation techniques.

But it was difficult and always has been for me. I didn't pick up social cues quickly, and on my first day of school, I pushed a kid for refusing to tell me his name. Couldn't he see that I was trying to be friendly, dammit? As I would later learn, hiding violence of this nature was my first mask, which does rather highlight that not all masks are necessarily bad. My brothers got me to do things by pushing me, so I assumed that was just how you got people to do what you wanted them to. Getting in trouble taught me that this was incorrect, and I adjusted quickly to the new rule. Pushing kids outside the home? Bad. Pushing kids inside the home? Good! Well, that wasn't necessarily the intended takeaway, but it's the one that I internalized nonetheless. Violence in my childhood home went unpunished, so it was the most logical conclusion for me to reach.

Making friends was always hard for me growing up. I have had few close friends that I didn't meet through mental health or academic spaces. I now have a handful of friends I met through work, but the point is that I only make friends when forced into tight quarters with others, forcing them to get to know me. My very first friends in grade school were, in fact, bought and paid for because nobody liked me, and I was quickly considered social anathema in that hierarchy. To be seen with me, my first friends demanded $10 per week, and my little trans autistic mind didn't realize that they were taking advantage of me. I'd figured that everyone must do that to gain friends. It literally never occurred to me that something was wrong there. I needed friends, and they were offering friendship at a small monthly surcharge. Weren't all friendships transactional, after all? I had no concept that this wasn't what everyone had to do to gain friends, though in time, I did realize that what was happening was wrong. I sought out new friends, some of whom would hang out with me in my rockin' game room at home but refused to acknowledge me in school.

As far as gender goes, I knew what was expected of me as a child perceived as male and performed those social roles to the best of my ability. Boys were always confusing to me — wild and rough, often violent and cruel, though even sensitive and kind boys never quite gelled with me. While I could keep up with them sometimes, I strongly preferred the company of girls, though girls often told me to go play with boys, and boys, mockingly, told me to go play with girls. I was very confused by this, and didn't understand why things were so divided along gender lines. And so, rather often, I just ended up buried in my books instead of interacting with other people at all. Words like "bookworm" followed me my whole life, which worked better for me than some others like "friendless loser" and "faggot." Bookworm seemed more appropriate, and I dug into the norms of a kid who spends all of their time having intellectual conversations with school librarians. Intelligence is gender-neutral, and I found that when I spoke a certain way that the impressive (for a ten-year-old) words I'd been collecting in my mind afforded me a kind of protection. Teachers tended to like me because I was demonstrably smart, driven in the subjects that interested me, and was hyperlexic in a way that made me amusing to them, if nothing else.

However, I masked my femininity from everyone, including myself, because society reacted to me so very poorly when I expressed it. Growing up, my brothers and older cousins often beat me for being queer, so I did my best to at least be "one of the good gays" and switched subconsciously between feminine and overcompensatingly masculine depending on whom I was around. When I came of age, I drank beer and ate steak, I played beanbag toss (cornhole, for you fellow Midwesterners), and took whiskey shots with my brothers at holidays. I did everything expected of me to be accepted as "one of the guys," albeit with a big gay asterisk. But that facade, that mask, became less and less accessible to me over time. Those things I did to mask began to clash horribly with mounting gender dysphoria, and the masks started to feel more like a pile of ill-fitting costumes that I placed on one after the other, without taking off the ones underneath. Naturally, I began to suffocate between the two extremes of masking and gender dysphoria.

It's certainly worth noting here that in a different world, I would have been diagnosed with "Asperger's Syndrome," rather than "Autism Spectrum Disorder." "Aspergers" has been largely phased out for being a problematic term named for Hans Asperger, a literal Nazi who created the scale by which autistics would be sent to work and used for their brilliance, versus which autistics were to be culled from the society for not being "high functioning" enough. Aspergers, high functioning, and low functioning are all labels that have been phased out in recent years due to how little they actually help autistics communicate their experience. Each ND person's needs are unique, and it's worth noting that autistic doesn't run on a scale from "Most autistic to least autistic" but on multiple scales of different needs and abilities from those of NT folks.

For instance, my autistic traits feature highly developed language (hyperlexia) and sensory perception, with moderate to low executive function and motor skills. While I can communicate in a way that was often identified as "gifted" when I was a child, this got me into trouble constantly for not being able to do what was being asked of me. I could communicate my feelings and intentions effectively (perhaps even too effectively), but I could never express why I was struggling, merely that I was struggling. I just knew that I struggled, and the answer from the adults in my life was always to try harder.

Symptoms like dyscalculia (number dyslexia), aphantasia (the lack of a mind's eye), auditory processing issues, noise sensitivity, among many others, went unnoticed or ignored because I masked them reasonably well. My hyperlexia and info-dumping tendencies were identified as positives that must indicate my "true" ability to function. Instead, I received quick diagnoses like ADHD, depression, and generalized anxiety disorder. These symptoms of the more significant problem were more accessible to outside perspectives than was the undercurrent of neurodiverse thought and action that has impacted every corner and crevice of my life.

— Finding a Place in the *Other* Boys' Club —

As my sexuality developed, I assumed that I was a gay man because I didn't have words to accompany the confusing feelings I had about my gender. "Dysphoria" wasn't a word that entered my vocabulary until my early twenties, and I had always associated trans women with "My Wife is a Man?!" episodes of Jerry Springer. I was effeminate, certainly, but not exactly hyper-feminine. So, while I aligned with gay men in the sense that I was attracted to men and found some semblance of safety in the gay community, it didn't immediately make sense to me that I was more like the women on those shows than I was to the gay men who used my body for sexual gratification.

So I dated gay men and presented myself as a feminine gay man because I knew somewhere in the back of my consciousness that it was more socially acceptable than the truth. With the vague feeling that there was some kind of storm on the horizon, I repressed the hell out of my transness because it just felt like that was what I had to do to survive. I quashed my reality and shoved it in a mental box where I also stored my childhood trauma, and there it lived with the rest of my traumas, slowly festering as a mental illness in what I would come to call my "trauma vault" through therapy.

It was only through meeting other trans people that everything began to click. I wasn't a man; I was a woman—a straight woman at that. I had wrapped myself up so much in a gay male identity that this reality first hit me as a great shock, and I hid it from everyone, including my trans friends. Living a lie seemed more manageable than coming out as a six-foot-tall woman. I was told my entire life that I was the spitting image of my father, and while this was always meant as a compliment, I took it as a curse and an insult.

But men told me I was handsome all throughout my 20s, and I rather liked having people find me sexually attractive. I enjoyed feeling like part of a couple, however much I secretly longed for a heterosexual relationship (though I now identify as bi/pansexual). So I let myself fall in love with a partner who could only ever love the idea of me in return. He loved a man that I could never be, and while my relationship with that person was both important to me and brought me joy, I define that time in my life as extremely abusive and traumatic. My ex-partner came to control many parts of my life, and I believe that he saw glimpses of what I was hiding — the storm that was, indeed, on the horizon, and he said and did things that were in an attempt to keep me in the closet, remaining a "man" for his benefit. He alienated me from my trans friends, whom he saw as threats, and told me several times that I was fortunate I wasn't trans because I'd make "such an ugly woman" (words also echoed by my mother a few times.) He would follow up such horrible statements with affirmations of what a handsome man I was and often critiqued my evolving style of dress under the guise of protecting me from the big, bad world. I do believe that, as my fashion sense feminized, he was genuinely terrified for me — but rather than learn to love me for who I am, he tried to control me and keep me from my truth.

As that relationship drew toward its inevitable close, I was the most unhappy I'd ever been in my life and was starting to find myself unable to mask my identity the way I used to. I couldn't just be a feminine man — it wasn't enough. Masking became inaccessible, and so I came to numb myself with drugs and alcohol, the ultimate thing that drove a wedge between myself and that partner. While I regard that relationship as extremely abusive, I also understand that I deeply hurt that man with my lies and drug abuse. I lied about the amount of cannabis I was using, which was bordering on Jerry Garcia territory, of Grateful Dead fame. I lied about how I was taking my prescribed Ativan. I lied about drinking during the day, and I lied about being the man my ex had fallen in love with. Concurrently, my ex hurt me deeply in turn by manipulating me into staying in the closet for as long as possible to keep up the facade of being in a happy gay relationship.

I came out to my ex during Pride Month of 2017 in an argument about my cannabis budget. He had discovered a vape pen that he didn't know I had. Confronting me about keeping such things behind his back, he demanded that I confess all of my sins, and so I did. I told him why I was numbing the way I was, and what I'd been hiding all of those years. The torn remnants of my gender mask fell away, and all that was left behind was a terrified transfemme girl who felt as though the storm had not just hit, but had destroyed my home and my relationship with it.

My ex and I didn't break up immediately, but it was soon clear that he didn't want to deal with me transitioning, which is fair, to be honest. He was not emotionally equipped to handle what I was going through, and I was ill-equipped to handle him and his own inability to hold his family's shared trauma. We were two hurting people who came together to hurt each other, and in that hurt, I grew and learned what I didn't need from a partner. I learned that masking myself for a relationship ends in heartache, and it's only been very recently that I've been able to start dating again as myself, free of masks and free of a facade. Honestly, I hold much resentment (that I'm working through in AA and therapy, thank you very much) toward this ex for how our relationship fell apart and how he treated me. Still, I would be remiss if I pretended that I didn't play a part in our coupling's toxicity.

In a whirlwind, I came out to my ex, to God, to my parents, to my friends, and, at last, the most burdensome mask I've ever worn fell to the ground and became unwearable. And so, I fled the city I had shared with a man who I had honestly and truly loved despite the ways in which we hurt each other. I chose to start a new life 3000 miles away from him and everyone else I love.

As one does.

Binary*ish?

So, where does my "binary-ish" gender come into play? I know that I've spoken a lot about myself from the perspective of being a trans woman and what it means to wear a gendered mask in a world that expects the wrong gender presentation of us. In a significant sense, my first coming out as a woman was incomplete. Because while I am, in fact, a woman, and I genuinely love being accepted among the feminine gender and other stereotypical portrayals and expressions of my womanhood, I also find gender to be confusing as all fucking hell.

So, this is all to say that masking can get super complicated when you are both queer and autistic. We can get wrapped up in the imaginary identities we've built up around us because there is comfort in a safe lie instead of building on a foundation of an unsafe truth. For autistic trans folks like myself, shedding a cisgender mask often means shedding our entire dry clean carousel of masks, as every mask we learned was also part of upholding our imaginary cisness. This means that, in addition to embracing our transness, we have to learn new masks that align with the gender that we truly identify with. We have to effectively re-learn how to act out our role in society, and this adjustment can be jarring and frustrating, to say the least.

So what does it look like when an autistic trans person refuses to mask anymore? For me, this results in a trans person who straddles both binary and nonbinary labels. If that sounds confusing to any neurotypicals reading this, it's far more confusing for neurodiverse folks to parse out. Extracting binary thinking when it has served us for so long can be jarring. While I am undoubtedly nonbinary and inherently under the trans umbrella in that regard alone, I am also a transgender woman and identify wholly with the "Male to Female" experience. These are simultaneous truths for me. I absolutely grapple with whether or not my binaryness is yet another mask to protect me in a society that is more ready to embrace my transfemme self than it is to accept that my gender is also autistic AF.

When I think deeply about it, I realize that if I'd been assigned female at birth (AFAB), I'd still identify as trans and not cis because I don't understand the social constraints of gender as they've been applied to me and others. I do question my nonbinary identity as it concerns my binary identity because I also don't understand nonbinaryness either. I don't fully understand binary transness, binary cisness, nonbinaryness, genderlessness, genderfluidity, genderqueerness, or anything else on the gender spectrum. Other people's experiences of gender confuse me, just as other people's experiences, in general, confuse me because my autistic brain doesn't let me know what it is to "imagine myself walking in another person's shoes."

Gender confuses the everlasting shit out of me in every way. While I may be pursuing a medical transition that aligns me with many trans women and transfemme nonbinary folk, I am doing so because my body doesn't match my brain. This is a physical health issue for me more than a gender issue, as I don't feel that my bodily dysphoria has much to do with identifying femme. My body and brain don't align, so I am pursuing certain things to align them as best I can. While I certainly understand these concepts of gender intellectually, it's as though there is a physical barrier in my brain between me and understanding these concepts outside of an academic sense, even as I earnestly apply some of these gender labels to myself. No matter what my gender identity is or how it may evolve in the future, I want certain secondary sex characteristics that I do not currently possess.

So, in true form, my identity as it unfurls becomes ever more complex.

You wouldn't be wrong if you called me a transsexual nonbinary queer woman; however, I don't prefer some of that language due to its obsolescence. The point is, however you feel about certain obsolete words, it's not wrong due to definition alone. I see transsexuality as labeling the changes I wish to make to my body. I see nonbinary as labeling my gender identity. Queer, in turn, labels my sexual identity. I understand that not all people who are trans and pursue a medical transition wish to label themselves as "transsexual," but I see some straightforward utility to the word for myself and myself alone. Even so, it's not a label about myself that I throw around regularly because I don't necessarily want everyone and their mother to know the exact trajectory of my transition.

Again, I am pretty sure that my gender is autistic. Some people even call it "autigender," a term that I don't *fully* identify with yet but probably will in due time, as I continue to embrace my neurodiversity and apply my autism diagnosis to a life fraught with confusion and alienation from others.

Gender is both a social construct and a stark reality of the world in which we live. Gender is everywhere, from obvious things like the kind of clothes and hairstyles we're expected to wear to less obvious things like how many exclamation points a woman needs to put in a professional email to avoid being perceived as "a bitch." Autistic and trans folks alike internalize these gendered social mores to an extreme degree, while cishet NT people just understand them as law and often cannot imagine any other mode of existence, even when the concept of the gender binary and nonbinaryness has been explained to them by a queer person.

Rather than just knowing it, autistic folks have to watch and learn from neurotypicals' behavior to figure out what/how to mask. For autistics, it can rather feel like cishet neurotypicals get a top-secret manual at birth on how to act that the rest of us were denied.

The Labels We Choose

I am an autistic nonbinary androromantic trans woman, and my journey to these five intersecting labels has been confusing and long. At 32, most of my life has been leading up to breaking down all of my masks and letting them live in the rubble of my defunct dry clean carousel. I cannot continue digging into ruins to seek validation. For so long, I have thought that there was something wrong with me and the way I think and process things. Being diagnosed autistic has opened my eyes to the fact that the way I perceive the world is merely different, not wrong. The way that I am is not incorrect; it's actually just how I was born and how my brain functions.

To drop an abstract concept that could easily spin off its own essay, this has enlightened me somewhat that what we each perceive as reality is subjective and informed by how our brains interpret and extrapolate data. Reality is HUGELY subjective. My brain might see something that yours never could, and visa versa. It is only through embracing experiences that are fundamentally different from our own that we can begin to see the full scope and beauty of the human experience.

I understand on some level that "binary-ish" could mean "nonbinary." But my identity and the nature of how I relate myself to gender doesn't fit that easily under either label, and I struggle to reconcile the nature of my medical transition with the fact that gender is a social construct that I shouldn't have to adhere to in order to be seen as valid. My abundant confusion with gender is part of who I am as an autistic non/binary-ish person, and these identities intersect greatly for me.

While scientists do not widely understand the phenomenon, it is clear that autistic people are disproportionally likely to be trans. What I am saying is that some of us lack the full picture of gender, and that's okay.

Much like my literal lack of a mind's eye (aphantasia), I very literally seem to lack the ability to perceive and understand gender outside of my disconnect with my physical body. So, while I know that I am trans because physical dysphoria is a huge part of my experience, I don't know what exactly my gender is because I cannot perceive it. It's there, somewhere, just out of sight. You could go searching for it, as I have, but life seems easier when I stop digging into the carousel of failed labels that I've masked myself in to get by and justify my existence to others.

I most desire to leave the reader with a bit more understanding of the fact that gender identity and neurodiversity as they intersect are complex issues. I don't have all the answers. For me, I know that coming to terms with my autistic gender both liberating *and* confusing as fuck.

If you're leaving this scratching your head, I think I've done the job of conveying a small taste of what's going on in my wonderful and confusing neurodiverse brain.

Sources:

https://www.ncbi.nlm.nih.gov/pmc/articles/PMC4067639/

https://www.spectrumnews.org/features/deep-dive/righting-gender-imbalance-autism-studies/

https://www.scientificamerican.com/article/autism-it-s-different-in-girls/

https://www.salon.com/2017/03/15/listen-black-female-and-autistic-hiding-in-plain-sight/

https://onlinelibrary.wiley.com/doi/pdf/10.1111/j.1083-6101.2006.00305.x

https://www.ncbi.nlm.nih.gov/pmc/articles/PMC6223803/

PART TWO

POETRY AND FREE-FORM

MALCOLM E. GOTTESMAN

TAYLOR LILITH

RHONDA D'VINE

ORION STEN

ETHAN JULIAN SEBASTIAN MOLINA

MADELEINE MCCOY

NA'AMAH OLEWNIK

LILLIAN DAGNY MAISFEHLT

MORGAN GAINNES

ULYSSES ARMEL

ROBYN RHEDD

ALESSA CATTERAL

MAARAW AMELL

REN THOMAS

LIS REGULA

MAL LEVENSON

EMERY HALEY

JACOB NASH

RORI PORTER

LALO CARLSON

NAT MINK

FEATURING THE POETRY OF
MALCOLM E. GOTTESMAN

Malcolm E. Gottesman is a Los Angeles-based trans nonbinary artist and writer. When he sent us his work catalog, needless to say, we were hugely impressed. Malcolm paints beautifully vivid imagery and emotion through poetic craft, and we are truly delighted to be featuring his work in TransFocus.

The following poems are selected from a larger compilation written throughout his life, titled *Bodies Unaccounted For*, which can be found on his website malcolmgottesman.com

RAISED BY A GHOST

The images of tooth and nail

painted on my back

flow out like food coloring

from my body sitting

in the bath.

I was searching for somewhere to be naked

like I used to be at home.

Like I used to be able to be at all.

I was searching for the feeling of sun on my skin

of goose bumps, ocean air,

grass on my shoulders and hips.

But now I'm naked on the bathroom floor

with the shower running,

so no one can hear my own water,

so no one will question my methods.

In the moments that I fantasize

about cutting open my chest –

I tilt my head back and imagine

there is a hand running through my hair,

a mouth right next to my ear:

"I can feel how much you're shaking,

I'll take the part of you that's hurting."

5 BILLION YEARS

I've been leaning this corpse against

walls and windows to ease the pain.

When the sun sets I long to go with it,

as the night comes I get nervous

slivers of data forced into my skin,

resigning me to destroy the evidence.

No other way besides erasing entirely.

A chemical bath of lips and whiskey.

Again the sun sets and I long to go with it,

but I let the night come and leave me sleepless.

A path that is clearly too short for my stride

leads only close enough to rising

to be far enough from dying.

So each time the sun sets,

I face west.

BOND

Human heat transfers so easily.

The smallest second of contact

gives a residual red wave to my

thermal image.

Games of speed and crash and brush –

just an excuse to feel the radiation.

The addiction is not to the poison.

I know you're coming back for me.

Here is the familiar point in the story

where I strip tease for you,

by digging my fingernails in

so hard,

by casting the skin from my body.

DISTANCE

Am I more arousing

when I bleed?

Is it easier to project,

to use me as a mold for flesh,

than to admit you enjoy

touching me?

INTERNALIZE

there is nothing but a **CUP**

cry into it and **DRINK**

PARTICIPATION TROPHY

Why do I have tape recordings

in my head

of sentences my abusers said

at completely inconsequential moments?

Why do I follow advice when I don't remember who gave it?

Why do I accept certain parts of reality as static

simply because they have been there

for so long?

Compartmentalization

is a powerful

fucking drug.

What a way to

alter perception

beyond any kind of repair.

Why do I have a compulsive phobia of

finishing,

always demonstrated

when I'm drinking my morning coffee?

When it gets less than an inch

from the bottom of the cup,

I return to the pot and start over, fill it up.

Block out the memory of seeing grains

waiting for me.

In the painful last swallow,

the never-ending last lap,

I give up to save my strength.

Live to fight another day

WHAT AM I?

I am
sixty seconds
from blackout.

I am
an hourglass
on its side.

I am
apology-flavored
lip gloss.

I am
ten deaths
for one life.

I am
the letters
you don't send.

I am
the nausea
of suspense.

I am
too old
to die.

I take my breaths from newborn babies.

I sleep on speeding trucks.

I drink the blood of shadowed gamblers

who owe you twenty bucks.

I eat the fallen lashes off your face

so your wishes don't come true.

I take shelter between your huddled bodies

so she won't feel close to you.

I am doubt.

PHANTOM ABSENCE

2D too long

lost my depth

in file conversion

brain overhaul

haven't slept

to have diversions

if shock hits your heart

can it start?

if there is care

must it come back to me

when the night is fraying

and I realize it's a dream?

how stone or soft

fantasies can become

when sinking in

drowning

in love alongside emptiness

I love alongside emptiness

TOXIC WATERFALL

bastardizing

the simplest oaths

of consistency

then whimpering

a petrified

apology

I'm awake but

I'm dying

pupils

dilating

mouth

masticating

a truth:

sickness

is coming

tenfold

taking

my firstborn

soul

this repetition

is necessary

for protection

from loving me

this tension

supports

a lifetime

that's killing me

YOU DIDN'T ASK WHAT'S WRONG

This is
the last time
I curl over and die.
Back against door frame,
bend knees,

slide.

——Automatic reboot. Yeah.
Like I always do. I'll handle it.
I'll rub my fingers raw.
Haven't you heard about
my temporomandibular jaw?

My neighbors must know me better
than anyone who knows my name.
My reputation proceeds me. I walk
backwards. I look you straight in the
gut, I play me like a game.

How naïve you must be to think anyone
could be this strong, could live this long
in a cheap suit two sizes too small.

BUT I'LL TELL YOU ANYWAY

There is no reason to keep lifting my feet.
You guilt me when I'm awake all night,
you berate me when I sleep.

This is not what I am. Taxes. Bills.
Obtainability. Alarm clocks. Listening
to the story about innocent bystanders killed
because I forgot to vote as soon as I turned eighteen.
Because my teacher is indoctrinated with statist bullshit
and I have to sit down, shut up and be quiet.
Because someone stole a piece of cardboard
I paid fifty dollars for.

Because it really is that simple, it really is that bad.
This. This thing. This is not what I am.
This assembly line. This mutilation. This slaughterhouse.
This trap.

You set it for me,
and I hate you for that.

- Taylor Lilith -

YOU DO YOU

After 29 years on this earth,

I realized my life had been a lie.

I was angry,

I had no past that I was certain was me

I had nothing I was certain was me

All I had was memories

from a person who I knew wasn't me.

I had no idea who "me" even was.

I decided honesty was important, so I came out

And then I came to you.

You told me you were supportive.

You voiced to me a phrase that I learned to hate,

"You do you."

And though you didn't know,

those words angered me to the point of tears

I had no idea what I was

Who I was

What I even found enjoyable

When I started making baby steps

into who I've always been,

You were upset.

You missed your brother

You missed your son

You missed your friend

But

"You do you"

When I changed my name

and unfastened myself

from the shackles of a man who

Robbed me of my past

Robbed me of my identity

A man I have every reason to despise

And I became a little more me

just by letting go of a name

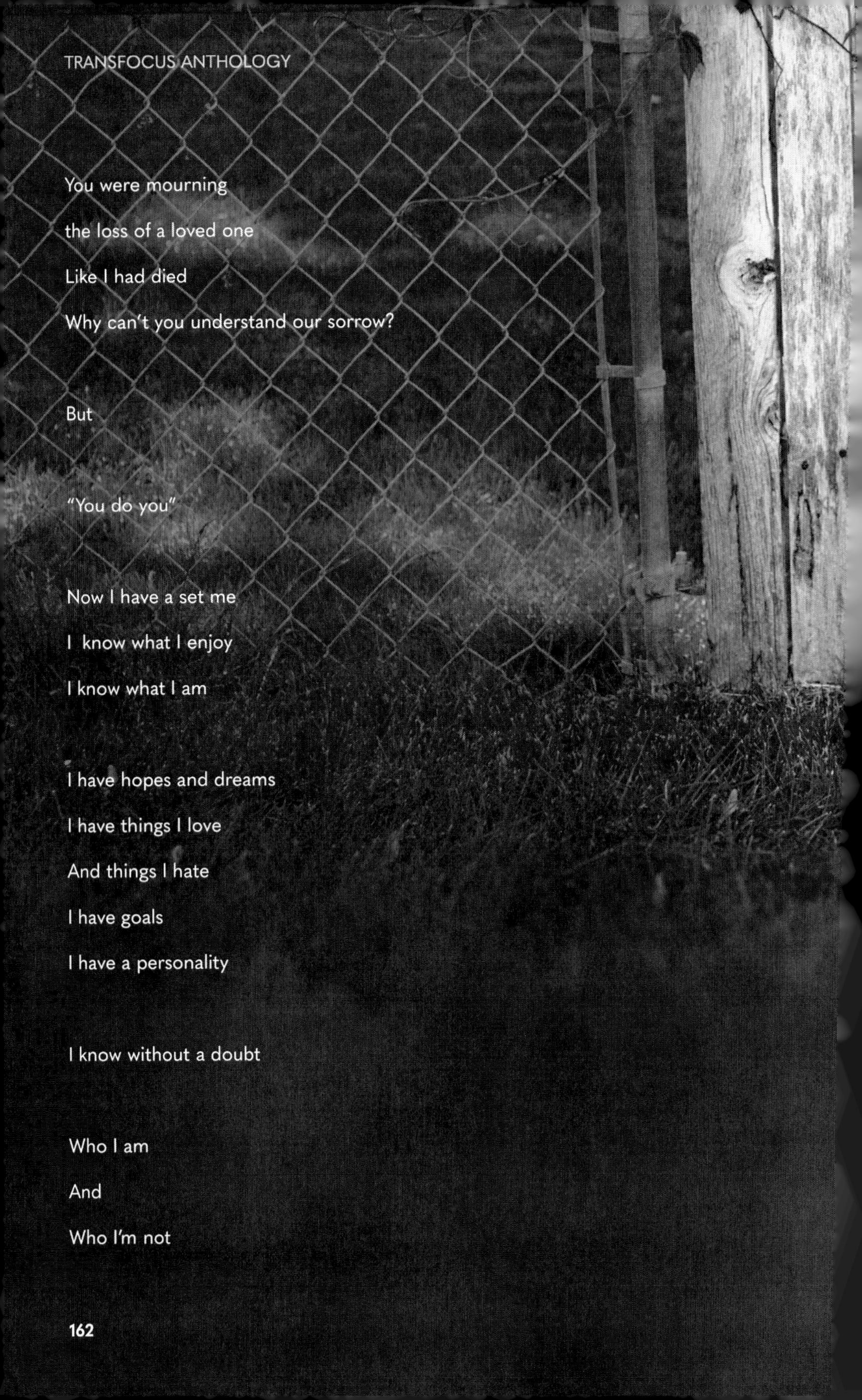

You were mourning

the loss of a loved one

Like I had died

Why can't you understand our sorrow?

But

"You do you"

Now I have a set me

I know what I enjoy

I know what I am

I have hopes and dreams

I have things I love

And things I hate

I have goals

I have a personality

I know without a doubt

Who I am

And

Who I'm not

Taylor Lilith

But you're still sad,

you're still mad

when all I did was what you asked

It's just that I don't think you know

what you were saying

when you told me over and over

"You do you."

- Rhonda D'Vine -

IT'S JUST SOOOO HARD

Content Notice: Anger; Intense Language

Don't tell me

Don't tell me how difficult it is to remember my name.

Don't tell me how difficult that is for you.

Don't tell me how difficult it is to use correct pronouns.

Don't tell me … anything about that. It's difficult? What is difficult?

Don't tell me how difficult is to not use the name

that every time I hear, hurts me inside.

That for every person who hears it stores it with the wrong pronouns.

That for every person who hears it plays the movie

of "man in a dress"

in their mind.

So do **not** tell me how difficult it is

to remember a name

and correct pronouns

when your error

causes me such pain.

It's difficult to discuss the issue with the fucking pussy-hat

having to discuss why the symbol of the image chokes you.

Even the woman who created it understood

that it is cissexist and trans-excluding,

for equating body parts with gender.

And yet it is used all over the place for women's liberation,

While not all women have pussies,

Not all vulvas are pynk, and not all people with vulvas are women.

And it's difficult to have to discuss why criticizing the pussy-hat

has nothing to do with pictures of vulvas.

Because fucking damned **yes!**

I'm **absolutely** for a relaxed approach of Vulvas.

Yes! Viva la Vulva!

I'd like to have one of my own after all!

(And here is the outing

so that you finally can get rid of the question

"what's in her panties"

which probably kept you occupied all this time

and distracted from the text.

Focus, folks!)

But it has to be possible to speak

about the liberation of vulvas

without **Every! Fucking! Time!**

telling trans women that they aren't women.

Without **Every! Fucking! Time!**

perpetuating biologisms.

Without **Every! Fucking! Time!**

equating body parts with gender identity.

It can't be that hard to break the cissexism,

Darn fuck!

So do **not** tell me how difficult it is

to remember a name and correct pronouns.

It's difficult to get told by relatives

that it doesn't matter which political party they get involved in

to annoy their mayor,

as long as it's not his party.

Difficult to hear, then, that they decided on a party

that says that you have "gender ideology" and "gender madness",

thus calling you a Persona Non Grata who wants to destroy society.

And it's difficult to be told that the party isn't that bad …

It's difficult to read within the software project

whose community was supportive of your transition during the last fifteen years,

to read within this community

that it's just an opinion

when a person denies using the pronouns of a person

and wants to go by chromosomes instead.

It's difficult to read essays on the origin of the singular they.

Essays on why chromosomes aren't unambiguous.

And not a single person pointing out that

You! Can't! See! Chromosomes!

Besides that, chromosomes are not identical with gender!

And chromosomes are **not** binary!

Besides that,

it's difficult to read how courteously and nicely

others deal with that person who denies you your existence

while you have been told not to be so short-tempered

with defending yourself.

So do **not** tell me how difficult all of this is for you.

It's difficult to have to say at the airport

that a rerouting of your flight through the United Arab Emirates

is far from OK.

Through a land where "cross-dressing" is forbidden.

A country in which I'm definitely read that way.

And it also happens here all the time.

It's also difficult to see the puzzled face behind the desk.

And it's difficult to think

for half a year about traveling to a conference in Brazil.

The country which has the highest murder rate of trans people.

To have to think about how you can present yourself there.

To have to think about how you can move around there.

To have to think about how likely it is for you to return from there ...

So do **not** tell me anything about it.

I do not want to know how difficult it is for you

while me, we, have to fight to live.

While me, we, have to fight to be loved.

While me, we, have to fight to be seen as dateable.

While me, we, have to fight not to get abused.

While me, we, have to fight to not be the targets

of physical or psychological violence.

So do not tell me anything about that,

because it makes me puke.

It doesn't let me sleep.

It wakes me up at four in the morning

and makes me write texts like this.

And I'm **darn! fucking!** tired

of not being able to sleep

because of your ignorance.

- Orion Sten -

AFTER THE FIRST SHOWER

After the first shower

the mirror's map rewritten

showing topography suddenly altered

No nipples, only skin

with the scars as winding rivers

carrying truth from within

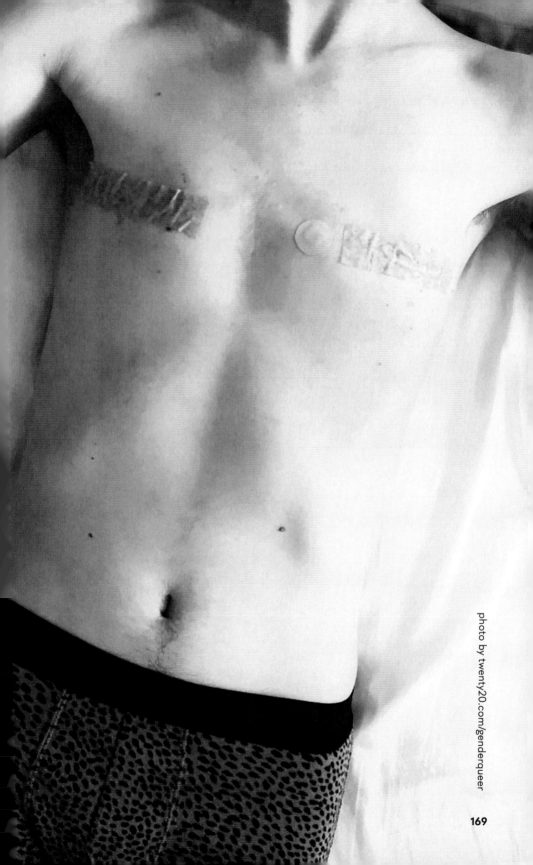

- Orion Sten -

WE THE TRANS PEOPLE SAY

Fuck the transhostile,

fake feminist

TERFs

and the talk

of male privilege

in a hunt

for trans women

Fuck the normal

status quo

humans

The cis concern

over trans kids' bodies

Fuck the christian

fear mongering

Fuck the allies

after asking

/so what's

down there?/

Fuck the endless

debate over pronouns

forging shackles

from grammar

Fuck the racist binary,

colonizers -

pillagers of cultures.

Fuck the gatekeeping -

the suffering internalized,

an open wound

still bleeding

TRANS IS BEAUTIFUL

- Ethan Julian Sebastian Molina -

LOVELY

Trans is beautiful

Trans is being

Loving yourself is challenging

Though very rewarding

Sometimes you'll cry and feel alone

It may even be hard at home

Feel like no one understands you

Though we are small percentage it's true

Never forget your worth

You're loved so so much

Remember you are still part of this Earth

Your identity shouldn't be kept hush hush

You'll break rules and show no pattern

It's called unique it's called different it's called trans

This poem has no pattern

We weren't made to belong and we stan

Sometimes you'll have a lot of challenges just stacked

Let's say you're brown or black

Let's say your sexual orientation is queer

You're beautiful and it's called intersectionality my dear

Not every trans person is white and hetero

Some of us have a lot lot more to show

- Madeleine McCoy -

A LATE START

First it came in moments when my sister's clothes I'd wear,

Then later as the angst I felt from wanting longer hair —

A little older, changes came that just felt so unfair,

I spent the next few years of life not really being there —

Alive but all the time believing nobody would care

At some point though my shell broke and then life came flooding

And once again came changes but this time they'd let me win

That deadly, looming feeling from before would start to wane,

And never in my living days would I be "he" again

- Na'amah Olewnik -

A STRANGER IN THE MIRROR

Content Notice: Mention of Blood

My reflection grows into a tsunami

of grief. I forget

my non-existence,

my missing jawline, chapped lips.

My mind is a rain cloud

hovering overhead, blurring the monster.

I throw my fists into red

boxing gloves, wrap the Velcro around my wrists.

Four ropes challenge me to a match,

My glove hits the black

and gray void, a punching bag releases

months of dust. Retracting my arm, pink scars

darken on my skin, once only covered

in freckles and pen doodles of stars

and hearts.

Mirrors live on the surface of walls,

haunt my protruding cheek bones

and taped knees. Hips cracked and worn

move towards the reflective glass, nothing more

than funhouse foil. Shards detonate around me,

a single hit, slivers collect into the foam on my hands.

I slide the gloves off my hands at the door,

glass embedded in my fingers

drips blood to the floor before locking myself

in a windowless bathroom.

The sink mirror

covered with cardboard,

nailed at the edges, don't forget to love yourself

written in black in the center, but even the faucet

reflected back to me.

- Lillian Dagny Maisfehlt -

INSTRUCTIONS FOR
FLYING A KITE

First, you should decide you're the type of person

who would like to fly a kite.

That turns out to be a lot harder than it sounds -

-you'll probably talk yourself

in and out of it quite a few times,

even if you already know the truth, deep down,

and asking for advice won't turn out to be much help.

People will say "kite flying is a ridiculous pastime;

you should just jog, like normal people,"

(even if they know you loathe jogging),

or, "that's so amazing! You're a wonderful kite flyer,"

despite your never having tried it in your life

(at least not in public),

or, most frustrating of all, "your afternoon; your decision,"

and of course those last

are the ones who are exactly right.

Next, you'll want to choose a kite.

The great big elaborate ones

with lots of tails in every imaginable color

or the realistic-looking dragons

or those multistringed fighting kites

will probably catch your eye,

and you'll be tempted to just go all out

from the very beginning.

But those fancy kites are expensive,

and complicated,

and high-maintenance.

A simple diamond or delta

or box is a good place to start

while you figure out what you're doing,

and you can always branch out

and explore from there.

Or not.

Some people just really enjoy

the straightforward pleasure

of flying a basic kite.

That's cool; it's a great big sky

with lots of room.

Once you've chosen your kite,

you need to assemble it.

There will be instructions included,

which are optional,

and occasionally confusing,

but helpful,

and as aggravating as kitemakers can sometimes be,

the good ones really do want

to see you get the thing off the ground.

You'll need a good place to fly your kite,

somewhere open, and safe,

is ideal.

Weather conditions should really be right,

clear skies, steady wind,

not storming.

You might not get those conditions right away,

and waiting sucks,

especially when you're excited,

and you've already been waiting so long

to even start this crazy enterprise

that you're not even sure will work.

Waiting is just no fun,

but trust me;

kite flying is best in nice weather,

on a flat, open space,

with no power lines around.

Now that you have your kite, and your space,

and your weather,

toss it in the air,

and run.

Be prepared to stumble more than once;

running in one direction,

and looking over your shoulder in the other

is trickier than it looks.

Don't be discouraged.

    Be prepared for gusts of wind out of nowhere

       that send your kite crashing

         before you have a chance to react,

          or have the feel of how to tug the string

           to set things right.

            Don't be discouraged.

    Be prepared for the breeze to stop entirely,

       and for your kite to come

                   fluttering limply back to earth,

     while you watch,

       powerless to do anything about it

                       but wait a little longer.

Don't be discouraged.

Or, be as discouraged as you want,

and kick and cuss and swear

and have yourself a nice,

cathartic bitchfest,

because none of this was as easy

as it looked before you started,

and it's just not fair.

But when you're done being discouraged,

pick up your kite, straighten the spars, throw it in the air,

and run.

Eventually,

the breeze will really catch it,

and you'll be playing out string,

and when the occasionally gusts happen,

it'll be high enough up that they won't really matter,

and anyway, you'll know what to do,

and then,

photo by @aaron-burden

Unsplash

almost

before

you know it,

you'll be flying a kite,

and the only thing left will be to enjoy it,

up there in the clear air,

for everyone to see,

just like it belongs there.

- Morgan Gainnes -

SUCH A PRETTY GIRL

You look at me and you think

'Oh, such a pretty girl'

You look at me

But you only see

the painted face I show to the world

What you don't see

Are the nights I spend

Hiding from my partners

Because if they touch me

It hurts

It doesn't physically hurt

Except it does

My stomach churns

And my skin crawls

Because my own body disgusts me

Because it is wrong

It is wrong by society's standard of women

But I'm not talking about that

I am talking about

Being trapped in the wrong body

And having to live in it the rest of my life

Because I can't fix it

No matter how hard I try

Morgan Gainnes

I can't

I bind my chest

I reshape my face

And still

'She' is said

'Girl' is called

And it hurts

People who claim to love me

Do not actually care

They respect me to my face

And drop the façade as soon as I'm gone

And it hurts

I hear the name that was given to me

And it hurts

I can't say it anymore

It sticks in my throat

And makes me sick

I correct you

'He,' I say

'Boy,' I say

And you don't believe me

Because I wear dresses

I don't wear dresses because I am a woman

I am not

I wear dresses because they make me happy

You ask me intrusive questions

And I answer honestly

Because I hope

That you can be honest with me

But you don't

You pretend to

'I gave you that name

because it meant something to me'

It meant something to me too

But now it just hurts

Everything you do behind my back hurts

And I wish you would listen

But you don't

Because you are dead-set

On your idea of me that exists in your head

She is DEAD

That is why it is called a dead name

She does not exist except in your own mind

She is gone

And I have taken her place

So when I correct you when you call my dead name

I'm not doing it to be spiteful or mean

I am doing it because that is not me anymore

But you don't seem to understand

You are so fucking focused on who I was

That you cannot see who I have become

And that sickens me

Because you clearly don't care

when all you see is

'such a pretty girl'

- Ulysses Armel -

THE BLUFF

me and scout, we scale

the bluffs bleeding before us, they weep

stones slicked in silty rain

two boys, we are exploring

their chest ribbed, with scars

my breasted lungs, let free

no breathing

just pants

one flat, other flesh

no acerbic comparisons drawn over skin

as we scramble further into our nature

they the jagged edges of rocks

my body the earth of any mountain

leaving behind plaid and torn tops, we grapple

the last of sandstone and bone, we catch less and less

boulders that whisper against wet hide, lost within

the growls, howls, bawls, laughs, hands

arms, necks, feet, we drummers

beat upon bellowing pecs at the precipice,

take turns playing chicken

between cracked trees and petrified river valley, we are forming

more than echoes of men

- Ulysses Armel -

BEARD TRIM

one thumb rubs the wires of my chin

his soft breaths groom

firm fingers to flatten rebel fur kiss the jaw

and bury my nose in those red cactus cheeks

these are beards

not him

masculinity at the end of a moustache

weighted which one of us the man

trans brittle and cis softie gays

his gentle noises

empathies

smooth hair

dancer body

laughter

love to my coarse admiration

faded anger heavy stock

bristles

need to feel

wholeness in those warm yelps

brown eyes forearms heart chambers

consider useless judge of men

compare him to any other part of our queer kingdom

- Robyn Redd -

DEEP THOUGHTS

Hidden in the soil of my heart

my true self grew roots and sprouted,

nourished by the waters of my soul.

But as she broke through the ground

Bursting through to the light,

I buried her in shame.

Scared I even tried digging her up to throw her away,

But her roots were deep in my soul.

Destroying her would destroy me.

So I distracted myself with video games that drew my attention away.

Ignoring her like a shadow, she remained by my side.

Still she sat and waited patiently for me to pay attention to her again.

I met my Beloved and still tried to ignore her.

I built my life as a house

And kept her outside, in a corner of my life.

A flower, hidden in the brush, she was.

But the one who is my Beloved saw her in me and asked

"What is this Secret you are keeping from me?"

I had to come to terms with my secret,

The true self I had hidden from the world.

I turned and confronted the self I refused to see.

I stared at the one I had tried to kill all these years.

I looked her deep in the eyes.

And she stared back at me with an inner beauty and smiled.

Nervously I shared my Secret with my Beloved

"Cast me out if you will," I said. "But there is something I need to say."

And so I ripped open my soul to reveal her

Expecting my Beloved to cast me in the cold.

But instead she smiled a painful smile,

"Why were you afraid?"

She took my hand and said to me sweetly,

"I love her too!"

She watered that place, helping it grow

She held me back from covering it with shame..

She whispered, "I had always loved you, all of you.

The piece I could see and the piece you buried in the ground."

Since then my Secret has become a part of me.

An important piece of who I am.

- Alessa Catteral -

SHE

When I die, bury me in a dress.
Braid my hair
And fill my bra with socks
(Like my first girlfriend did
When I borrowed her dress).
Paint my nails, if you like,
For the first time
And the last.

Save your shallow,
Breathy definitions of love,
For your empty words
Have no power
And do not care,
Not as the silent earth cares.

Delve deep into
The loving ground,
Not for things that shine
And glimmer in the lamp light,
But for space.
Sweet, precious space.

A whistling, a breathing
A sighing within the void,

A relaxation, and an expectance

Of a space I can occupy.

A quiet world

In which to be complete.

Finally - and irrevocably -

Myself.

Leave me there,

Embraced in the invisible,

In the arms of trees,

And grasping the only flowers

Anyone ever gave me.

Leave me -

And your memories of me, too.

Forget them - they were never true anyway.

Don't tell tales of me

You who never knew me

At all.

Leave only

A single stone

Only

A single word

To tell

Who I was

Or may

Have been -

'She'

- Alessa Catteral -

RIVER

Dysphoria is not only a monster

Waiting for you to switch off the light

And close your eyes

So that it can reach up,

Clawing at the blankets

Keeping you warm -

The comfortable clothes

Of your being.

It is also a river,

Running through the Underworld,

Which our dead must cross

To find some peace

And simple solace

It is a river flowing with the salt water

Of quiet sadnesses,

Carrying the visions of lost possibilities

Running like a vein

In your mind.

It is the rain.

Rain, upon your skylight

Alessa Catteral

After midnight.
It reminds you of the places
Where you are too much, or
You are not yet whole,
Not yet.

It is a voice
Like the wind,
Whispering
'Not enough'
In your ear.

Dysphoria may not rampage
Through your life
Breaking glass
And bruising skin.
Sometimes, it is simply there
A silent, ghostly presence
Passing through your home.
Casting shadows on all you love
Turning cherished things
Slightly
- Oh so slightly -
So you barely notice
That they no longer catch the light.

Dysphoria is a quiet river
whispering falsehoods

- Maaraw Amell -

HAIR SO BEAUTIFUL

the hair everyone wants,

the hair nobody wants to tame.

object of lovers'

and strangers' affection,

always causing a double take.

full-bodied and straight.

tangled in just the
right way,

for them.

shave it off,

take it away.

heavy and dark,

falling to my shoulders.

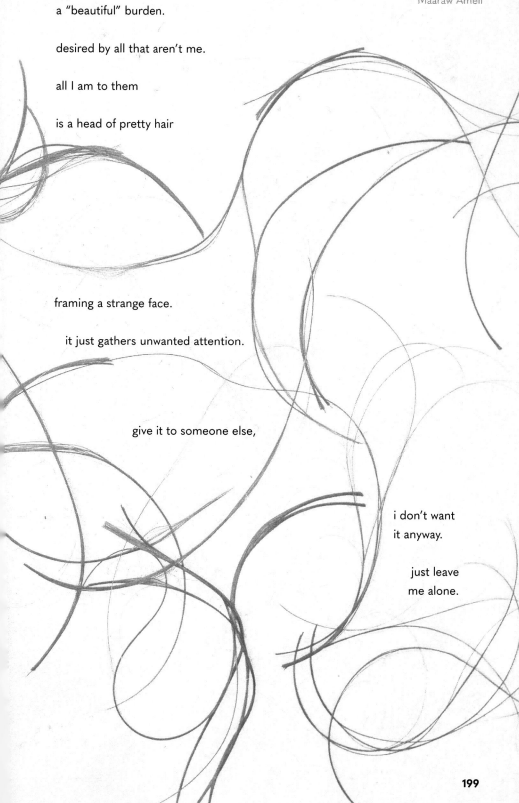

a "beautiful" burden.

desired by all that aren't me.

all I am to them

is a head of pretty hair

framing a strange face.

it just gathers unwanted attention.

give it to someone else,

i don't want
it anyway.

just leave
me alone.

- Ren Thomas -

TIPS FOR BEING AN ALLY

1 Stop asking us for our 'real' names,' or what our names 'used to be'.

2 Don't tell us how much you're struggling with pronouns.
We're struggling a lot more.

3 Use our pronouns and names around others, not just around us.

4 We are not 'transgendereds' or 'transes' or slurs that
'you can't say anymore.' We are people.

5 Stop obsessing about what is in our pants.
It's none of your business.

6 Stop saying that being trans is an illness.

7 'Transtrenders' don't exist.

8 Don't tell me it doesn't matter what people call us;
we'll always be 'XYZ' to you.

9 Don't be surprised when we don't want to come home for the holidays
if you've been resistant to accepting the reality of us.

10 .... They're not 'just jokes.'

11 .... There are some words you're not allowed to say.

12 .... Stop telling us we're being dramatic when so many of us are dying.

13 .... Don't tell us that racism and sexism don't factor in.

14 .... The chromosome argument has been proven incorrect.

15 .... We have always existed. Just because this is the first time you've heard of us doesn't mean this is the only point we've been here.

16 .... Binary genders aren't the only ones that exist.

17 .... Just because you're genetically related to us does not mean you are family.

18 .... Sometimes we get tired of having to be the fount of all trans knowledge. We do not owe you any sort of explanation. Educate yourself with resources by and from trans people.

19 .... Gender is fake. Anyone can wear makeup.

20 .... Respect our existence, or expect our resistance.

- Lis Regula -

AN IMMODEST PROPOSAL

My dear, when I met you
I was not looking

But I found someone who shared my dreams,
my experiences, my philosophy.

When I met you I was complete in who I was and am

But I found someone who made me even more, made my life overflow with love.

When I met you I was not lost

But you took me in hand and led me to a place
better than I had imagined could exist.

When I met you I was content

But you made me hungry for more even as you slaked my thirst,
left me yearning while at peace.

You are the man of my dreams,
conjured forth in a time of roiling upset,
And filling my mind with sunny tomorrows.

You are the calm in the storm,
easing my nerves with your honeyed voice,

And making my eyes sparkle at the thought of you.

You are my rock, providing stability and roughness
that has so often been lacking in my life,

And yet soft enough to melt my heart daily.

You push me to be a better man,
challenging me to think harder and to delve deeper,

And yet giving my life a place of respite and reprieve.

For all these reasons and more, my heart,
I ask you to please give me these gifts of yourself-
Will you take my hand in yours
as we make this journey called life?

Will you work by my side to keep up our hearth and home?
Will you walk toward me when the day is done
and it is time to rest?

Will you hold me close in good times and bad,
so that we might be support for each other?

Or put simply, my love, will you be my husband,
to have and to hold, 'til death do us part?

We stood on that beach, one sunny weekend,
Proclaimed ourselves as we are- men in love and free.

Gazing deeply, holding hands from start to end,
No brides to see, even if some would say that's you and me.

Two broken boys, with hearts that need to mend,
Lifting each other up for all the world to see.
With so many people that we call friend
And what we have left of our family.
Falling in love is simple,
but staying there takes hard work.
With the world against us,
in the shadows we'll no longer lurk.

Two broken men, side by side,
looking out at our life ahead,
Reminding the world
that trans love is true and sacred.

- Lis Regula -

MY VOW TO YOU

Mj, my dear heart, we stand here today, two broken boys, two men who by many measures should not have made it, to pronounce our love and devotion to each other in front of our family and friends. In a time and place such as now, when fascism creeps into everyday conversations and hate crimes are on the rise, love can be a protest. Yet here we are, not just living but loving, not just surviving but thriving when our existence makes too many people nervous.

In our time together, I have grown to better know what a passionate, caring, dedicated, and intelligent man you are. I have also learned so much about myself. Though the last eighteen months have been tumultuous to say the least, our love has grown. You have been my shelter in the storm of life, my rock in the roiling sea, my soft respite in this hard, harsh world. I have learned that no matter what craziness might get tossed our way, I want to face it with you.

I never imagined myself to be the kind of kind to find true love. I wasn't sure that true love was a thing, to be honest. Meeting with you gave me hope that there were better people in the world than I had imagined in a long time, and getting to know you changed the idea that I could be loved and love someone like this, the way they do in fairy tales.

I have a hard time now; seeing a future without you in it, and looking at the time before we were together makes me wish that you were there as well, in spite of the potential of creepiness and weirdness. You are worth it! Finally, sharing my life with someone means sharing all of it, good and bad. That's what I'm here today offering to you with these rings, beloved. I vow before creation that I want all of you, and in exchange, I offer all of myself.

There are days that this will not be enough- one of us will want more than the other has to offer at that moment- but I vow also to keep learning to do more and better at loving you, and I have faith that you will do the same. No matter what, I'll continue choosing you, forgiving you, and loving you for the rest of my days.

IN LOVING MEMORY

OF MJ ECKHOUSE

- Mal Levenson -

THE AUDACITY OF THE STATE

I decry the notion of the state having a say

What supreme gender fuckery has thee

In any attempt to assign me

Beautiful glorious me

Anything at all

No hospital has knowledge of my body

No parent has more than I to say

Not a person may comment nay think

A thing that I have not thought for myself

Be it girl or boy or starchild

I am assigned nothing

Only I am given the leave to assign for me

Not trans nor cis nor anything to you

Not anything but me and the assemblage

That I gift to myself

In my recognition of personhood

I gift myself all

And take nothing from

Those dicks those raging controlling

Useless

Modifiers

Who

Seek

To

Control

Through

Definition

I resent it all and I shrug it all away

Be I more nothing to you than you are to me

Accept that I am me and only

Define me as me

On a long journey to remove the need

For control

And in that empty space

Here I am

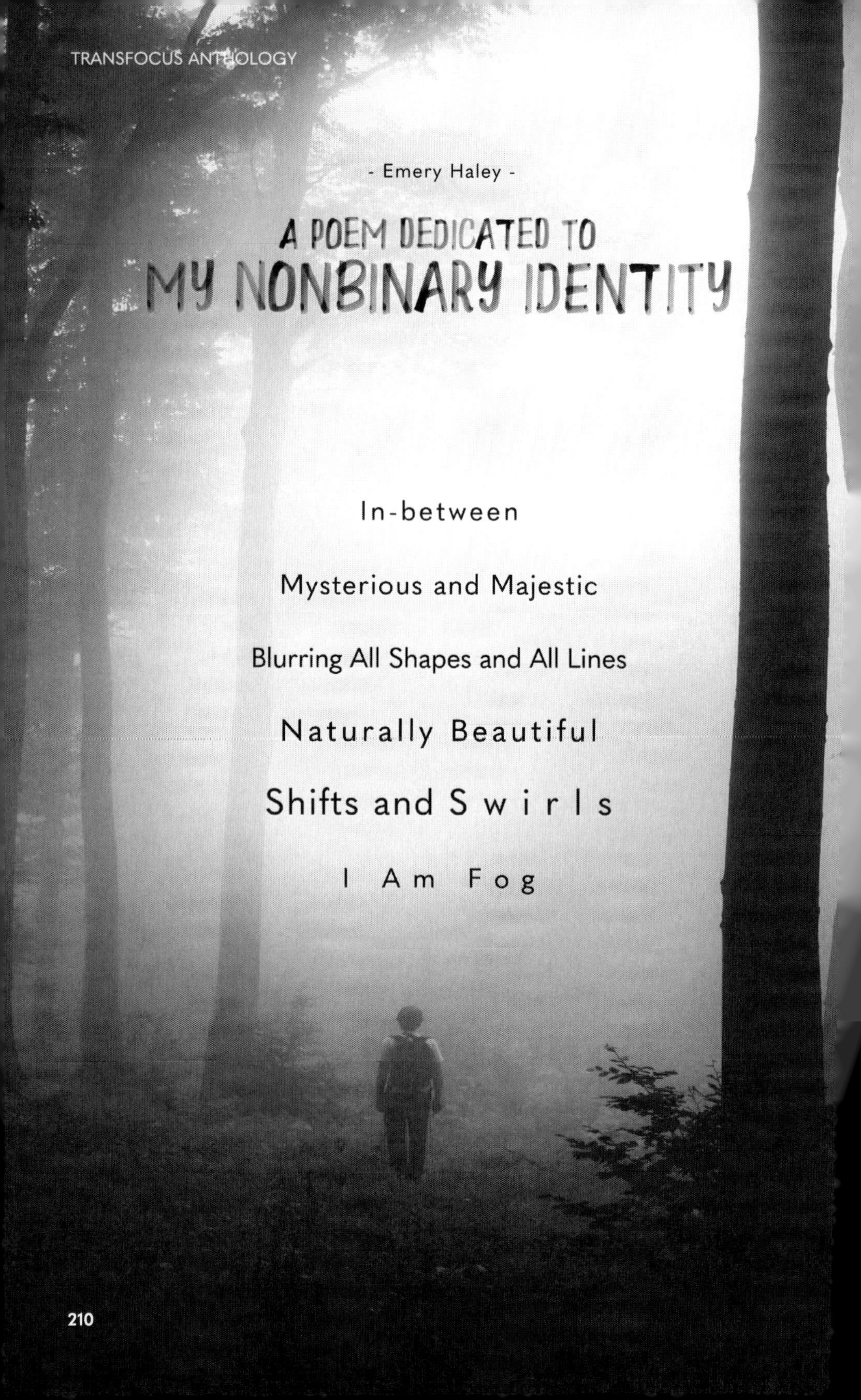

- Emery Haley -

A POEM DEDICATED TO MY NONBINARY IDENTITY

In-between

Mysterious and Majestic

Blurring All Shapes and All Lines

Naturally Beautiful

Shifts and S w i r l s

I Am Fog

Emery Haley

BE THE CRYPTID YOU WISH TO SEE IN THE WOODS.

—Source
Unknown

- Jacob Nash -

GRAY, GRAY

Black, White

Gay, straight

Male, female

Gray, Gray is where I live

In the small dark crevices and shadows

hidden for fear of what we call life

Not seen for who you are or how you love

but as if you do not matter

Who do you love, who will love you?

I cry out to the only constant in my life,

my God in whom I trust

He sees me for who I am,

He knows my heart,

and how I am capable of loving

All society sees is the shadow,

the hollow of my being,

not who I am but what I am not

Not in or out but pushed aside to try

and live some kind of life in this world

What kind of life CAN be lived

Slipping through the cracks,

not fitting in the pieces of your life

Society squashes your dreams
Life ebbs and flows and I fight,
I fight to swim up stream
I fight against the darkness in this world,
the darkness in my heart as I fight
The fight to live,
the fight to be,
the fight to love and be loved by just ONE

God is with me in my darkness
He is with me in the shadows,
in the crevices where no one will go,
HE IS
THERE!

I am afraid to love,
for love is not always there
What is love anyways?
I only know of the love of my Father
I once knew love.....
or at least I thought I did
Love is not suppose to be conditional,
apparently being human is
You can not BE unless you are like me,
at least that's what THEY say
I am not anyone but everyone
I am not black or white,
male or female,
gay or straight
I do not fit into societies mold
I am ME

- Rori Porter -

THE WEIGHT OF YOUR TONGUE

Content Notice: Suicide, Violence, Slurs, Suicidal Ideation

Tonight   I am overwhelmed
                 with the dishonesty of the testament
                 and the carelessness
                 with which piety preaches.

I am ashamed to admit   that words
                                    can pierce my body like daggers

                 My resolve torn,
                 scars naked,
                 raw for the world to see

Hands shaking violently
words flow   as blood from a decanter

                 If I can manage to shake
                 one of the daggers from my back
                 another takes its place,
                 using the last wound
                 to sink in deeper   deeper than before.

I cannot take more damnation,
                 about my morality,
                                    my life,
                 the sin of my flesh,

He said, "In God We Trust."

He said, "Fags burn in Hell."

He said, "Love the sinner, hate the sin.."

He said,

He said,

He said,

STOP.

Stop the flow of poison,

the unfelt weight of ignorant tongues,

The damage they can cause,

the lives they can steal.

Twisted minds form churches,

schools,

homes.

Where I am nothing but the tranny girl

who dares not cross the threshold.

Where I am nothing but a faggot boy

who rots in flame,

whose soul will cry out forever

Stop.

Stop.

STOP.

I may be young,

but I am not naïve   of pious bigots who preach

the word of love

but fail to live it.

Preachers spouting only words of   hatred

longing,

of altars stood upon
as soapboxes.

Of men
who would brand the queers
to appease their god.

A scarlet letter,
burned into my chest and into their eyes,
a scarlet letter   carved into my mind.

They could burn me alive,
but it won't add truth to their words.

Nor will it make it any less so
that I love

as much as I hate them.

They may not have pulled the trigger,
or knotted the rope,
or put the bottle of pills into the child's shaking hands...

...but words
can be the finger on the trigger.
Words
kick the chair aside.

Words

        shove pills down the throat,

        one by one until they're gone

        and the world of an innocent fades away

        with naught but pious words in their head.

If I am to survive this pyre   of books,

        and bodies,

        and pets,

        and possessions

as sickly ashes fall from the sky like fresh snow

it will not be the thought of what,

        but whom,

is blanketing the cold, hard earth

that will tear me away,

        giving me the strength to run

from men   with bibles and bullets.

But if I don't,

        and I am caught in the fire of those abyssal,

        pitiless eyes

I hope you catch a piece of me on your tongue as it falls

        so you can taste who I am,

        who I was,

        and who "nothing but a tranny"

        could be.

- Lalo Carlson -

TO BE INCOMPREHENSIBLE

today i mourn the time i wasted

explaining my infinite beauty to those

whose eyes and feet are locked to the ground

no longer do i desire to be understood

rather, look at me like you look up at the cosmos

stare with awe at my vastness, gasp at my brilliance

see me and know that you cannot know everything

because you will not know my depths

i want to be regarded

like the mythos of the ancient world

i want centuries of scholars to argue over my meaning

i want to be the basis of poetry and painting

because just as the primordial gods shaped the earth

with passion, vigor, and glee

i too am molding reality in my own ever-shifting image

Lalo Carlson

i am not a product for consumption

i will not make an appearance on daytime television

my name will not be spoken at the dinner table

you can find me in the dreams you wake from sweating

in the alleys you won't turn down

in the questions you won't ask yourself

because you live in fear of the answer

- Nat Mink -

HAZE

My gender has always been a haze

Like static I could never clear,

I am a collection of ones and zeros

Until I'm not.

Nat Mink

Until I can put it into words and be heard

I want to scream into the void,   *but am I not the scariest void of all?*

Am I not society's version of me?

I'm not a boy and I'm not a girl, I'm something in between

I'm living on a perpetual edge my entire body aches to scream

that I'm nonbinary.

is it okay that I don't know where I stand on

the land of they\them?

living in a world between masc   and femme.

Needing to belong,

but belonging nowhere.

PART THREE

ART AND ACTIVISM

MILA JAM

GEORGIE PUDLO

EM WESTHEIMER

RORI PORTER

ASH DANIELSEN

ROXY VALLE

JORDY ROBINSON

MARS WRIGHT

ROSALIE DERK

PAGE PERSON

SQUEAKY BLONDE

ANDY PASSCHEIR

MILA

ARTIVISM & PUTTING MY BODY ON THE LINE

Content Notice: Nudity, Descriptions of Violence

The purpose of the 'Stop Killing Us' movement is universal. It's predicated on violence and murders toward trans women, yes; however, this is for marginalized women, immigrants, young people, kids – it doesn't say "Stop killing us trans women" necessarily. Because I am trans, there is an obviously specific narrative, but it's about something we can all relate to – that killing people for who they are is not fashionable. It's not cute. Especially when there's no reason, and that is what we experience as trans people and trans women who have been murdered, in relationships or "situationships" with their murderers because of their desires. And it

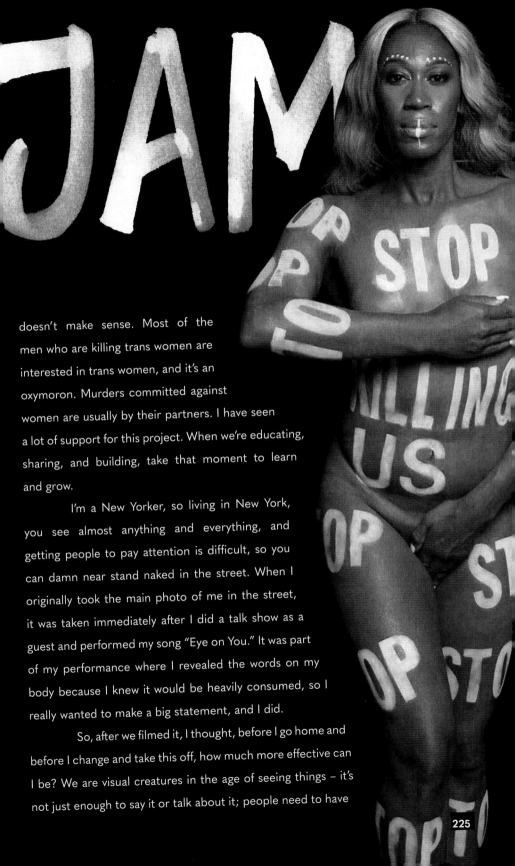

JAM

doesn't make sense. Most of the men who are killing trans women are interested in trans women, and it's an oxymoron. Murders committed against women are usually by their partners. I have seen a lot of support for this project. When we're educating, sharing, and building, take that moment to learn and grow.

I'm a New Yorker, so living in New York, you see almost anything and everything, and getting people to pay attention is difficult, so you can damn near stand naked in the street. When I originally took the main photo of me in the street, it was taken immediately after I did a talk show as a guest and performed my song "Eye on You." It was part of my performance where I revealed the words on my body because I knew it would be heavily consumed, so I really wanted to make a big statement, and I did.

So, after we filmed it, I thought, before I go home and before I change and take this off, how much more effective can I be? We are visual creatures in the age of seeing things – it's not just enough to say it or talk about it; people need to have

225

something to see and resonate with, so I thought, well, "I'm going to stand in the street." I really thought it over; should I post this? I mean, I'm nude, but the message is so much more important than my naked body. That accompanies what this is about – my body. In moments like that, I just have no fear and go for it. That's the artist in me. I needed to make a statement with this.

Honestly, I have a level of safety because of where I live, but there are all different nuances in our privilege, but for women who are trans and black in the south living in Mississipi, or Lousiana, or Georiga, dealing with people who are ignorant and don't know how to handle them, that is different than where I live in a major city like New York. I just want to be able to shed light on that and share what's it's like; even if it appears to be easier for you or me or anyone, there is still a level of discord we have to deal with that is unacceptable. The merit of our character is constantly overlooked because of who we are. In the future, I hope we move toward that.

I just want to reassure all of these kids out there that you are not alone. There are people like you who are out, living and being uplifted, and it's possible to be respected and revered and make a name for yourself. Constantly move forward mentally, constantly think about the positive, and no matter how much negative energy there is underneath, we constantly counteract that with our views on who we are, what we want, what we wish for and hope for.

That self-motivation is one of our greatest gifts. We have to be so self-motivated and so aligned with ourselves to drown out other people's issues and drama with us to pierce through the darkness and find some sort of light. I'm here to say that there is light, there is a way, and you just have to hang on and give yourself permission to hang on, even if it's to cry, even if it's a dark moment under the covers – find a way to push through it. That's why I make music, and if any of my music can help you, that's what it's about. Just encourage and inspire.

Your resilience can come from those others hating you. I believe it builds character and strength, and armor that others may never have. On the other side of that, if and when you are able to move beyond your parent's home and perspective, or however they treat you, you can equip yourself with the strength to take on almost anything. We are warriors. The only way to become a warrior is to be able to combat adversity and to stand above it, and come out on top of it. I believe that you do that by

strategizing the life that you want to live – researching and reading the life you want to live and following the people who you are uplifted and inspired by. If you follow me or look up to me, know that I have people that I look up to as well – it's just a consistent cycle of positive energy. It isn't always easy, and it isn't always going to be easy, but you have to love yourself and know that there are other people out there like you who love themselves so fiercely that no one can tell me who I'm not. It's about survival. It can be hard to keep on, but the world needs you.

I think the world is changing. Even though there's a lot of madness, there's change. It's about finding the change here and there and seeing the moments of change in media. We have to fund the change in conversation in acknowledgment, in making space for people and inclusivity, and there are little pockets of change; we just have to grasp them and push them together, so they make one big change. Until then, take a day at a time, and if you have somewhere decent to lay your head, and I know there's a lot of kids who don't, each day to wake up is a new day to reset your goals, your wishes, your intention, your determination.

We are the gift. Not everybody recognizes that, and some may never recognize that, but you just have to know it. We have a lot to bestow upon people – wisdom, ability, creativity, energy, light, and cultural history. There are so many versions of our history that have only done anything but uplift humanity. We just have to continue knowing that we are the gift.

Follow me on Instagram @themilajam, I'd love if you streamed my music on Spotify or iTunes or apple music, and I do read my messages even if I don't respond; I do read everything that gets to me. I'm just sending everyone some love and some jam. Stay in the loop, and let's stay connected.

"WE ARE THE GIFT.

JUST HAVE TO CONTINUE KNOWING THAT WE ARE THE GIFT."

- MILA JAM

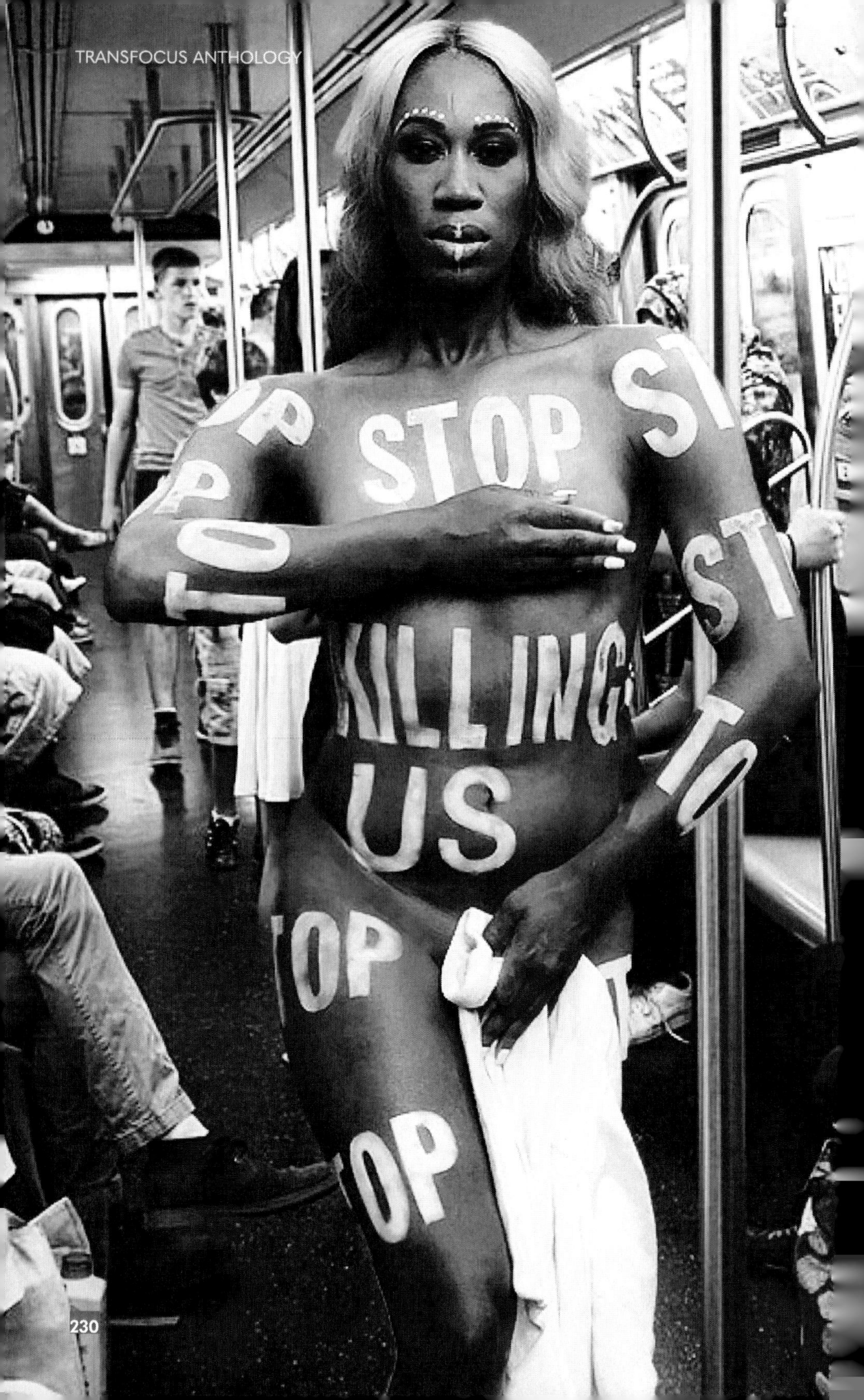
STOP
US

@THEMILAJAM

- TransFocus Editors -

THE IMPORTANCE
OF REPRESENTATION

For most of our lives, trans folks haven't been able to see themselves adequately reflected on television or in movies. Many trans people's first encounters with a trans character were in films like Dressed to Kill, about a transgender murderer, or Sleepaway Camp, about a transgender murderer, and Silence of the Lambs', about a trans murderer, or in Psycho, which is about, you guessed it, yet another trans murderer. These early instances of trans women depicted in film imprinted an image upon society of trans folks as deranged, psychopathic murderers who pretended to be women to lure their victims into a false sense of security. Needless to say, calling this "representation" is a bit of a stretch.

In some more recent films with well-meaning trans storylines, trans women have been played by cisgender men, like Jared Leto's Rayon in Dallas Buyer's Club and Eddie Redmayne's portrayal of Lili Elbe in The Danish Girl. These movies become particularly problematic when said cis men won academy awards for them and walked up on stage with beards while wearing suits, painting the picture that trans women are just men playing dress-up. A man walking up on stage to accept an award for playing a trans woman on screen directly puts trans women in danger by allowing the public to think that we are just acting or otherwise deceiving them.

Transmasculine representation, on the other hand, is far more lacking. One of the most notable and recognizable trans films (if it can even be called such, given that no trans people were involved in its production) is Boys Don't Cry, with Hilary Swank playing Brandon Teena, who is sexually assaulted before being tragically murdered. Many trans people can cite that movie as the first time they realized that being out might mean getting killed. While it's based on a true story, whether the film is groundbreaking or disgustingly exploitative is a hotly debated subject to this day.

Glenn Close similarly plays the titular character in the film Albert Nobbs, further painting the picture that trans men are just women dressing up in men's clothes. While these films may have been groundbreaking in a certain sense, they also put actual trans people at risk by insinuating that we are just acting out our "preferred" genders and are not "really" the genders we say we are. Time and time again, cisgender actors win awards for playing trans or queer roles, and it's a matter of immense frustration that they can land these roles while trans actors get passed over in favor of a cis person who is considered "more worthy" of Oscar bait.

To highlight the difficulty trans people have in finding trans representation in media, it's worth noting that when we searched for sources about trans representation, one of the only articles we could find was written by the senior editor of TransFocus herself, Rori Porter.

Representation becomes truly groundbreaking when actual trans people are given a chance to play trans people on screen. Television shows like POSE, Orange is the New Black, The OA, Star Trek Discovery, Mrs. Fletcher, Grey's Anatomy, Euphoria, The Chilling Adventures of Sabrina, Supergirl, Billions, Transparent, The Fosters, Shameless, Queen Sugar, and Sense8 all feature transgender characters played by transgender actors. Conversely, movies like A Fantastic Woman, Assassination Nation, Saturday Church, Happy Birthday Marsha!, Man Made, Port Authority, and Tangerine are rare examples of films that feature trans characters played by trans actors. This is by no means a complete list, and some of these shows and movies contain sensitive material, so we advise caution in seeking these out.

What's most important about these films and TV shows is that the trans characters have more personality than just being trans in most of these cases. In POSE, for instance, we see a hugely diverse cast of trans women who are traversing the world as fully realized people. Being trans impacts their lives, of course, but there is more to their characterizations than just being trans.

Examples of trans representation in cartoons are scarce. The cartoon Steven Universe features genderless or nonbinary aliens who are often coded female but are portrayed as feminine, masculine, or androgynous. In addition to a bevy of genderless aliens, Steven Universe notably features a canonically intersex character in the form of Stevonnie, a fusion of boy and girl characters Steven and Connie. There is also nonbinary representation in the Netflix cartoon Kipo and the Age of the Wonderbeasts' in the form of the character Asher Berdacs, though they are a relatively minor character. In general, Kipo focuses heavily on diverse representation in its characters, and we can likely expect more focus on trans folks from the show in the future.

When shows get it right, it is often rather shocking to trans people, given how very poorly trans representation has been handled for most of history. Most trans people don't expect representation in media at all, and good representation comes as a welcome surprise. Your average American says they don't know someone who is out and trans, and that's also often true of trans people when we first come out. For that reason, we turn to media to see who out there is like us and what it means to live a trans experience. When we look to media and see murderers or characters portrayed by cis people, it can be highly frustrating.

Even worse is if we grew up watching shows like Maury, Jerry Springer, and Ricky Lake. Many of our first encounters with trans people in media were shows that hosted trans people with headlines like, "My girlfriend is a man?!" or "Is It a Boy or Is It a Girl?" Well, we've got news for you, Jerry; sometimes it's neither or both, so hah.

Perhaps even worse is the movie Ace Ventura Pet Detective, in which a woman is revealed to be trans, and all of the men who were attracted to her begin vomiting. The adult cartoon Family Guy similarly includes a character in an episode getting sick when he discovers that a woman he slept with is trans, in a scene that features several excruciating minutes of projectile vomiting. And don't even get us started on South Park, which features a character who transitions, detransitions, transitions again, becomes a lesbian. In a later episode, a random trans woman using the restroom sexually assaults a mentally disabled child. Yeah. South Park sucks.

When a lot of us were growing up, these instances were the only "representation" that many of us had, and internalizing such media can have a deleterious effect on trans folks. Many of us couldn't see ourselves in the media we watched and therefore didn't think we were trans because the way trans folks were depicted didn't make sense. Comedy is comedy, sure, but when the "joke" has a measurable impact upon the community about which it's been made, it stops being comedy and is just transphobia. Comedy that punches down isn't comedy at all; it's bullying. Just because an act of bullying doesn't have a direct victim doesn't mean that it doesn't have a victim at all. Many of us were significantly impacted by poor excuses for representation, and content creators can and should be held accountable for inserting bigoted nonsense into the zeitgeist. We can't precisely hold Alfred Hitchcock responsible for his numerous transphobic works, but we can undoubtedly deplatform transphobic creatives like Seth MacFarlane, Trey Parker, and Matt Stone, who have demonstrated time and time again that they view the trans community as easy pickings for their crude and transphobic brands of comedy.

"The L Word" also failed miserably in trying to introduce trans representation. Many viewers were excited when they introduced the character Max, but he quickly devolved into a gigantic jerk after starting hormones. For that matter, the writers seemed to be taking out their hatred of trans men on the character, having him get pregnant by his partner, who then dumps him, with another character later telling Max that "he's going to make a great mother." The L Word's writers unwittingly played directly into the "no happy ending for the queers" trope, something they should have been especially sensitive to while writing a queer show. Max's depiction was a side effect of not having enough (or possibly any) trans people in the writer's room, and the show reflected how cis lesbian culture in the 90s viewed trans men in their community. It is primarily due to Max's characterization failing so miserably that allowed future writers to learn from these mistakes, but by that point, the damage was already said and done. If we had buckets of good representation at our disposal, the occasional shitty instance wouldn't make such a significant impact, but as trans representation is sparse at best, and every single depiction of a trans person in film or television matters greatly. Even with a show from the 90s, some poor trans kids will watch it and internalize what they are seeing.

Whether we're being portrayed as murderous villains, raging testosterone-addled assholes, or the victims of violent crime in several thousand (give or take) episodes of CSI, these depictions hurt and negatively impact the trans community. These tropes are still occurring as recently as the 2017 French movie La Mante, in which a trans woman is portrayed as a murderer yet again since we apparently didn't get enough of those movies in the 70s. There are few things more disappointing in a film than enjoying a flick only to find out that the big gag at the end is that the murderer or villain is a trans woman. You'd think we as a society would have left this dangerous and ill-informed trope in the past, but the "transfemme ax murderer" depiction is alive and well. At the time of this publication, it was featured perhaps most recently in notoriously transphobic J.K. Rowling's mystery novel, "Troubled Blood," in which the book's villain dresses up in a burqa to kill his victims and hide in plain sight, giving us a rare double-dose of transphobia topped with Islamaphobia. The TV show Pretty Little Liars similarly played into the "Trans Villain" trope by building up viewers for seven seasons to conclude that *gasp* the trans girl was the villain *all along*. That bit of representation would've been better left on the table.

We as a community are far more likely to be the victims of crime than the perpetrators, so there's just no excuse for depicting us this way anymore.

Not that there's much value in constantly depicting us as victims either. Except in telling true stories, media that paints us as victims harms the trans community by reinforcing the narrative that our lives are short and tragic. Few shows tell good stories about trans people, and unfortunately, they are rare exceptions to the rule. We are blessed to have beautiful shows like POSE, Euphoria, and Star Trek Discovery on the air today that allow us to be complex people. We are diverse and beautiful human beings with more stories to tell about us than those tired old narratives that have been retold hundreds if not thousands of times before.

Representation matters because every trans kid deserves to see themselves depicted in a positive light. We deserve to see characters who triumph and live happy lives so that we, too, can find ourselves in characters and stories that help us escape from the real world. Media that reflects our lived experiences is essential, and while Orange Is the New Black is groundbreaking, it's also sad that one of the only instances of mainstream trans representation features a Black trans woman who's in prison for fraud. For that matter, that show ends with Laverne Cox's character receiving little resolution to her story arch, leaving her locked up in solitary confinement for several episodes before being ultimately written out and seldomly featured therein.

It's 2021, and the trans community deserves better. Trans kids deserve better. We can only hope that Hollywood continues to see the error in their ways and casts trans people in trans roles that uplift, cherish, and honor the trans experience and what we as a community have to offer the world.

QUEERING CONGRESS
WITH A TRANS VOICE

MAEBE! FOR CONGRESS 2022

PROGRESSIVE DEMOCRAT FOR CA-28

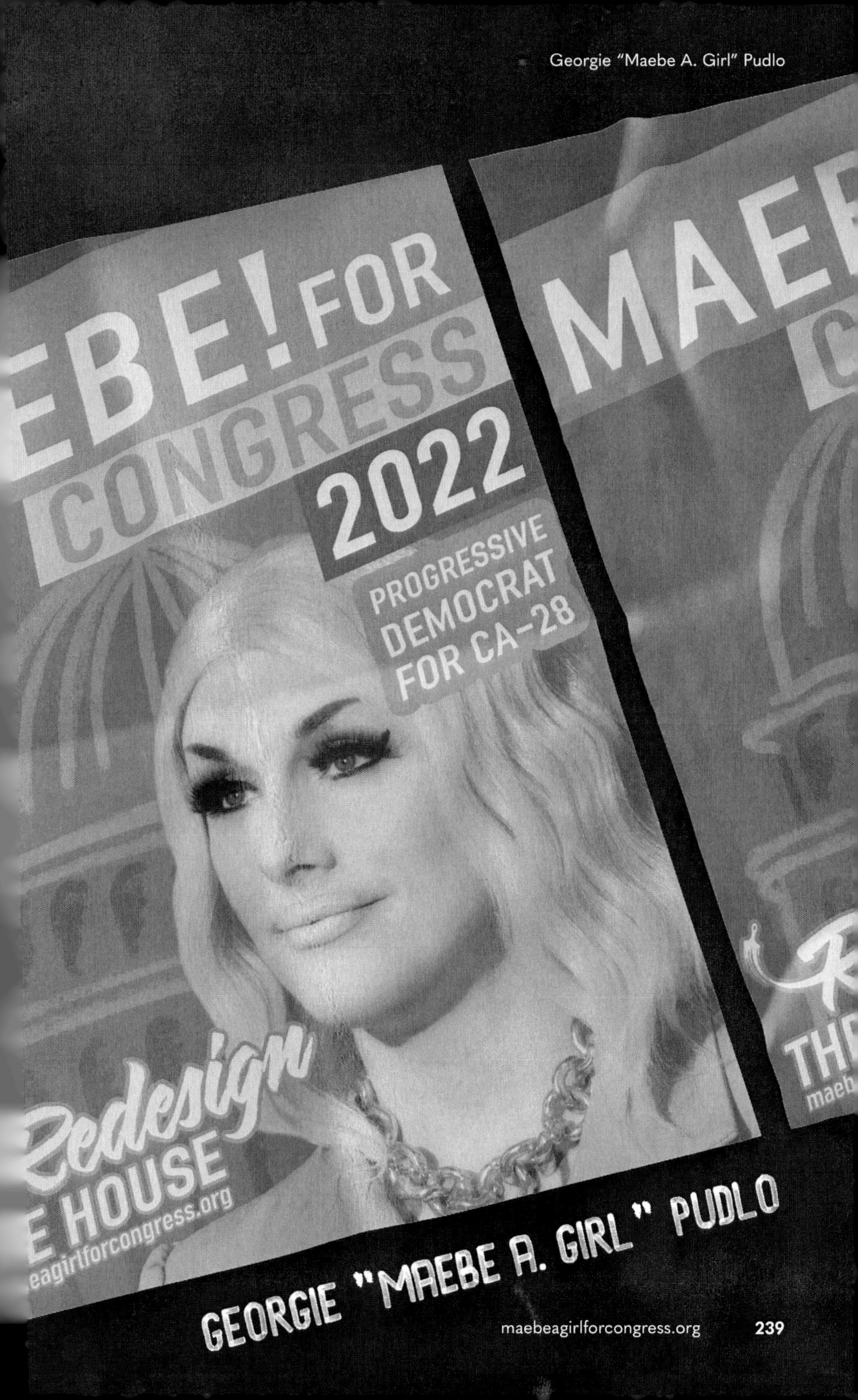

EBE! FOR CONGRESS MAEB

2022

PROGRESSIVE DEMOCRAT FOR CA-28

Redesign E HOUSE

eagirlforcongress.org

GEORGIE "MAEBE A. GIRL" PUDLO

after Trump was inaugurated, I started doing a lot of political numbers, and so a lot of my performances we based on real-world events that I was trying to communicate in my performances. My political numbers were very satirical, and I wanted them to be educational but also entertaining. I realized that a lot of people weren't paying attention, so I thought, you know, this might be a good way to get people to start paying attention.

People started referring to me as a "political queen," and the more I thought about it, I thought, well, why not run for office? As far-fetched as it sounds, anyone can dream and make it a reality.

Get on that Poll,

I consider myself to be very progressive and far left, so some of the things I'm impassioned about when it comes to politics are fair representation, diversity, equity, and inclusion in our government. I think at the very basis of it all, that is so important, and I don't think we currently have fair representation. When you look at congress, and you see the physical makeup of it, it's still mostly older, wealthy, white cis men. If you look at our nation, that's not what our nation looks like, that's not what our cities look like, that's not what our neighborhoods look like. So that's really important to me. LGBTQIA+ representation is a big one for me, but at the same time, I think that's a big misconception that that's my main priority. I think a lot of people assume that because I'm a trans person and a drag queen that's in office and running for higher office that that's my priority, and it absolutely is one of my priorities, but I have a lot of others that are very important to me, such as alleviating homelessness and assisting our unhoused neighbors. Medicare for all, the green new deal, so a lot of my passions in politics revolve around enfranchising the disenfranchised. Sort of being a voice for people who are and have historically been on the lower rungs of our society.

Being elected one of the first genderqueer people and the first drag queen ever elected to public office was really exciting. When I ran for Silverlake City Council, I decided to run under my stage name. "Maebe A. Girl is not my legal name, believe it or not. But I go by Maebe, and I didn't know people would vote for me or not. My hope was that people would look at my platform, and my goals, and my vision for the community, and if they agree with me, hopefully, they'll vote for me. I hate to say I was surprised to win, but anybody in that position is, especially as a first-time candidate.

So I was really excited when I won, and I didn't realize that there were no drag queens in public office. In fact, it was brought to my attention when I read an article that came out about me. I was obviously excited by that and thought it was really cool, but I also found it kind of disappointing because I feel like drag performers are inherently political. The nature of gender nonconformity is a political and social statement, so I was kind of surprised to see that there were no drag queens and very few trans people in. I will say in the past two years, I have seen an incredible number of trans people not only run for office but also get elected, everywhere from city positions to state. I think it's only a matter of time before a trans person is finally elected to congress, to our highest levels of government. Still, I think it's really sad and unfortunate that there's never been a trans person as a representative. How can we really trust that our government is looking out for us when we're not even part of the government?

"HOW CAN WE REALLY TRUST THAT OUR GOVERNMENT IS LOOKING OUT FOR US WHEN WE'RE NOT EVEN PART OF THE GOVERNMENT?"

I definitely questioned when running, are people going to vote for me? And they did. I think that my advice to trans people looking to go into politics is to absolutely follow your dreams. Nothing is out of reach for anybody just because they're a trans person or are interested in drag. Drag especially can be fun and silly, and I think a lot of times we don't affiliate that idea with something as serious as politics. But politics also doesn't have to be super serious – politics can also be fun and engaging. I think it's one of those things where, because we have this idea of what a politician is – an older cis white, wealthy man – we often think that it's out of reach for us, but nothing's out of reach – nothing is out of reach for trans people.

"WE HAVE THIS IDEA OF WHAT A POLITICIAN IS —
AN OLDER CIS WHITE, WEALTHY MAN.
WE OFTEN THINK THAT IT'S OUT OF REACH FOR US.
BUT NOTHING IS OUT OF REACH
FOR TRANS PEOPLE."

A lot of things are coming up for me, and I'm seeking my reelection for th neighborhood council, so I've been getting ready to announce my campaign for that as well as my next campaign for congress. We ended up doing a lot better than I eve thought we would do for a first-time congressional run. We lost by less than 1% or 1114 votes in a congressional district with more than 75000 people. We came really, really close, and this time around, we're doing a lot of planning, starting sooner than last time, and hopefully, this time, we get the results we want to get, which would be a win. I think it would be so cool to finally have a trans person in congress, and hopefully, that will happen this time.

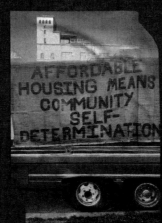

But if not, it's still okay – I think it's so important just to have the visibility of a trans person running for office, and I think it's so important to a lot of younger people who are going to be eligible to vote, or eligible to run for office themselves, and I think putting enough examples out there will hopefully encourage the youth to continue on and change the world and do the things that people like me might not be able to do. So if it's not me, I just hope it's a trans person soon, and I think that it will be. It only takes one personto inspire the masses and the next generation to take up that cause and go for it.

" IT ONLY TAKES ONE PERSON TO INSPIRE THE MASSES AND THE NEXT GENERATION TO TAKE UP THAT CAUSE AND GO FOR IT "

— GEORGIE "MAEBE A. GIRL" PUDLO

- TransFocus Editors -

WHAT IS DRAG
& WHY IS IT IMPORTANT?

There is a common misconception that drag is the domain of cisgender gay men, but drag is an art form with room for everyone and all walks of life. We have come a long way from the origins of the word "drag," which was likely first used in British theater slang in the 1900s, though its exact origins are largely disputed. Some incorrectly say that drag stands for "dressed as a girl," but the word was not used in this way until recently. In the 1990s ballroom scene in New York City, drag was popularized by trans women of color, who would "put on their drags" and perform for trophies, ala "Paris is Burning."

While cis gay men are some of the most familiar and famous drag queens out there, trans women of color have been doing drag for as long as drag has existed. At the same time, cis gay drag queens and trans drag performers were once closely allied. In the 1970s, even drag queens who didn't necessarily identify as trans or cross-dressers fought on behalf of both. Drag was a more political art form in the 1970s than today, and the idea of trans queens being excluded from the scene was absurd. There was strength in numbers, and trans women and cis gay drag queens fought side by side. As drag culture was "virtually disowned" from the gay rights movement of the 70s, there was a necessary joining of forces between trans folks and cis gay drag queens.

Today, however, cis gay drag culture and trans drag culture are often pitted against each other. A certain "supermodel of the world" who shall not be named once equated trans women in drag to athletes abusing steroids in the Olympics, insisting that trans queens had some sort of advantage over cis queens.

In the 1990s, cis gay (and sometimes straight) drag started to become more mainstream, with movies such as To Wong Foo, The Birdcage, and Mrs. Doubtfire becoming big box office hits. The Broadway Musical RENT! is also an example of an early representation of drag in the character Angel, though whether she is trans or a drag queen is widely debated. These movies imprinted drag as a cis gay male art form upon the cultural zeitgeist, and trans women were largely excluded from this definition.

In the case of Angel from RENT, she is almost certainly trans and not a drag queen, as the creator defines her. She is rarely seen "out of drag" and uses she/her pronouns throughout the movie/musical. By all accounts, Angel is most likely a trans woman who occasionally goes stealth for safety. During Angel's funeral, Mark stumbles on her pronouns -- first saying "he" and correcting himself to "she." That she is written as a drag queen illustrates a sincere misunderstanding by the writer of RENT, Jonathan Larson, regarding the difference between drag queens and trans women, which is honestly only to be expected. It was the 90s, after all.

In some way, separating trans women from drag queens was necessary, as transness is not drag. Trans people are not cross-dressers, because to crossdress means that one dresses in a manner in which they do not identify. However, some drag queens ARE trans, a reality that has been largely ignored in favor of a "cleaner," trans-free image of the drag scene and what it means to be a drag performer. In the cultural sense, drag became a sterilized version of the queer experience for straight, cisgender audiences. In the especially queerphobic 90s and early 2000s, drag was a "safe" way of dealing with queer culture, given cis people's fascination with cis gay men dressing up in women's clothes. It was only seen for its camp, fun side, conveniently ignoring the reality that some drag queens are trans and are women and that there is a whole culture surrounding drag kings, too. Nathan Lane, Robin Williams, Wesley Snipes, Patrick Swayze, and John Leguizamo became the faces of drag in the 90s, despite being cis straight men, except for Nathan Lane, who is a cis gay man. Cis men dressing in drag allowed drag to become mainstream and made way for cultural acceptance of the gay rights movement, given the association with gay men and fun, friendly drag culture. Many bachelorette parties have been held at drag clubs, largely because of this sanitized "I want a gay drag bestie" image that Hollywood created.

When we look at To Wong Foo and RENT, we see characters that seldom get out of drag. This has caused some severe confusion with cis people as to what drag is and what transness is. Noxeema, Vida, and Chi-Chi in To Wong Foo are rarely seen as men, and Wilson Cruz's Angel in Rent rarely comes out of "drag." This leads many trans viewers to believe that these characters are, in fact, trans and were merely written by cis straight men who didn't know what the difference between drag queens and trans women is. Drag queens simply don't stay in drag 24/7, and they certainly don't seek to be seen as women, as we see most particularly in To Wong Foo. A cis gay male drag queen's entire identity is not drag; they take off the clothes and the wig at the end of the performance. A trans drag queen is a showgirl who peforms in drag spaces, and while they do remove their outfit at the end of the day (rhinestones can get heavy), it's usually to slip into more comfortable women's clothes.

Furthermore, it's worth noting that these early depictions of drag in movies are hugely problematic and unrealistic. Most cis men cannot just hop into drag and "pass" as cis women. The fact is, Noxeema, Vida, and Chi-Chi as they are depicted in To Wong Foo are most likely trans women AND drag queens. They were merely depicted as drag queens due to the writers not knowing the difference. A movie about transgender people was bound to be more taboo and less likely to gain an audience than a movie about cis gay men in drag during that particular era in American cinema.

This all brings to mind the movie "She's the Man," in which Amanda Bynes dresses as a man and is immediately accepted among one of the guys. Any newly out trans guy can tell you that this is simply not how it works. Anyone with eyes can tell that Amanda Bynes' character, Viola Hastings, was a woman (given that she identified that way) or was at least assigned female at birth. In all actuality, she would be clocked immediately, leaving trans men everywhere screeaming at the television. These movies unknowingly erase the struggles that many trans men and women face every day when we're clocked. Cis culture thinks that a change of hair and wardrobe instantly means one can walk the world in a different gender, but that is not remotely close to what trans people experience. Many of us never "pass," and certainly don't pass when we're freshly out of the closet and just begin presenting in our actual genders.

Some drag performers are kings, and some are nonbinary majesties. This fact is largely ignored and does not attract the same level of fervor as cis gay male drag queens. The drag scene today is not just cis gay men. Your average drag scene does not look like the West Hollywood drag scene. Take a skip to downtown LA, and you have nonbinary performers, drag kings, trans queens, trash queens, tranimals, drag monsters, and more.

The drag community is hugely diverse, and the stereotype of a cis gay male in drag is a part of that, but it isn't the whole picture by any means.

Drag is important because of a common phrase in the community. "Drag is a gateway drug." Meaning, drag often leads to transness. Drag is a comfortable and safe community for one to explore their gender identity, and while some popular TV hosts may disagree, drag is demonstratively trans. Trans women have been there since the beginning, from Paris is Burning to Drag Race.

However, not all trans people do drag, and not all of us love it because of how conflated transness has become with drag in the mainstream. Trans women are often referred to as drag queens, whether we do drag or not. Similarly, drag queens are often referred to as a particular trans slur, highlighting just how far our culture has to go before accepting all of us for who we are. The trans drag community is simply not responsible for the fact that some cis gay men use an art form that we created to make a mockery of womanhood.

Many trans folks are hugely offended by the Drag Race franchise because it so often makes fun of our reality. For instance, the issue of "tucking," wherein a person tucks their genitals to create a smoother appearance in the panty-area, is constantly brought up as if a drag queen or trans woman's tuck is anybody else's fucking business. On that show, drag performers are told to go "untuck backstage" in between runway shows and deliberation, which is a mighty personal thing to tell someone to go do. In the 13th season Gottmik, a trans man, was cast on the show, yet they still tell the queens to go "untuck backstage." And don't even get us started on how problematic the word "fish" is as slang for "feminine."

All in all, drag is significant because art is important. Everyone deserves a safe space to explore gender without scrutiny or assumptions about their identity. So many of us find ourselves through the art form of drag, where we can dress in our preferred manner freely before ultimately coming out as trans. Cis people also find the freedom to fuck with gender through drag as an art form, which is also important.

While it's essential to distinguish between drag and transness, it's also necessary to make it clear that trans women of color invented drag, and cis gay men who perform in drag better know it.

I'VE BEEN A FIGHTER FROM DAY ONE

Em Westheimer / Siri

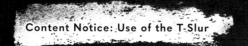

Content Notice: Use of the T-Slur

I fought the ballet teacher over not getting to wear a tutu. I fought with teachers over using the single-stall bathroom. I've fought off grown-ass men who couldn't keep their hands to themselves. I've fought the follicles of my hair. I've been through more bleach, relaxer, extensions, hot iron burns, and tragic box dyes than Paul Mitchell HERself.

If I'd had trans-affirming parents, community, teachers, extracurriculars (including sports, believe it/not), mentors... I don't know. I'd be less depressed, less anxious, and have less acne probably. Maybe I wouldn't have ended up in abusive relationships or tended towards self-destruction the way I did from 13 to 23. Good therapy, stable housing, healthcare (including access to medical transition), an affirming community, equal access to education, and bright career prospects are the cures for trans depression, not NOT being trans. Because that's not an option. We /all/ tried.

Em Westheimer

I can say with 100% certainty that coming out and dealing with others' cruelty was easier and more worthwhile than denying my reality to myself and pretending to be a boy. Going from being a young *maybe gay??* white boy to a "FUCKING DISGUSTING TRANNY, KILL IT WITH FIRE" and internalizing all of that was easier than lying about who I am. It's been said that a trans girl is never more clockable as trans than when she's still trying to pass as a boy, which was undoubtedly the case for me.

Ultimately, I wasn't "born trans." I was born myself, a human, like everyone else. The fact that nobody accepted me just as I was and forced me into roles I didn't fit into with violence and manipulation, forcing ME to have to do the work to RE-discover my true self, having to transition - is what makes me trans. Transness, like gender, is a social construct. I'm not nearly so different from cis people as either of us would like to admit. But the GOP isn't ready for that convo.

I am incredibly grateful to have met myself. I love me. Big things are coming. I have a bright future. We're here, we've always been here (although not in the humbled state you find us now), and we'll be here until the sun blows up and takes us all out.

- *Siri* -

They/Their
or She/Her in drag

Em Westheimer

259

NONBINARY DRAGPRINCESS SIRI

SIRI is the drag alter-ego of Los Angeles-based nonbinary performer, Em Westheimer. Known for her digital drag show "FAKE SMART," Siri has carved a name out for herself in the L.A. drag community and beyond.

Follow them on Instagram @Siri_Ew

Em Westheimer

NONBINARY DRAGPRINCESS SIBI

DROWNING IN INK

RORI PORTER

As a graphic artist, I tend to labor over minute details and strive for absolute pixel-perfect flawlessness in my work. When I turn to forms of media that I don't typically engage in, I try to allow myself the freedom to be a little, well, sloppy. As such, the following is an art series about letting loose and, contrary to the title, is about making sure that I don't drown in the self-imposed expectation of laying down perfect ink on the page. I believe that there is beauty in letting the ink drip down the canvas, spraypainting with rough stencils, or letting motion blur imply a sense of depth and emotion.

These pieces are quick works of ink, mixed media, and photography that convey snapshots of what it feels like to be trans from my perspective while recovering from addiction, including a letter to my friend Abby who overdosed in August 2020.

For more of my work, you can visit my website at **RoriPorter.com**

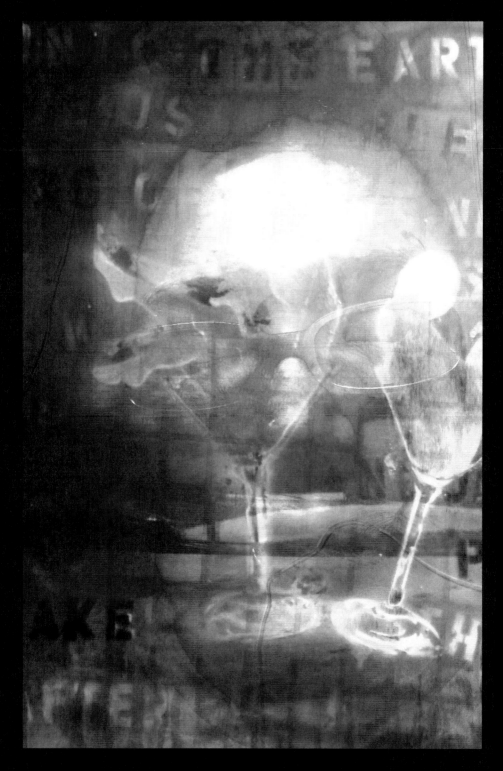

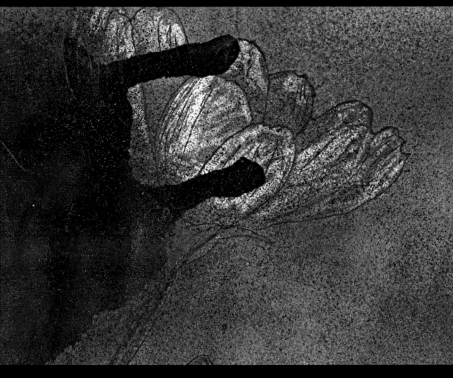

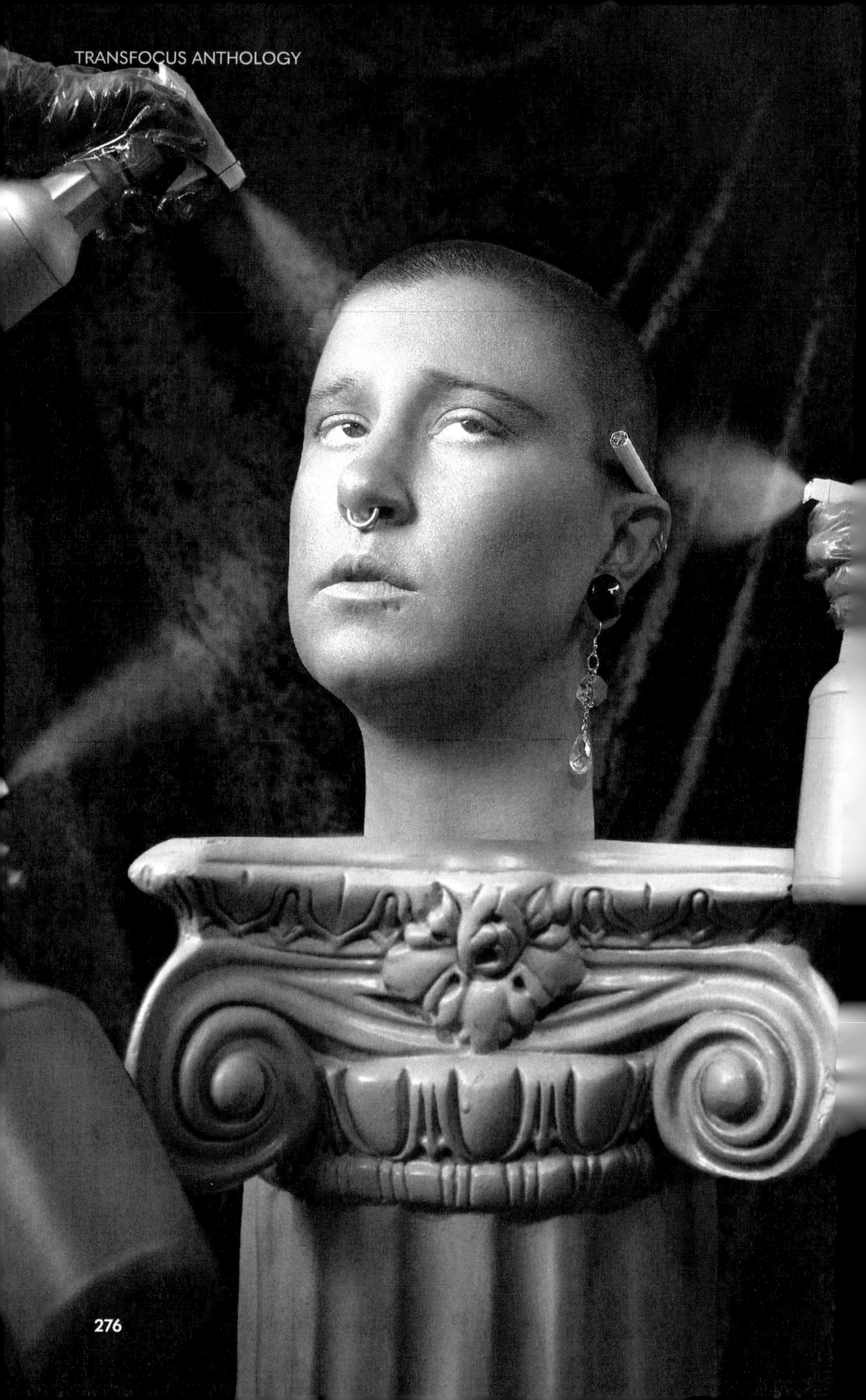

SEARCHING FOR WEAKNESS

ASH DANIELSEN

This series of self portraits is photographed on days in which I inject myself with testosterone.

Contents of the series reflect how I'm feeling on that particular day, and will serve as a way to catalog the progress during my transition.

You can view more of my work by visiting

ashdanielsen.com

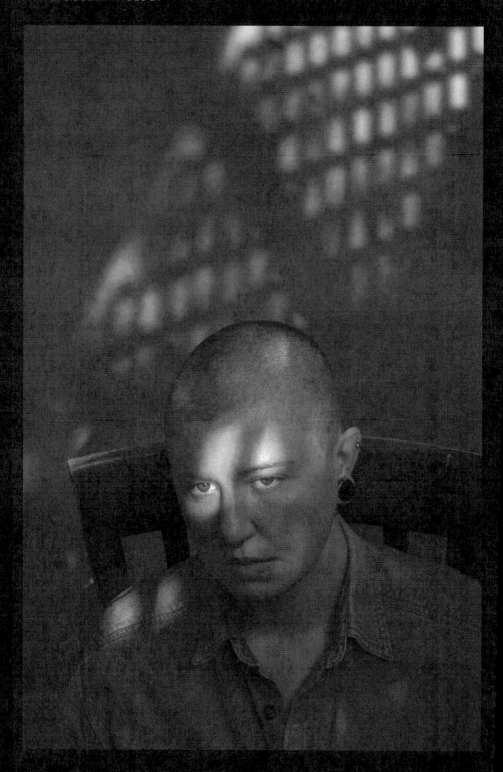

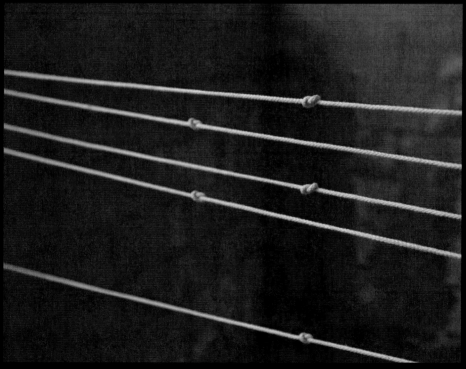

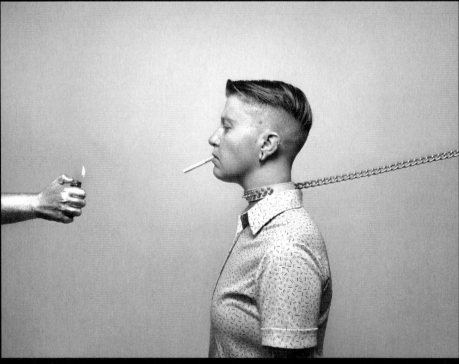

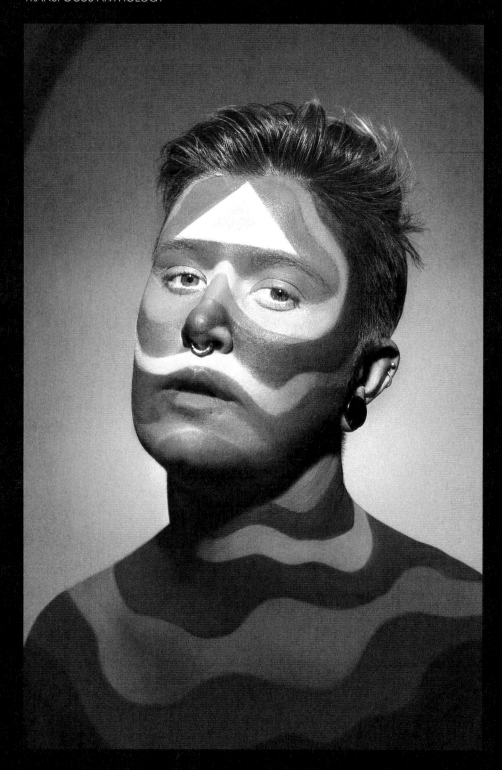

A MANIFESTATION OF TWO SPIRITS

ROXY VALLE / JOHNNY SIN-ROSA GENTLEMAN

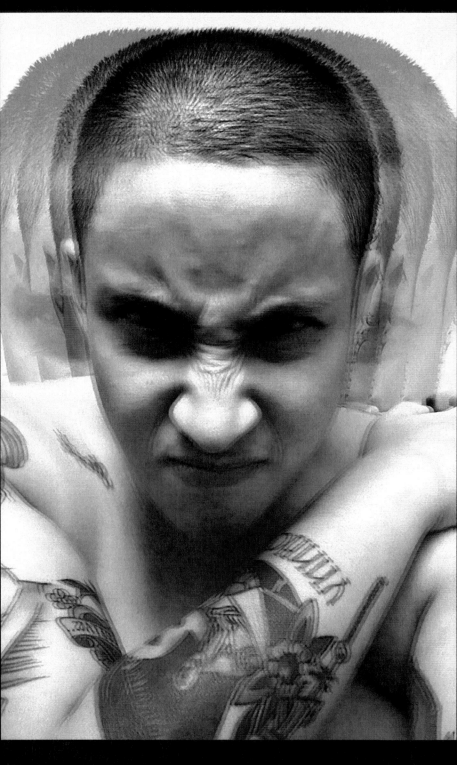

Roxy Valle (They/Them) is a Latinx, Two-spirit/ Non-Binary, Transmasculine drag king located in Los Angeles under the name, Johnny Sin-Rosa Gentleman. They started their artistic journey at the age of 12 when they discovered the art of hip-hop dance and went on to perform for almost a decade. Since then they have explored photography, cinematography, screenwriting, and currently work in the Film and TV industry. But one of their true passions come from their nightlife persona and the Downtown LA Drag Scene. Their drag is a statement that AFABs (Assigned Female At Birth) can be gentlemen too. The vision for their drag is to show that masculinity can be within everyone, that bringing Latinx and BIPOC representation and issues need to be put in the forefront, and to bring to life that happiness that comes from nostalgia and showmanship. They aspire to bring visiblity to transgender and nonbinary folx in the drag community and give them a spotlight for their art. They perform on numerous virtual drag shows around the world on Twitch TV, produce numerous drag shows on their Kings of the World Twitch Channel, and can be seen performing in numerous drag shows in the DTLA drag scene.

follow @johnnysinrosagent on Instagram

TRANS FASHION

Jordy Robinson

Jordy Robinson

299

TRANS JOY IS RESISTANCE

Mars Wright (he/him) is a Trans artist and Activist who is dedicated to spreading Trans Joy and radical self-acceptance. You can find his work on Instagram and TikTok **@mars.wright** and online at **marswright.com**

MARS WRIGHT

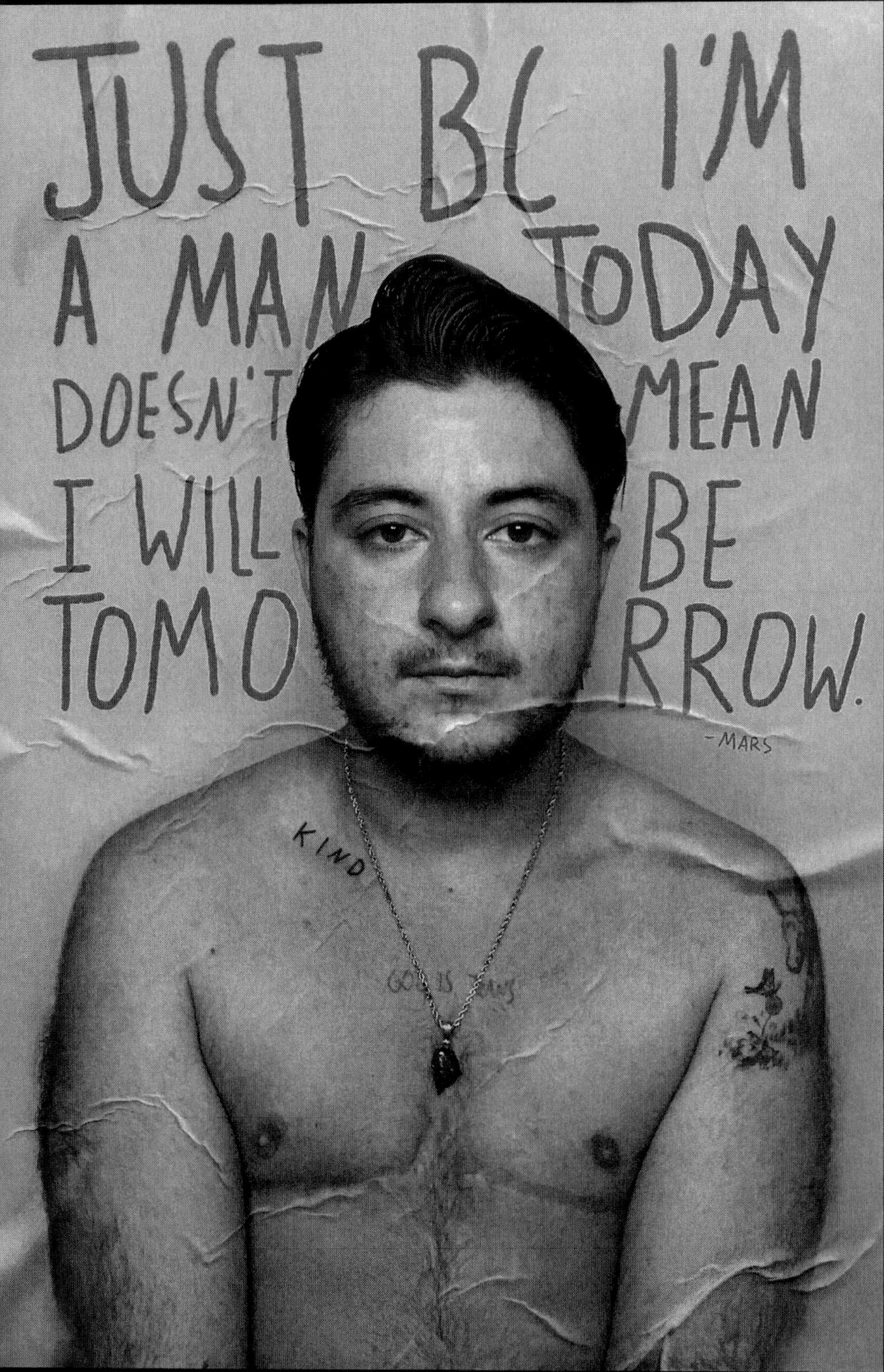
JUST BC I'M A MAN TODAY DOESN'T MEAN I WILL BE TOMORROW.
-MARS
KIND

LET'S GO ON A TRIP TO MY HOMETOWN AND HOLD HANDS IN ALL THE PLACES I FELT UNLOVABLE.

—MARS

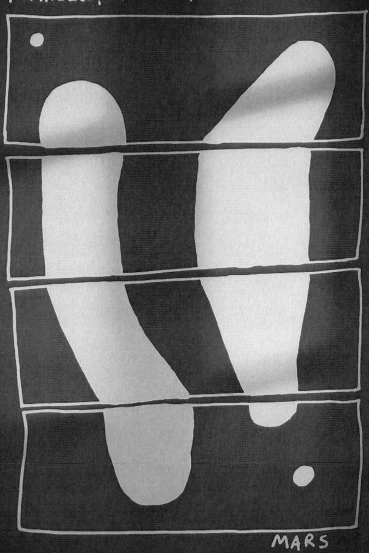

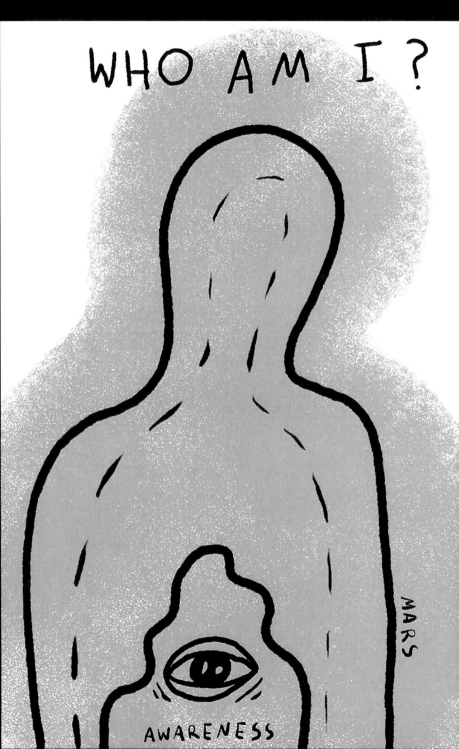

NONE OF THIS

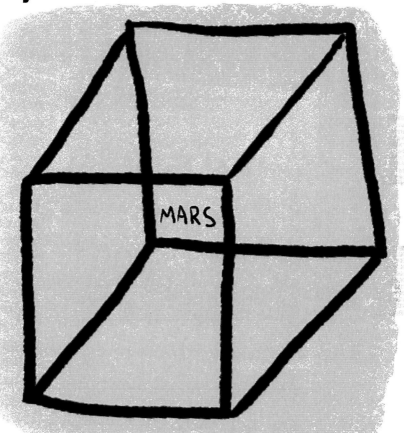

MARS

IS REAL...

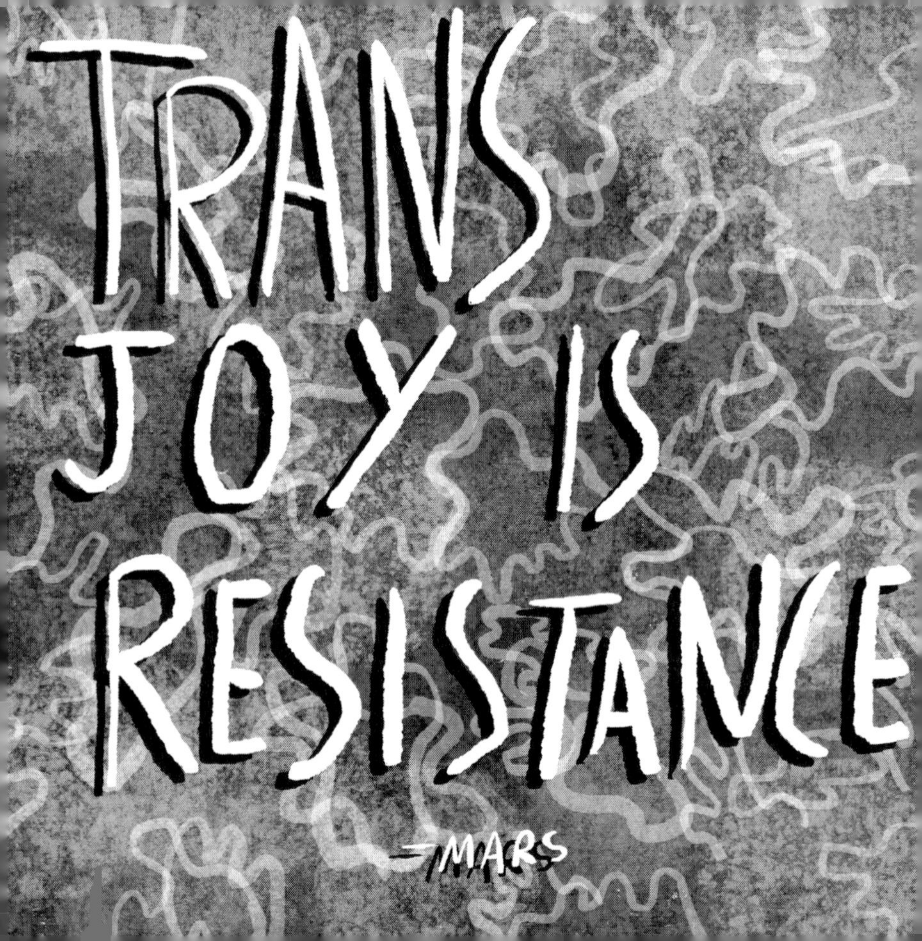
TRANS
JOY IS
RESISTANCE
—MARS

QUEER MAN ♥!

—MARS

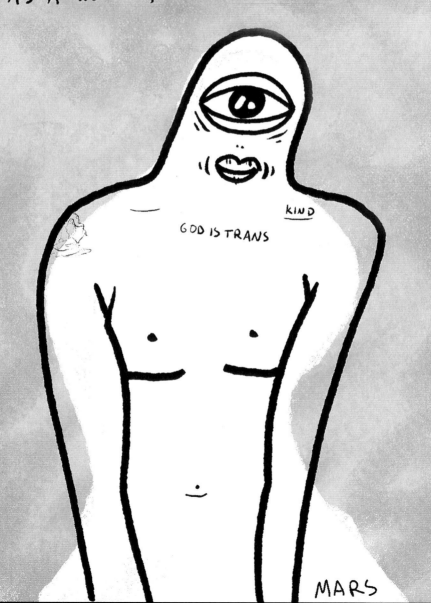

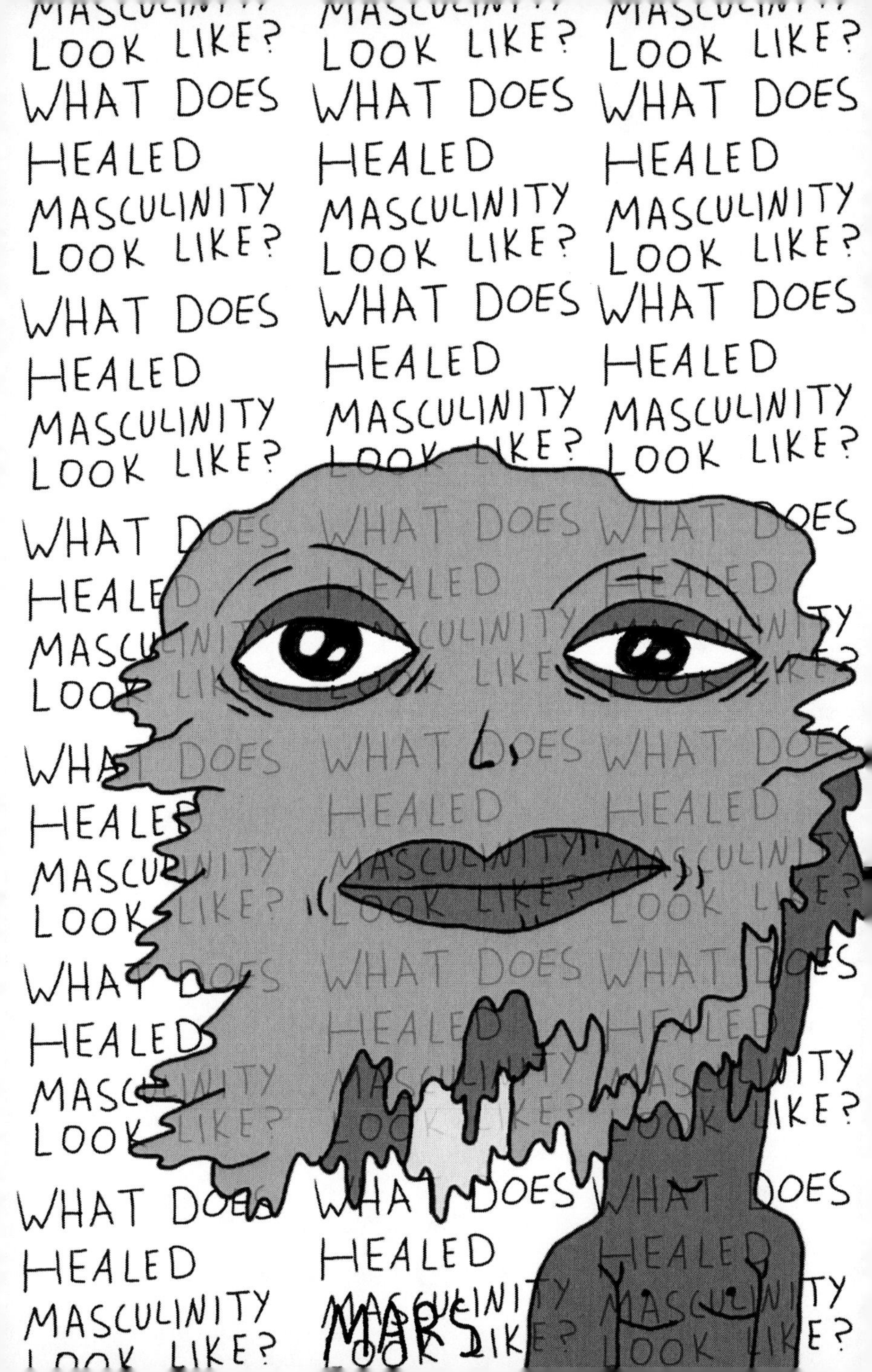
WHAT DOES HEALED MASCULINITY LOOK LIKE?
MARS

DID YOU KNOW?

A COMIC BY ROSALIE DERK

TRANS DRAG
TRANS ART

PAGE PERSON / M. PAGE GREENE

When I started my medical transition two years ago I also started performing on the drag scene. I had mostly been a behind the scenes type person until then and suddenly wanted all the visibility I could get. I utilized my background as a painter to find my drag face and to create a new reality to step into. For me, being trans is just another way to use my creativity to reshape my existence into something that resonates with my experience as a gender fluid individual.

follow @page__person on Instagram

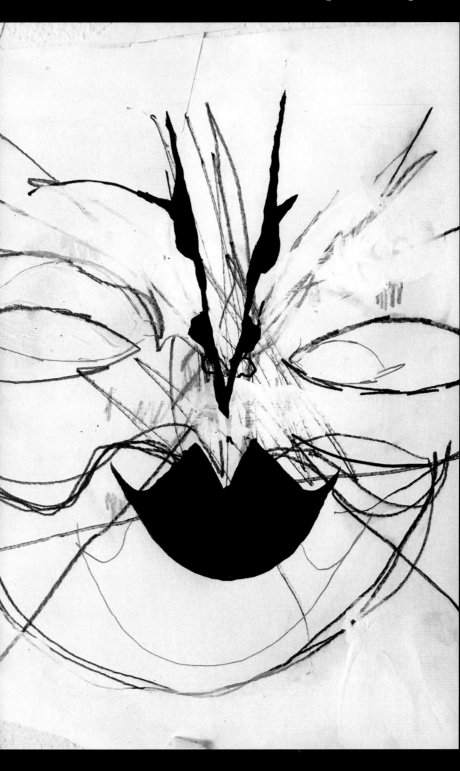

TRANIMAL INSTINCTS

the origins of Squeaky Blonde

Content Notice: Use of the T-slur (Historic Context)

For many years I lived a double and triple life hiding from myself and others. I was constantly searching, constantly seeking to find the truth of my own identity. I'd been searching for my own people for many years and was still living as a cisgender, heterosexual man until one glorious Tuesday evening in the summer of 1996. I stumbled into The Stud bar in San Francisco on the corner of ninth and Harrison. There is a massive sign on the side of the building, in a fantastic font I had never seen before, spelling out the word "Trannyshack."

I thought to myself, "wow, what is that and who is inside? What happens in there? Are those my people? I guess I'm gonna have to find out.."

And from the moment I walked through those doors to the moment I stood on that stage for the first time a year later, I knew that I had found a place to call home, a place where I was safe among others just like me. The Stud was a dark and shabby rundown wood-built bar that had had its heyday during the 70s, 80s, and the mid-90s when I first found it. The inside was very rickety and felt like the inside of an old ship. There was a small dance floor and a pool table, and at the end of that dance floor was a makeshift stage where some of the most beautiful women I've ever seen in my life took to the stage for the midnight cabaret show.

Suddenly, I heard the theme song to The Muppets roaring from the loudspeakers and echoing throughout the club. Droves of queens, punks, skaters, sex workers, leather daddies, twinks, drag queens, club kids, trans women, bull dykes, lipstick lesbians, and folks off the street all rushed into the club, knocking into me as they pushed their way toward the stage. They had all rushed in as soon as they heard the speakers blare that song. I later realized that it was the club's theme song and the signal to the midnight show's opening. I knew the show is about to begin and, within moments, a tall, gorgeous Amazonian priestess stepped onto the stage and announced herself. In the cutest nasally voice, she told us her name was Heklina, and she said she had named herself after a volcano in Iceland, where she had been raised.

She had such a quick wit, a sharp tongue, and an undeniable knack for the gift of gab. It made her one of the most enthralling hostesses I've ever laid my eyes upon, and from that moment on, I knew I had found my people, my home, my sanctuary. And one day, I would be on that stage as the woman I was meant to be and had always dreamed of being. In the club that night, I knew everything had changed for me.

There was so much love there; so much joy and excitement and glamour in that room. I knew I was safe and free to be whoever the hell I wanted, even if it was only for a few hours, one night a week. There, I could be myself, behind those closed doors with the most bizarre array of beautiful creatures of the night. I studied their lips and how they overdrew them with lip liner and said to myself, "Wow... I want mine to be just like that." It was as if I was picking out body part by body part from a catalog of girls who had already transitioned. They would walk through the club with exposed breasts, showing off their brand new freshly acquired assets and flaunting them like gorgeous peacocks.

I knew I wanted to be like one of those beautiful women who called themselves The Gorgeous Ladies of Trannyshack. While it's taken me almost half a century to get to that place, I never gave up and never faltered. I never looked back and stand before you today as a woman. A woman that I love, the woman I was always meant to be, and this, my friends, is the story of how I became complete and how I found myself in the body and mind of the glamorous showgirl and chanteuse that I am today. I found the ultimate gift that was waiting for me all along; she was right here behind my eyes the whole time; it just took me a few years to realize it and accept, embrace and embody her in all her full glamour and glory.

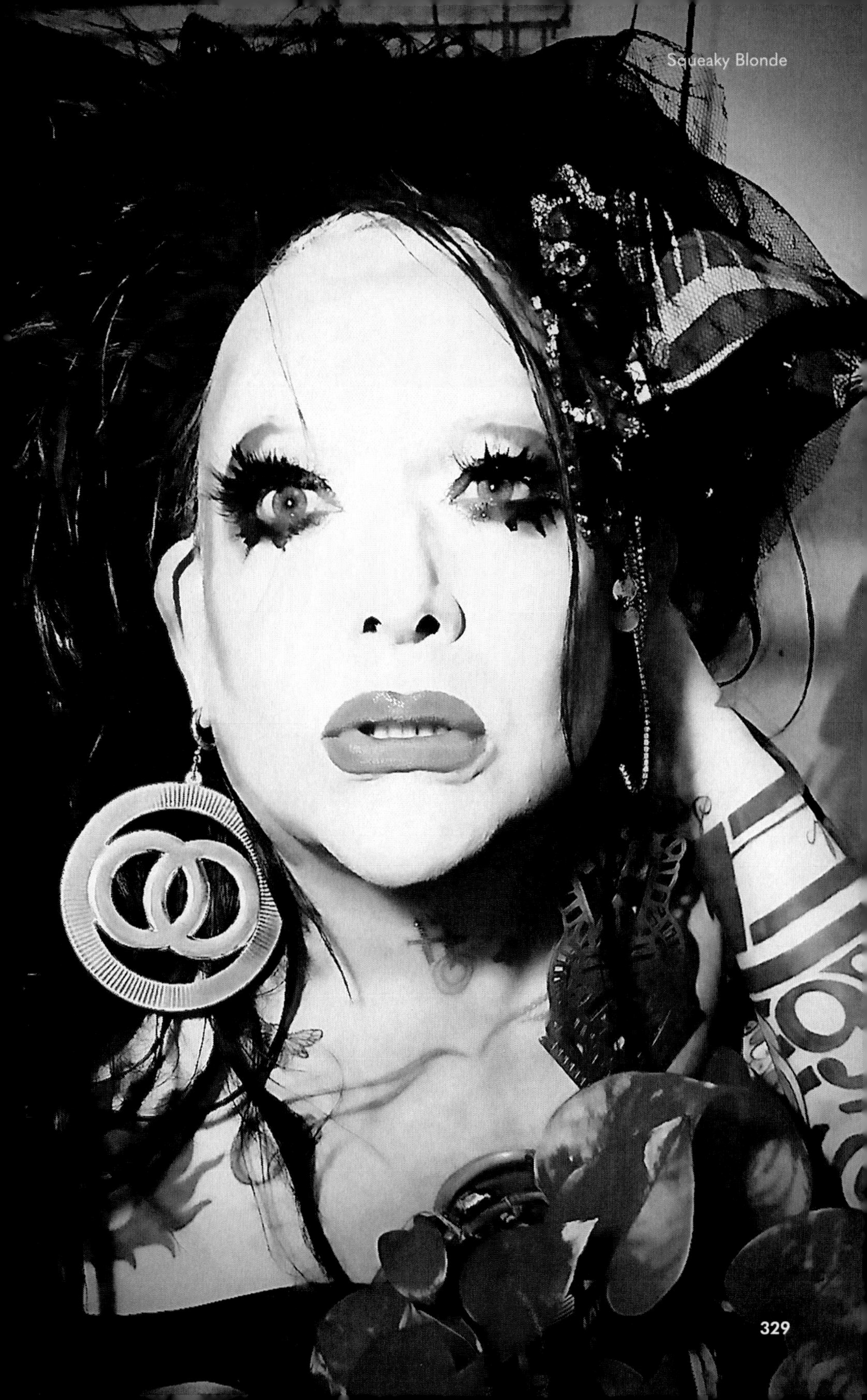

- Andy Passchier -

RAINFOREST

Content Notice: Transphobia, Slurs

BEING TRANS IN THE WORLD CAN BE HARD

...BEING TRANS ON THE INTERNET CAN BE EVEN HARDER

COMMENTS RAIN DOWN
FROM ANONYMOUS CLOUDS

YOUR PRONOUNS
ARE RIDICULOUS

YOUR GENDER
IS BULLSHIT

YOU'RE SICK

TRANNY

GOD WILL
PUNISH YOU

FUCK OFF

DISGUSTING

SOMETIMES IT'S A DRIZZLE,
EASY TO IGNORE

SOMETIMES IT'S A STORM,
HARDER TO AVOID

OTHER DAYS IT FEELS LIKE
YOU'RE BEING SWEPT AWAY
BY A HURRICANE

MAYBE YOU THINK IT
WILL DROWN ME

OR WASH ME AWAY

AND I'M TURNING INTO
A FUCKING RAINFOREST

Andy Passchier is a non-binary illustrator originally from The Netherlands, currently based in the USA. They work as a freelance illustrator working on children's books and other projects, and draw comics in their free time on the Instagram account @andyrogyny. Andy lives with their two cats, loves to travel, draw, eats lots of sushi and enjoys all things spooky and Halloween.

Check out more by Andy on Instagram @andyrogyny

TRANS 101
COMMONLY USED WORDS

* an asterisk next to a word indicates that the term is outdated or problematic in some way and should only be used in limited contexts

AFAB/AMAB: assigned Female at Birth. It can apply to trans men or nonbinary people. Assigned Male at Birth -- Can apply to trans women or nonbinary people.

AGAB: assigned Gender at Birth. This is the gender that is marked on one's birth certificate, in most cases male or female.

Agender: refers to a person who experiences no gender or an absence of gender.

Ally: a person who supports and goes to bat for trans people, even in our absence. They listen when trans people speak and do not talk over us.

Androgyne: a nonbinary gender identity associated with androgyny or the desire to be androgynous. A gender identity that is simultaneously masculine and feminine, though not necessarily in equal measure.

Androgynous: the quality of being neither masculine or feminine, or both at the same time. Stems from the root words "Andro" (masculine) and Gyne (feminine)

Autigender: also sometimes called Autismgender or Neurogender, autigender refers to an autistic person whose gender identity is typically not male or female and falls somewhere under the nonbinary umbrella. Autigender is not autism as a gender, but is instead, when one's gender identity is so heavily influenced by autism that one cannot separate the two. Autigender can stand alone or can be combined with another gender identity. For instance, one can be an autigender trans woman, or an autigender demiboy, etc.

Bigender: to experience two genders either simultaneously or varying between two. It can mean one experiences gender as male and female or as male/female and nonbinary.

Binary: refers to binary gender -- Male and Female. Binary is often used to explain the erasure of nonbinaryness.

Boi: African American Vernacular English (AAVE) that typically refers to a Black AFAB person who presents themselves in a masculine manner, though "Boi" can also refer to a Black AMAB person who presents in a feminine manner, whether cis or trans. It is a spelling that is often, but should not be, used by non-Black people. Its use by a non-Black person is considered appropriation and is strictly discouraged.

Bottom Surgery: refers to genital surgeries, such as vaginoplasty, orchiectomy, phalloplasty, or metoidioplasty.

Butch: refers to an identity or gender expression, and can be used as a noun or a verb, depending on how it's used. One can identify as butch, or one can be butch in a physical sense. It is most commonly associated with masculine queer or lesbian women and is also distinct gender identity and expression and does not always mean that one identifies as a woman.

CAAB: Coersively Assigned at Birth. an alternative to AGAB to explain how others forcibly applied one's assigned gender. Often refers to the intersex experience surgeries performed upon infants.

CAFAB / CAMAB: Coersively Assigned Female at Birth or Coersively Assigned Male at Birth. Alternative to AFAB/AMAB. Can refer to an intersex person whose sex characteristics were altered at birth.

Chaser: a cisgender person who explicitly seeks out sexual relationships with trans people, particularly trans women. In contrast to people who date trans folks, chasers harass and exploit trans people for their personal pleasure and never actually want a relationship with a trans person. They may even hide their attractions from others and are often the perpetrators of violence against trans women of color.

Cisgender / Cis: means that one aligns with their gender assigned at birth. Stems from the Latin root word "cis," which means "on this side of."

Cisgender Privilege: the privilege that cisgender people possess because their gender identity aligns with their assigned gender at birth. For instance, cisgender people are often considered "normal" and do not experience discrimination, hatred, or violent threats due to their gender identity, whereas trans people frequently do.

Cissexism: like transphobia, cissexism is the erasure and/or discrimination or expression of hatred toward trans people.

Coming Out: to "come out" about one's LGBTQIA2+ identity and share that part of themselves with friends, family, loved ones, and others.

Cross-Dressing/Cross-Dresser: refers to someone who dresses and presents themselves as a gender aside from the one in which they identify. Most often refers to a cis man who dresses in women's clothing, but can also refer to a woman who dresses in men's clothes. Trans people are typically not cross-dressers, as a trans woman who dresses femininely or a trans man who dresses masculinely are presenting in a manner in which they do identify. Cross-dressing specifically refers to dressing "across" from one's actual identity, and can be a part of one's identity, aesthetic, or is sometimes sexual in nature.

Deadnaming: to use a trans person's birth or given name, rather than the name they have chosen and use for themselves.

Demiboy/man: refers to someone who identifies as partially a boy or man, or otherwise masculine. Can refer to either an AFAB or AMAB person.

Demigirl/woman: refers to someone who identifies as partially a girl or woman, or otherwise feminine. Can refer to either an AFAB or AMAB person.

Drag: a performance art form, stemming from the acronym "Dressed as a Girl." However, modern drag encompasses all genders and expressions and can be performed by anybody. Many trans men, trans women, and nonbinary people perform drag in their preferred gender expression, albiet typically with more flare than they express in every day life. Cis women and men can similarly perform in drag, as it is an expressive art form and has little to do with gender identity.

Dyadic: refers to non-intersex people

Enby: the shortened form of "Nonbinary." It stems from "NB," which used to be commonly used as an acronym for nonbinary, but has fallen out of use due to the acronym more commonly referring to Non-Black people of color.

Facial Feminization / Masculinization: refers to a number of surgeries to feminize or masculinize one's facial features, such as jaw contouring, hairline advancement, cheek implants, etc.

Femme: short-hand for feminine. Can serve as a descriptor of identity, an identity label itself, or as an identity-modifier, as in the case of "transfemme"

FTM*: an outdated term that means "Female to Male." While some still use it to identify themselves, it should not be used by others. Has fallen out of favor in preference for AFAB

Gender: refers to a person's experience of identity as related to male, female, nonbinary or other expansive gender identities

Gender Dysphoria: a feeling of discomfort and incongruence with one's gender assigned at birth. .

Gender Expansive: refers to the whole of the trans and gender non-conforming community and all identities therein.

Gender Expression / Presentation: how one presents themselves to the world, which may or may not directly align to their gender identity; How one communicates their gender identity to others.

Gender Identity: how one thinks of their own gender and related to themselves. Gender identity is personal and can therefore not be dictated by others, and is entirely separate from one's sex.

Gender Neutral: refers to anything that is not defined or separated by gender.

Gender Non-conforming: any individual who does not conform to stereotypical gender roles as they pertain to their gender assigned at birth.

Gender-Critical Feminism: a hate movement that is characterized by a sincere hatred of trans people, especially trans women. Gender critical feminism is a misnomer, however, as they are neither critical of gender, nor or they feminists. They effectively see women as walking uteruses and believe that biology dictates gender, despite all evidence to the contrary.

LGBTQIA2+: an acronym that means Lesbian, Gay, Bisexual, Transgender, Queer, Intersex, Asexual, Two Spirit. The + stands for anybody who is questioning their gender, as well as all gender expansive and sexual identities not mentioned or yet defined.

Macroaggression: typically a major display of transphobia. For example, "Trans women shouldn't be allowed in women's restrooms. I don't want a man in a dress around my child." See page 62 for a broad explanation on transphobic macroaggressions.

Masc: shortened form of "Masculine."

Microaggression: typically a minor statement betraying one's transphobia and/or ignorance of trans people. For example, "So, you used to a girl?" or calling a trans woman "buddy" or "dude."

Misgendering: to use the wrong pronouns for a trans person, ie: the pronouns that align with their gender assigned at birth.

Genderfluid: a gender which can vary over time, either between male and female, or between male/female and other nonbinary identities. The variation can be rapid, frequent, or gradual. Many genderfluid people experience different genders dependent upon circumstance.

Genderqueer: both an identity and an umbrella term for gender expansivity. They can be trans or cis, and some define genderqueer as an alternative to trans or cis entirely and use it as a third option between or outside the two. It often carries similar meaning to nonbinary, and can refer to anybody who feels that they have a non-normative experience with gender.

HRT (Hormone Replacement Therapy): refers to the medical intervention in which a person takes hormones to in order to either masculinize or feminize their sex characteristics. Hormones come in a myriad of forms, including pills, injections, and transdermal patches or creams.

Intersex: a person born with "ambiguous" sexual characteristics, including any combination of reproductive organs, genitalia, hormone levels, chromosomes. Some intersex people identify as transgender, but many do not. Because genital surgery is often performed on intersex infants nonconsensually, many are raised not knowing what happened to them at birth and only discover that they are intersex later in life, if ever. One can also have a myriad of intersex traits unrelated to genital configuration.

MTF *: an outdated term that means "Male to Female." While some still use it to identify themselves, it should not be used by others. Has fallen out of favor in preference for AMAB

NB *: sometimes used as an acronym for "Nonbinary," but given that it is typically used to mean "Non-Black," it has fallen out of favor. "Enby" is now considered correct to avoid confusion between the two.

Neopronouns: Neo pronouns are any pronouns that have been created recently, typically in the last 200 years. Examples of neopronouns include Xe/Xir/Xyr, E/Em, Ae/Aer, Co/Cos, Ve/Vi/Vir, Per, Hu, Ze/Zir, Fae/Faer, etc. Some people also use "It" pronouns, but given that this can be hugely derogatory when used for the wrong person, we generally *do not* recommend using "it" pronouns for any person unless they very specifically request you to do so.

Nonbinary: Describes any identity that does not fit the male-female binary. Can refer to an individual's identity or can be used as an umbrella term for all gender-expansive identities.

Omnigender: refers to experiencing all genders, but defining them as one. Stems from the Latin root "omnis" meaning "all.

Outing/Outed: similar to "Coming Out," but typically with the implication that someone has come out on another's behalf. Do not out anybody who does not wish to be outed.

Passing*: to "pass" as cisgender.

Queer: in antiquated use, meant "strange" or "weird," and has been historically used as a slur against the LGBTQIA community. In its reclamation, it is a catch-all that can refer to the entire LGBTQIA+ community, or can be used to describe a specific gender identity, sexual orientation, or gender expression that does not adhere to cisheteronormative society.

Sex: refers to one's sexually dimorphic biology and includes ones hormone levels, genitalia, chromosomes, and secondary sex characteristics like breasts, hips, body hair, and voice pitch.

TERF: "Trans-Exclusionary Radical Feminist/Feminism" refers to gender critical feminists, or rather more appropriately, Feminism-Appropriation Radical Transphobes, or uh... FARTs.

Top Surgery: Breast augmentation in the form of surgical implants in AMAB individuals, or double mastectomy or periareolar (keyhole) surgeries in AFAB individuals.

Trans Antagonism: effectively another way to say "transphobia," but with the implication that one is purposefully antagonizing trans people and is verbally acting out their transphobia.

Trans Man: an individual who was assigned female at birth but whose gender identity is male

Trans Woman: an individual who was assigned male at birth but whose gender identity is female

Transfeminine / Transfemme: a term used to describe a transgender person who is generally assigned male at birth. Typically, but not necessarily, feminine in presentation.

Transgender / Trans: describes someone who does not identify with their gender assigned at birth. Stems from the Latin root word "trans" which means "across"

Transition / in transition / transitioning: refers to the state of altering one's social surroundings to accommodate their gender identity (ie. social transition); or medically transitioning one's sex characteristics.

Transmasculine / Transmasc: a term used to describe a transgender person who is generally assigned female at birth. Typically, but not necessarily, masculine in presentation.

Transmisandry: Cissexism/transphobia toward trans men. It is worth noting that "misandry" toward cis men is not a prominent issue worth noting. Transmisandry is specifically necessary to address because trans men face transphobia specifically for being trans men.

Transmisogyny: cissexism/transphobia toward trans women

Transphobia: the hatred, derision, prejudice, and discrimination of trans people

Transsexual*: an outdated term for a trans person. Is sometimes still used by a transgender person who identifies strongly with their medical transition. Not recommended for use except by those who identify strongly this way.

Transvestite*: a label used regularly as synonymous with "Cross Dressing," this largely regarded as derogotory and is not used by many people.

Trigender: translates to having three genders. Could be any combination of male, female, or nonbinary gender identities

Two Spirit: a culturally-specific identity label used by some North American Native Americans to refer to individuals who fulfill a traditional third gender and was created to replace an outdated and offensive term "Berdache," which, roughly translated, refers to any LGBTQIA person, especially those who are effeminate by a western standard. Two Spirit typically means that one has a male and a female spirit or soul. The term was created at the Indigenous Lesbian and Gay International Gathering in 1990, and was chosen to distinguish between Native American/First Nations people from non-Native peoples. It serves as both a sexual identity and gender identity, depending on how one chooses to use it. Use of the identity by a non-Native person is a form of blatant appropriation and is strictly discouraged.

TRANSGENDER

NONBINARY

GENDER-EXPANSIVE

TRANSFEMME

COMING OUT

DEMIGIRL

AGENDER

AMAB

AFAB

GENDERQUEER

BIGENDER

DEADNAME

TRANSMASC

AUTIGENDER

QUEER

DYSPHORIA

EUPHORIA

FEMME

ENBY

DYADIC

CISGENDER

MASC

346

TRANSFOCUS

TRANSFOCUS
GENDERFLUID
DEMIBOY HRT OMNIGENDER QUEER ANDROGYNOUS
EXPRESSION
TRIGENDER
GENDER TRANSITION
TWO-SPIRIT
IDENTITY INTERSEX TRANS HE/HIM
NEOPRONOUNS
BUTCH LGBTQIA2+
ALLY SHE/HER
THEY/THEIR OUT
TRANSFOCUS

- Rori Porter -

Editor of TransFocus

FOREVER MY SISTER, ABBY ROSE FIALA

JULY 16, 1990

AUGUST 25, 2020

We met in a therapy group for girls like us, and I was immediately drawn to your kind spirit and sensitive nature. You spoke so rarely, but when you did, you had something profound or affirming to say. You took up so little space and gave it readily to others who needed it just as much as you did. Wearing Tinkerbell shoes and a polka dot bow in your hair, you were quiet but also bubbly and sweet. Always selfless, always concerned with the wellbeing of others, I took your calm and strong presence for granted.

When I was struggling, you came to my home to console me and make sure that I would be safe. You reached out to me in times of stress and shared moments of joy with me when they came. I miss your voice. I miss your presence. I miss the calm assurance that you lent to others, letting us know that everything would be okay.

The pandemic hit, and you were on the frontlines. Working in lab tech, you went to work every day that the rest of us were stuck in quarantine. As we complained about isolation, you were made to risk your life in a hospital. We asked how you were doing, but you always said you were fine. You were sober from a substance I can hardly begin to understand the gravity of and what grappling with that must have been like for you. For over a year, sober and moving forward. Sober and working on yourself. Sober and making it to that transfemme therapy group every single week.

I admired your sobriety and, in some ways, envied it. I looked up to you and respected your journey so fucking much. You were beautiful, sober, and kind. You had qualities I wished to have. And then, you pre-lapsed. You hadn't used yet, but you were dreaming of it. You confided in us that you were looking up your substance of choice on the dark web, and I was scared for you, but I also felt that you were so much better than the rest of us -- sober and staunchly so. So much stronger than the rest of us. Sober in a group of girls who were all numbing themselves.

And then one week you didn't come to the group, and nobody thought much of it. One week missed in two years of consistent attendance seemed like a blip. Maybe you were sick. Maybe you just needed to work. We didn't think twice. We had no idea that you had succumbed to addiction and were gone from this world.

I wish I had followed up with you after you confided about your searches on the dark web. I wish I had been more concerned and took it seriously. I wish I had said I love you one more time. I wish I had done something. But that's not how things panned out, and now you're no longer here, and your absence leaves a hole in the group. We took you for granted. I had to tell our group's facilitators what happened. They didn't know. I assumed they would have, but they didn't, and I bore the news to everyone. They needed to know what happened so they could prevent it from happening again. Something had to be done.

If there's an afterlife, I hope you can see how I tried to turn your absence into action. I was angry, and I called every damned person at the LGBT Center I could find to tell them that we needed a trans women's addiction recovery group. Now. Urgently. Expediently. It wasn't fair that you'd have had to confide in cis gay men to get the help you needed. It wasn't fair that there wasn't a place for you to air your struggles with addiction. It's not fair that you're not here anymore. But I took that lack of fairness and got sober. I petitioned in your honor. I tried to make your passing and my anger and mourning mean something. I've continued to try to make sure that what happened to you doesn't happen to any other trans girl in our community who wants help. But even if that help had existed, I just don't know if you would have taken it. You were... stoic. You endured so much and suffered in silence. I got sober for me, but I also got sober for you.

I miss you so much, Abby. I will always I love and cherish the time I had with you, and I will never forget the girl in the Tinkerbell shoes.

- TransFocus Editors -

ADDICTION AND RECOVERY

Addiction; Mention of Drugs; Ideation

Addiction is a serious and complicated subject for many people and is especially so for LGBTQIA+ folks. An alarmingly disproportionate number of people in our community live with and suffer from addiction, with social pressures, discrimination, abuse, and mental health issues resulting in many of us turning to drugs and alcohol to numb our pain. According to AddictionCenter.com, roughly 20 to 30 percent of LGBTQIA+ people abuse substances, compared to 9% of the cisgender, heterosexual population. We face stigmatization of sexual and gender diversity, hate crimes, abuse, death threats, rejection, shame, unstable employment or housing, oppression fatigue, minority stress, unwanted reliance on sex work, and internalized queer/transphobia. These are all factors that contribute to a significantly higher rate of addiction in our gender-diverse communities. LGBTQIA+ people are also disproportionately likely to experience major depressive disorders, anxiety disorders, suicide attempts, and higher stress levels than the general population.

When we don't know how to cope with all that life throws at us, drugs and alcohol can be especially appealing. We numb ourselves with substances that help us escape and repress the realities of our condition as humans in a transphobic and queerphobic world. Many trans people cope with substances to avoid the fact that we are trans, favoring repression to coming out and living our truths. But substances can only numb us for so long, and eventually, the issues we're dealing with break through the surface of that numbness. Suddenly, our problems are no longer able to be brushed under the rug with the aid of drugs and alcohol. When we reach that threshold, the substances we used to numb ourselves can even start having the opposite effect, amplifying our pain and making us feel more deeply. When this happens, drugs and alcohol are an insufficient covering on a gaping wound that needs sutures, not a dollar store bandaid.

Many trans people choose to get sober in the same breath as coming out as trans, but a significant number of us turn to substances to cope with being an out trans person in a world that mistreats and abuses trans people. Minority stress is a prominent component in substance use in all marginalized populations. As a community, we face devastating levels of discrimination in many parts of the world when compared to the rest of the population. We see bills passed to prevent us from accessing gender-affirming healthcare, targeting our especially vulnerable trans children, and bills proposing a limitation of our rights to play in organized sports. Even if we are not directly impacted by these laws passed to restrict our freedoms, it can be hugely discouraging and even traumatizing to constantly see the oppression of trans people as the cornerstone of many political agendas. Unfortunately, transphobia is everywhere. We can try our damnedest on social media to avoid transphobia, but it pops up time and time again. Our rights are often casually debated amongst people who have no vested interest in trans issues, as though trans people are an abstract concept and not a reality of human existence. We are all too often treated as a discussion or a debate rather than the vibrant and diverse community we are. Ultimately, we are just people, and being discussed as though we aren't in the room is exhausting. The point is, there are a multitude of reasons why a trans person might turn to substances to ease their pain. While all addicts should be treated with compassion and dignity, cis people should be especially sympathetic to trans addicts.

Choosing to get sober isn't easy for anybody who experiences addiction, as it means facing everything that we've tried so hard to ignore for most, if not all, marginalized communities. When we choose to get sober, it's not just a choice to stop using -- it's a choice to feel everything we've been trying not to feel, and we suddenly experience a deluge of every emotion we've used drugs and alcohol to repress. Sobriety means finding new ways to cope with transphobia, invalidation, hatred, and abuse. For many of us, access to a therapist is grossly cost-prohibitive, making finding a place to unpack that which drives us to substances entirely inaccessible. For those of us with access to proper healthcare, finding trans-affirming medical professionals can still be difficult, if not impossible, leaving us to cope with addiction independently.

In the digital age, however, we are fortunate. A strange, positive side-effect of COVID is that recovery meetings are more accessible than ever before. Trans-led and trans-affirming recovery groups are everywhere, no longer forcing trans folks to settle for cishet sober spaces that can often be hostile places. When we choose to get sober, it is of great importance that we surround ourselves with a sober community. While some people can get sober without any outside help, that is unfortunately not the case for most addicts. Making friends with other queer and trans addicts is crucial in moving on from substances and choosing a sober lifestyle. A sober support network is one of our most valuable tools in recovery.

If you are reading this and you are struggling with addiction, the one thing we wish to do is impart a sense of hope. There are options for you out there, and if you wish to get sober there is a way to do so. The sober community is bright and diverse, and there is a way beyond any barrier that keeps you from seeking sobriety. For instance, suppose the religious undertones of Alcoholics Anonymous turn you off. In that case, there are non-religious meetings and even recovery settings inspired by the teachings of Buddha that you can attend. You can find trans-led meetings, women-led meetings, nonbinary meetings, and any combination therein. There are even meetings out there that are for everybody under the sun, except for cis men. Whatever your requirement, there is a sober gathering that will meet your needs.

If you wish to get sober, there is a path to do so. There is always hope, and if you are struggling with addiction, just know that you are not alone.

If you require help finding trans-led addiction recovery meetings, feel free to email **addictionrecovery@transfoc.us** and we will assist you in getting the assistance you need, regardless of where in the world you are located.

You can also call the SAMHSA (Substance Use and Mental Health Services Administration) helpline at 1-800-662-HELP (4357) for help with accessing resources.

Trans Lifeline or Mermaids UK can also assist you. Flip to pages 316 - 317 for how to contact those specific services.

If you are based in Los Angeles, the LA LGBT Center has Addiction Recovery Services that will suit your unique needs, including 12-step meetings, anonymous online chat support, outpatient programs, harm reduction programs, meth recovery, women's meetings, and individual therapy. Visit **lalgbtcenter.org/health-services/addiction-recovery-services** for more information.

TRANS
ADDICTION
RECOVERY
IS
IMPORTANT

Margie's Hope

Margie's Hope is the manifestation of Jacob and Erin Nash's dream to help transgender, non-binary, and gender expansive individuals who need assistance. Named after Jacob's mother, Margie Nash, in September of 2011, the Nash's took the steps to make their dream a reality by hand-picking the founding Board of Directors for Margie's Hope.

Since then, Jacob and Erin have devoted their time and energy to creating the framework that will enable Margie's Hope to open its doors to transgender people throughout Ohio and neighboring states. Margie's Hope currently has five different support programs that work to empower the transgender and gender expansive community in various ways:

TransAlive:

A support group for transgender, non-conforming and non-binary individuals and their loved ones and friends. Facilitated by transgender individuals themselves, it offers support, guidance, and resources to all those who come.

Margie's Kids:

A group to give transgender, non-conforming and non-binary children and safe space to hang out and support each other. Leaders who facilitate the gr transgender individuals, clinical workers, and allies within the community.

Margie's Pride:

A support group for any parent or guardian of a trans child to share and talk about their children in a safe, judgment-free environment. This group conveniently meets the same time and place as Margie's Kids, so there is no need to find a sitter!

Together We Can:

A space for partners and spouses of trans individuals to meet and discuss their relationships together in a safe space environment.

Margie's Closet:

Provides clothing and accessories for free to the trans, non-binary and gender expansive community.

Margie's Hope also provides diversity trainings specializing in transgender and gender expansive individuals. They have trained over 50,000 people around the country on the needs of this marginalized population. Whether it be a large company where an employee has just come out as transgender or to a congregation that wants to support the transgender/non-binary community, they specialize the training in order to meet any organization's specific needs. Margie's Hope trains for-profit and nonprofit organizations and companies alike.

Margie's Hope is continuing to build relationships daily. Join them on their journey as they grow and evolve into life-saving programs that will assist the trans community of Ohio.

Trans Lifeline is run by and for trans people.

Trans Lifeline is a grassroots hotline and microgrants 501(c)(3) non-profit organization offering direct emotional and financial support to trans people in crisis – for the trans community, by the trans community.

Trans Lifeline connects trans people to the community support and resources we need to survive and thrive.

We envision a world where trans people have the connection, economic security, and care everyone needs and deserves – free of prisons and police.

The Trans Lifeline hotline is available 24/7

If you are in crisis or need someone to talk to, make a call.

You are worth it.

US (877) 565-8860
Canada (877) 330-6366

translifeline.org

Mermaids has been supporting transgender, nonbinary and gender-diverse children, young people, and their families since 1995.

Mermaids supports transgender, nonbinary and gender-diverse children and young people until their 20th birthday, as well as their families and professionals involved in their care.

Transgender, nonbinary and gender-diverse children and teens need support and understanding, as well as the freedom to explore their gender identity. Whatever the outcome, Mermaids is committed to helping families navigate the challenges they may face.

Helpline Open Monday to Friday, 9am to 9pm
Call 0808 801 0400

Textline Open 24/7
Text MERMAIDS to 85258
for free 24/7 crisis support all across the UK.

mermaidsuk.org.uk

- TransFocus -
CONTRIBUTORS

Alessa Catterall (she/her) is a musician, dreamer, and poet. She lives in the wilds of Scotland and dreams of a kinder, more peaceful world for us all.
[pg. 194, 196]

Alex Adams (he/him) is an autistic trans man from Northamptonshire, UK. He studies game design at university.
[pg. 54]

Andy Passchier (they/their) is a non-binary illustrator originally from The Netherlands, currently based in the USA. They work as a freelance illustrator working on children's books and other projects and draw comics in their free time on the Instagram account @andyrogyny. Andy lives with their partner and two cats, loves to travel, draw, eats lots of sushi, and enjoys all things spooky and Halloween.
[pg. 330]

Ash Danielsen (they/their) is a Los Angeles-based photographer. Juxtaposing acid-trip colors with melancholic characters, they draw a surreal picture of what it means to be alive in this day and age. There is beauty through all of the confusion, and through all of the wonder, there is suffering. They long to depict that, and you can check out their website at AshDanielsen.com.
[pg. 276]

Branok Ryland Fuller (xe/xem) is a barista working on going back to college to pursue a career in LGBTQIA+ counseling. Xe spends most of their time daydreaming about having the career of xyr dreams and living with their partners and children. Xe has dreams of becoming a freelance writer.
[pg. 115]

Cassiopeia Violet Drake (all pronouns acceptable) is a 25 year-old non-binary transgender woman from Houston, Texas. Fae works as a professional penetration tester/computer hacker and in faer spare time, fae writes screenplays and stories featuring queer characters, with her ultimate goal being to tell good queer stories to a wide audience. Outside of that, fae enjoys being active in the trans community and advocating for trans rights.
[pg. 116]

Charlie Chowdhry (he/him) is a writer and student from Scotland. Between studying for his university degree and starting his fiftieth hobby during the pandemic, Charlie is in the process of writing a novel. He hopes to publish it in 2021 but has been working on it since 2017 and says of it, "Who knows when it will see the light of day?" Charlie's muse is Lottie, his dog -- whenever he is experiencing writer's block, he goes to give her pats.
[pg. 30]

Dr. Natalia Z. PhD. (she/her) is a clinical psychologist who specializes in serving the trans community. She works solely with adults who are questioning their gender identity or individuals who want to undergo gender transition but don't know where to begin. People who often come to see her have been struggling with Gender Dysphoria for a number of years, finally making the decision to reach out for help. Check out her website and block at DrZPhD.com
[pg. 39]

Ethan Julian Sebastian Molina (he/him) Ethan Molina is a queer, Indigenous- Chicano activist from Pacoima. He started getting into organizing in middle school when he became a youth leader at Somos Familia Valle. There Ethan learned how to do public speaking, networking, committee work, and more. Later on Ethan became a media manager at PAC solidarity, and works on improving the community that surrounds him. He wants to help future generations of trans and gay BIPOC individuals.
[pg. 173]

Elliott Draznin (they/their) is studying business at the University of Cincinnati. They are the president of their Jewish sorority and are frequently found at Hillel and the LGBTQ Center on campus. Their dream is to be a social entrepreneur, creating nonprofits that help Tikkun Olam - repair the world.
[pg. 16]

Em Keevan (they/their) is a twenty-two-year-old non-binary writer. They aim to publish their fiction novels soon, and have other non-fiction works planned out.
[pg. 104, 106]

Em Westheimer/Siri (they/their), known by their drag name Siri, is a drag performer based in Los Angeles. California. They host their own digital drag show, "Fake Smart," on their Instagram @siri_ew. They regularly perform in the Downtown, Los Angeles drag scene, and beyond.
[pg. 254]

Emery Haley (they/their) is a nonbinary person from Alabama. They are currently pursuing their Ph.D. in Cell and Molecular Biology in Michigan. Outside of the lab, Emery enjoys hiking, yoga, attending art festivals. Otherwise, they enjoy staying home with tea, a good book, and their cats.
[pg. 210]

Ezekiel K. (he/him) lives in Greenwich, London, where he is currently attending university.
[pg. 72]

Georgie "Maebe A. Girl" Pudlo (they/she), better known by their stage name "Maebe A. Girl," is a drag queen and local politician based in Los Angeles California. Georgie successfully ran for Silverlake City Council in 2019. They ran for congress in 2020 and just announced their second bid, running to represent California's 28th District in the 2022 congressional election. Their Instagram is @maebeagirl
[pg. 238]

Jacob Nash (he/him) is the founder and president of Margie's Hope, the manifestation of his dream to help transgender people who need assistance. Jacob is a consultant, adjunct professor at Case Western Reserve, a published writer and a seasoned, engaging presenter committed to training both providers and community activists on cultural competency. He has delivered training's to thousands of people around the country and has also presented to the Public Relations Society of America on proper language and pronoun use when writing about the trans community.
[pg. 6, 212]

Jenny Sansom (she/her) has been described as a quick-witted odd soul, and a kind-hearted flowerchild with an old soul. Her hobbies are drawing, reading, and writing. She finished her first book and should hopefully be out on kindle within a few months. It's called "The Life of a Resoucer and How it Ended." It's a fantasy novel series involving a gay transwoman who is pushed beyond all limits to take care of her family.
[pg. 74]

Jordy Robinson (she/they) is a transfemme fashionista based out of Los Angeles, California, and are inspired by Japanese art and anime, translating that into their fashion.
[pg. 298]

Lalo Carlson (he/him) is a Latino trans man born in Colorado who now calls LA home. He is an artist and activist who focuses his poetry around his experiences with gender, sexuality, race, and family.
[pg. 218]

Levi Thrower (he/they) is a Black trans man living in Los Angeles, California. He has overcome homelessness and is recently completed his EPA certification in HVAC. In his free time, he likes to listen to true crime podcasts and Black culture podcasts like The Read, and is also an avid fan of RuPaul's Drag Race and the Teen Mom franchise. When the world's not in a panorama, he frequents music festivals like Bonnaroo, Coachella, Voodoo, and Tropicalia.
[pg. 26]

Lillian Dagny Maisfehlt (she/her) is a trans woman living in Connecticut, USA. She began her transition in late 2015 and began living full-time as a woman in February 2017. Their poetry entry for TransFocus was written in 2017 to reflect her transition experience. Lillian is an academic librarian, visual artist, occasional musician, and proud mother of three children (with hopes for another on the way).
[pg. 178]

Lis Regula (he/him) is an out trans man married to the love of his life, MJ Eckhouse. He teaches human anatomy at a Catholic university and finds other small ways to change the world (usually for the better). Besides his husband and son, he loves the outdoors and reasons to be hopeful. He lives in Kent, Ohio.
[pg. 202, 205]

Lys Morton (he/him) is a prairie boy, Island bound. His work has been featured in The Nav student press, Incline magazine, Disabled Voices Anthology (edited by sb. smith), and Portal magazine. "There's No Privilege in Passing" is a section of his upcoming non-fiction collection that explores trauma and transition. He lives in Vancouver Island, Canada. You can follow him at facebook.com/LysWritesNow
[pg. 60]

Maaraw Amell (they/their) is an amateur artist and writer living life downside up. They are a trans nonbinary person and spend every day reading.
[pg. 198]

Madeleine McCoy (she/her) is a transgender woman who has been out and transitioning for about two years. She is a passionate person with many hobbies and interests, including music, writing, and foreign language studies.
[pg. 174]

Madeleine Voltin (she/her) is a transgender woman currently residing in Austin, Texas. She is an educator, daughter, and partner.
[pg. 96]

Malcolm E. Gottesman (he/him) is a poet and writer based in Los Angeles, California. He writes a lot of things, but poetry has always been a staple. His style is confessional but surreal. He openly identifies as a non-binary, bisexual man, and themes of gender and queerness are presented heavily in his work. He is a prominently featured writer in TransFocus because of his writing quality and the passion that he expertly lays down on the page. Malcolm is a force to be reckoned with, and he is an artist to look out for. The poems he provided to TransFocus were selected from a larger compilation written throughout his life, titled Bodies Unaccounted For, which can be found on his website malcolmgottesman.com.
[pg. 140]

Mal Levenson (they/their) is an unpublished menace, queering society and breaking down capitalism through small acts of kindness and rebellion. Look out for their soon to be released book of poetry, "Here I Am", to be published in 2021. Their Etsy shop is etsy.com/shop/SpookyHausCoOp

[pg. 208]

Mars Wright (he/him) is a Trans artist and Activist who is dedicated to spreading Trans Joy and radical self-acceptance. You can find his work on Instagram and TikTok @mars.wright and online at marswright.com

[pg. 302]

Mila Jam (she/her) is an NYC-based pop recording artist & transgender superstar; she is known around the world for her stage performances and one-of-a-kind music videos. She toured internationally with the Broadway musical RENT; performed alongside James Brown, Mark Ronson, Laverne Cox, Travis Wall, Jody Watley, Lady Kier (Deee-Lite) and Natasha Bedingfield. Appearances include the BBC's "The Lilly Allen Show," MTV & MTV NEWS with special features on The Huffington Post, MTV.com, OUT.com & Perezhilton.com. She is the Odyssey Nightlife Awards Breakthrough Artist (2015), the GLAM Nightlife Awards Best Video & Dance Artist (2013) and the talk show host of an original YouTube Talk Show Series titled 'I'm From Driftwood'. Their art piece "Stop Killing Us" has made waves across the world, and they were gracious enough to speak on it and provide photos for publication in TransFocus.

[pg. 224]

Miles Mayes (he/him) is one of TransFocus' youngest contributors. By the time this comes out he'll be a senior in high school, and has been "out" as transgender to his friends for about two years now. He has very supportive friends, and a supportive boyfriend. Miles wanted to share his small coming out story and what he plans on doing after high school.

[pg. 120]

Morgan Gainnes (he/him) is a transmasc individual from Portland, Oregon. He likes yelling at movies and spending time with his chosen family.

[pg. 184]

Na'amah Olewnik (they/their) is a college student from Illinois studying mathematics and pursuing art & literary publications on the side. Na'amah hopes to continue living out their creative passions while also continuing their educational goals.
[pg. 176]

Nat Mink (they/their) is an aspiring writer out of Houston Texas, and spends most of their time focused on intersecting their queer identity with their disability and mental health. [pg. 220]

Orion Sten (they/their) is a nonbinary trans person doing paid work as a library assistant and unpaid work dismantling ableism and transphobia. Owned by cats (numbers vary), and shares life and love with both an anchor partner and several crushes. A gamer and a space nerd, they spend a lot of time in their head or staring out into space contemplating eternity.
[pg. 170]

Page Person/M. Page Greene (they/their) is a nonbinary artist and drag performer based in Downtown Los Angeles, California. They frequently create art and drag out of what others consider trash, upcycling plastics that would otherwise be thrown away. They use their platform to make a statement about sustainability and single-use plastics. Their Instagram is @page__person (with two underscores.)
[pg. 318]

Ren Thomas (he/him) is a 22-year-old artist based in Florida. He started using writing at a young age in order to cope with mental illness and trauma. He's since branched out into visual arts, and music. Ren has a bachelor's degree in the Psychology of Religion, which he can rant about for hours on end, and a slightly concerning fascination with true crime. He spends way too much time playing video games, and gets along better with animals than people.
[pg. 78, 200]

Rhonda D'Vine (she/her) is a transfeminine activist from Austria. She works on Free Software and often does her poetry in haiku style, either in English or German, which she also presents at poetry slams.

[pg. 164]

Robyn Redd (she/they) enjoys hiking and camping in the mountains with her wife, four kids, and three dogs. When she's not enjoying the outdoors, she can be found in front of a computer screen, writing and gaming with her kids.

[pg. 192]

Roni Shapira (they/their) is, among other things, a freelance graphic designer, a huge nerd, an incredibly awkward person, and a lover of all cats. They recently finished their army service in the Israeli Defense Forces.

[pg. 22]

Rori Porter (she/they) is the senior editor of TransFocus and a freelance graphic/web designer and writer. She grew up in Canton, Ohio and started her career in Akron before interning in Chicago and moving to New York City. She now lives in Los Angeles with her partner, three cats named Alby, Minerva, and Jojo, a geriatric chihuahua named Daisy, and a turtle named Prince of the After World. Her portfolio website is RoriPorter.com, and their writing can be found at RoriPorter.Medium.com

[pg. 2, 90, 125, 214, 262, 348, 370]

Rosalie Derk (she/her) is a Los Angeles-based comic artist who started drawing and showing her art off for the first time in 2020 during the pandemic. She is a big fan of Dungeons and Dragons and Magic the Gathering and can often be found role-playing as a wood elf priestess. Her Instagram is @rosalie__alyssa (with two underscores.)

[pg. 316]

Roxy Valle / Johnny Sin-Rosa Gentleman (they/their) is a Latinx, Two-spirit/ Non-Binary, Transmasculine drag king located in Los Angeles under the name, Johnny Sin-Rosa Gentleman. Their drag is a statement that AFAB individuals can be gentlemen too. (...)

(...) They perform on numerous virtual drag shows around the world on Twitch TV, produce numerous drag shows on their Kings of the World Twitch Channel, and can be seen performing in numerous drag shows in the DTLA drag scene. You can follow @johnnysinrosagent on Instagram.

[pg. 290]

Squeaky Blonde (she/her) is a trans woman and drag queen living and performing in Los Angeles, California. They got their start at the Trannyshack Club in San Francisco, California, and have been performing since the mid-90s. Their Instagram is @ squeakyblonde

[pg. 326]

Taylor Lilith (she/her) is a line cook who lives in Northern Colorado. She enjoys philosophy, science, anime, video games, reading, writing, drawing, and chilling with her friends. She is currently working on her first novel.

[pg. 160]

Ulysses Armel (he/him) is a white, Midwestern non-cis cub who writes poetry. Some of his work appears in anthologies like Lilies Volume 7: Lily Bulb, Lovejets: Queer Male Poets on 200 Years of Walt Whitman, and Pan's Ex: Queer Sex Poetry

[pg. 188, 190]

Zoey Sanford (she/her) is a development exec, screenwriter, writer, and standup comedienne based out of Los Angeles. She is one of the founding members of TransKind L.A., and her writing can be found at IamZoeyRose.com

[pg. 39]

THANK

A.	Chowdhry Family	Jason
Aaron	Cole L.	Jay S.
A.J.R.	Danny P.	Jaymie H.
Alessa C.	Darren L.	Jef C.
Alex A.	Debbie K.	Jess
Alexis P.	Dr. Serenity S.	Jess S.
Alice R.	Drew J.J.	Joanna L.
Anastasia P.	Dublin M.	John M.
Anonymous	Duell M.	Kai
Aren B.	Ellen M.	Kathleen B.
Autumn G.V.K.	Ellie D.	Kathleen R.
Avery R.	Elliot D.	Kay
Bernd L.	Em K.	Keladry G.
Brian H.	Emery H.	Kelly M.
Brooke B.	Eric B.	Ken F.
Camille D.	Erin S.	Kian A.H.
Cecil F.	Jade G.	Krem A.
Cedar K.	Jaeden E-O.S.	Lakodak
Chloe A.	James L.	Lara B.

YOU!

TO OUR KICKSTARTER BACKERS!!!

Lauren H.	Nikkie F.	Takkory
Lillian M.	Olivia M.	Talia
Lily Z.	Orion S.	Tasha T.
Lis R.	P.F.A.	Taylor L.W.
Lucy L.	Quinn	The Creative Fund
M. V. Ho	R.Soares	Theo Q.
Maddie A.	Rataplani	Tiffany G.
Madeleine P.	Rhonda D.	Tracy
Marcos L.	Robin D.B.	Valyrie M.
Mark S.	Rosie P.	Violet F.
Mary C.	S.	Wilhelm A.
Matthew T.	Sal M.	Xander G.
Megha B.	Sara G.	Zac
Michael Wilkie	Sarah W.	Zo S.
Mike L.	Signy M.	Zoe J.
Mindy S.	Skyler E.J.	
Morgan J.	Spirit Healer Mage	
Morgane B.	Su P.	
Myla Calhoun	Tabitha S.	

- TransFocus -

ACKNOWLEDGEMENTS

Without all of you, the book you hold in your hands wouldn't exist. You have given us the ability to donate to our trans charities, the Trans Lifeline US/CA and Mermaids UK and, as we launch in traditional publishing venues globally, we will be one of the only charity-driven projects in this space. I am incredibly proud of that. Ultimately, nobody should be profiting from our community but ourselves. There is no more valuable resource to us than saving and bettering the most vulnerable lives amongst our ranks. You made this possible and I cannot thank you enough for believing in this project.

Trans people have so few venues through which to speak, and I feel strongly that TransFocus has served as a place where our voices can be heard. We made this happen together and we created a platform to amplify the voices of over forty trans people, many of whom have never been published in print before. Thank you for giving this project a chance, and thank you for sticking with it to the end.

A shout-out is very much in order for Charlie, whose support on the backend in the beginning of this project made my life much easier. Your help with the website and our online community was invaluable to the project, and I am so grateful to have met you. Thanks for all the time, dedication, and love you contributed to TransFocus, all while balancing your studies. You're an OG. I hope you know you're a rockstar, and I can't wait to read your work someday. Keep on pushing toward that dream.

Special thanks go out to all of our authors and artists for your fantastic work. We wouldn't be doing this without your help, and I am in awe of what y'all made here. I hope you know that I am incredibly proud of all of you and the passion you each put into your contributions. We went through some changes to get to the book you are featured in, and I am so grateful that you stuck with it and kept submitting.

I also have to thank my friends who encouraged me to keep going on this project when I was going through hell during the better part of 2020. Kieran, Em, Malcolm, and Mo, your encouragement and support of this project have meant the world to me.

Big thanks to my fiancé and partner in crime, Levi, who put up with and supported me through many late nights as I worked on wrapping up the editing and design of TransFocus. Your constant affirmations helped me keep going when I wanted to call it quits. I love you so very much and I cannot wait to call you my husband. You'll probably disagree, but I know that I am the lucky one.

Thanks to the Los Angeles LGBT Center and the Los Angeles Gender Center for keeping me healthy and sane. Thank you to Tyler, Angela, Toby, Melissa, Forest, Scott, Sarah, and others whose names I may be forgetting. You helped me find my path to sobriety and none of this would have been possible without that.

Thanks also go out to Mila Jam and Georgie "Maebe A. Girl" Pudlo for granting me interviews so we could include what you do in this beautiful book. Thanks also to Dr. Natalia Z. Ph.D. for sitting down with me to discuss the state of trans healthcare so I could write and edit from a more informed place, and thank you to Zoey for facilitating that discussion.

Thanks to Jacob for his beautiful introduction that helps set the tone for the book. Your hard work is so appreciated, and I am glad that I got the opportunity to work with you. You're one of my first trans role models, and I feel honored to be including your intro and original poem in this book.

To the readers: working on TransFocus has been the privilege of a lifetime, and I hope this book is as much a source of light and hope for you as it has been for me.

And last, but certainly not least, thank you to my community. You are caterpillars and butterflies, and you are all beautiful and worthy of love. This project is for you. And, wherever you are, I am sending all of my love to Abby and MJ. I dedicate this book in memory of what you meant to me.

Everyone's support for this project means more than I can say.

Thank you, thank you, thank you!